The
Reference Shelf ®

Representative American Speeches

2009–2010

Edited by Brian Boucher

The Reference Shelf
Volume 82 • Number 6
The H.W. Wilson Company
New York • Dublin
2010

The Reference Shelf

The books in this series contain reprints of articles, excerpts from books, addresses on current issues, and studies of social trends in the United States and other countries. There are six separately bound numbers in each volume, all of which are usually published in the same calendar year. Numbers one through five are each devoted to a single subject, providing background information and discussion from various points of view and concluding with a subject index and comprehensive bibliography that lists books, pamphlets, and abstracts of additional articles on the subject. The final number of each volume is a collection of recent speeches, and it contains a cumulative speaker index. Books in the series may be purchased individually or on subscription.

Library of Congress has cataloged this serial title as follows:

Representative American speeches. 1937 / 38–
    New York, H. W. Wilson Co.™
        v. 21 cm.—The Reference Shelf
Annual
Indexes:
    Author index: 1937/38–1959/60, with 1959/60; 1960/61–1969/70, with 1969/70;
1970/71–1979/80, with 1979/80; 1980/81–1989/90, 1990.
Editors: 1937/38–1958/59, A. C. Baird.—1959/60–1969/70, L. Thonssen.—1970/ 71–1979/80,
W. W. Braden.—1980/81–1994/95, O. Peterson.—1995/96–1998/99, C. M. Logue and J.
DeHart.—1999/2000–2002/2003, C. M. Logue and L. M. Messina.—2003/2004–2005/2006,
C. M. Logue, L. M. Messina, and J. DeHart.—2006/ 2007– , J. Currie, P. McCaffrey, L. M.
Messina.—2007/ 2008–2008/2009–2009/2010, B. Boucher.
    ISSN 0197-6923 Representative American speeches.
    1. Speeches, addresses, etc., American. 2. Speeches, addresses, etc.
        I. Baird, Albert Craig, 1883–1979 ed. II. Thonssen, Lester, 1904–III. Braden, Waldo
    Warder, 1911–1991 ed. IV. Peterson, Owen, 1924– ed. V. Logue, Calvin McLeod,
    1935– , Messina, Lynn M., and DeHart, Jean, eds. VI. Series.
PS668.B3   815.5082   38-27962
                                                                      MARC-S

    Library of Congress [8503r85] rev4

Cover: Dr. Anne Schuchat, Assistant Surgeon General of the United States, and the Director of National Center for Immunization and Respiratory Diseases at the Centers for Disease Control and Prevention, testifies at a hearing on Protecting Employees, Employers and the Public: H1N1 and Sick Leave Policies on November 17, 2009. Credit: House Committee on Education and Labor

Visit H.W. Wilson's Web site: www.hwwilson.com

Printed in the United States of America

Contents

Preface

Throughout 2009 and 2010, Democrats, Republicans, and members of the newly formed conservative Tea Party clashed on a number of issues, ending hopes that the bitter partisanship of recent years might give way to greater national unity. Much of the debate centered on President Barack Obama's efforts to reform health care and the financial services industry—topics we explore in the first two chapters of this, the latest edition of *Representative American Speeches*. Both legislative initiatives generated intense media attention and highly emotional debate, and the speeches selected reflect the wide range of views—and tones—heard as the public considered these issues. In subsequent chapters, we look at nuclear disarmament, disaster preparation and response, and the changing field of philanthropy.

Obama wasn't the first president to try overhauling the U.S. health care system, but in a September 2009 address to a joint session of Congress, he vowed to be the last. In the speech that kicks off this volume, the president unveils a plan he says would better protect the insured, extend benefits to millions of Americans without coverage, and prevent health costs from continuing to skyrocket. He also raises the possibility of a "public option"—a controversial government-run insurance plan Democratic proponents would ultimately be forced to abandon. Even without the public option, the legislation proved contentious, and on March 23, 2010, Obama signed into law a bill that had passed through Congress without the support of a single Republican lawmaker.

Appearing at a TEDMED conference just a few short weeks after Obama's congressional address, Intel Fellow Eric Dishman stepped outside the political fray to consider some other health care issues. In his speech, he insists that efforts to rein in health care costs will be futile unless the United States makes use of emerging technology and changes the locus of health care delivery from hospitals to homes. In March 2010, as the health care bill was finally coming up for a vote, Speaker of the House Nancy Pelosi compared the legislation to Social Security and Medicare. In a speech included here, she also quotes Senator Edward Kennedy, who wrote that "access to health care is the great unfinished business of our society." Republicans remained staunchly opposed to the bill, and in the chapter's next speech, House Minority Leader John Boehner inverts Obama's "Yes, We Can" campaign slogan, rhetorically asking whether his Democratic colleagues could claim to have arrived at their health care legislation via honest means. "Hell no, you can't!" is his reply. Joining this chorus of disapproval was former Florida representative Thomas Feeney, who maintained that the law violates the Commerce Clause of the U.S. Constitution. Stuart M. Butler, of The Heritage Foundation, meanwhile, claimed that many of the promises made by proponents of the health care reform bill were unrealistic. He predicted the law would negatively impact the health care system in ways supporters had not anticipated.

After the world financial system came close to imploding in the fall of 2008, many raised the call for reforming the system and imposing stricter regulations. During the debate over the legislation, pundits gave varying assessments of the causes of the crisis. In a July 2009 speech before the National Press Club, Representative Barney Frank, chairman of the House Financial Services Committee, blames "non-regulation" and outlines several reforms he'd like to see implemented. The following spring, Republican senator and Minority Leader Mitch McConnell had his say, telling Senate colleagues that the Democrat-backed reform bill then under consideration would only make matters worse and fail to prevent future taxpayer-funded bailouts of private companies. Just days later, Barack Obama took to the podium at New York's Cooper Union, describing the proposed reforms as "not only in the best interest of our country, but in the best interest of the financial sector." Though the president's plan was ultimately approved by Congress, many—even in Obama's own party—withheld their support, including Senator Russ Feingold of Wisconsin. In his address to his colleagues, Feingold claims the Senate bill is inadequate, as it fails to address the question of how to dissolve companies that are considered "too big to fail," or too interconnected to be allowed to do so. Richard Shelby, ranking Republican on the Banking, Housing, and Urban Affairs Committee, attacked the bill on other grounds, blasting the partisan process that led to its creation. Closing out the chapter, Shelby highlights several important areas on which he insists "the bill is silent."

Turning from domestic to international affairs, the next chapter of this volume considers the issue of nuclear disarmament and arms control. Even as Iran and North Korea moved toward gaining the capacity to launch nuclear strikes, proponents of disarmament continued to call for downsizing nuclear arsenals. Speaking at The Heritage Foundation in February 2009 and drawing on her experience working on disarmament issues under former president George W. Bush, Jackie Wolcott highlights perceived weaknesses in current multilateral institutions and recommends alternatives. In a more inspirational vein, President Obama, in a spring address in the Czech capital of Prague, calls for "a world without nuclear weapons." That summer, Sam Nunn, a former senator and current CEO of the Nuclear Threat Initiative, offered further details on how to move toward that vision. Paula DeSutter, former Assistant Secretary of State for the Bureau of Verification, Compliance, and Implementation, spoke later that summer against the New START treaty then under consideration—the first nuclear arms control agreement between the United States and Russia in almost a decade.

While commentators argued about how humanity might prevent nuclear self-annihilation, Mother Nature offered stern reminders that humans aren't alone in their ability to create widespread destruction. The two-year period covered by this book witnessed several major natural disasters, including floods in Pakistan and earthquakes in China and Haiti. What's more, 2009 saw the international spread of a novel flu: the H1N1 virus, also known as swine flu. While not as deadly as was feared, H1N1 resulted in a number of fatalities and raised questions about controlling the spread of dangerous contagions. The Centers for Disease Control and Prevention (CDC)'s Anne Schuchat testified on Capitol Hill in November 2009, and in the address that opens this chapter, she describes her organization's efforts to understand the disease and deter its spread.

On January 12, 2010, a magnitude 7.0 earthquake hit Haiti, leveling much of Port-au-Prince, the nation's capital. Secretary of State Hillary Clinton addressed the United Nations (UN) in March 2010, and in the remarks reproduced here, she discusses efforts by the United States to help Haiti "build back better" and improve its vital infrastructure, which had been lacking even before the earthquake. Clinton encourages international donors as well as the Haitian government to rise to the occasion. Addressing the Congressional Black Caucus, Paul Farmer also discusses the situation in Haiti, calling for a strengthening of that country's public sector. Three months after the Haiti quake, an explosion on the Deepwater Horizon, an oil-drilling rig under lease to BP in the Gulf of Mexico, caused one of the worst ecological disasters in history. Tony Hayward, then a chief executive at BP, appeared before Congress in June 2010, and in his address, the final entry in this chapter, Hayward conveys his contrition and pledges to make the situation right.

We end this year's volume with a series of speeches centering on philanthropy, a field very much in flux. In June 2010, Bill and Melinda Gates joined Warren Buffett in calling on the nation's billionaires to pledge at least half their fortunes to charity, either during their lives or at the time of their deaths. In the speech that leads off this chapter, Atlantic Philanthropies CEO Gara LaMarche explains how and why his organization is undertaking a similar challenge and attempting to "spend down" its assets and cease operations. Next up, Professor Steven Rathgeb Smith says in a speech at Georgetown University that the United States has reached a critical moment in the relationship between government and philanthropic organizations. He lays out a detailed history of that relationship to buttress his point. Taking a markedly different tone in his address to the National Press Club in October 2009, actor and rap artist Chris "Ludacris" Bridges describes the activities of his own Ludacris Foundation, which he started with the help of his mother and which focuses on children and communities. In the speech that closes this book, Ben Cameron, project director for the Doris Duke Charitable Foundation, makes the case for why arts organizations are also deserving of financial support. Cameron insists that ". . . within this world of infinite possibilities, there is infinite value to be found in the arts."

Brian Boucher
December 2010

1

Health Care Reform

"Here and Now We Can Meet History's Test"[*]

Barack Obama

President of the United States, 2009– ; born Honolulu, HI, August 4, 1961; early education in Jakarta, Indonesia, and Honolulu; B.A., Columbia University, 1983; J.D., Harvard Law School, 1992; first African-American president of the Harvard Law Review; *community organizer and civil rights lawyer in Chicago; senior lecturer, University of Chicago Law School, specializing in constitutional law; state senator, representing the South Side of Chicago, Illinois State Senate, 1997–2004; U.S. senator (D), Illinois, 2005–2008; author,* Dreams from My Father: A Story of Race and Inheritance *(1995, reprinted 2004);* The Audacity of Hope: Thoughts on Reclaiming the American Dream *(2006).*

Editor's introduction: In this speech, delivered to a joint session of Congress, President Obama presents his case for an overhaul of the U.S. health care system. He points out that the United States is the only wealthy nation to allow so many of its citizens to go without health insurance, and in which those who are insured are vulnerable to losing their coverage or going bankrupt if they or someone in their family become ill. After discussing rising health care costs, which place an ever-growing financial burden on the public, the president lays out three goals for health care legislation: that it offer security and stability to those who are currently covered, allow those without insurance to obtain coverage, and slow the rate of growth in the cost of medical care. He also addresses criticisms of his plan—among them, that the new system will feature so-called death panels to deal with the elderly and infirmed, offer insurance coverage to illegal immigrants, fund abortions, and amount to a government takeover of health care. The debate over health care had boiled over into open rage at townhall meetings throughout the country in the months leading up to the president's speech. This anger even flared up during his address, in an unprecedented outburst from Rep. Joe Wilson (R-SC), who shouted, "You lie!" when the president asserted that undocumented immigrants would not be covered under his plan.

---

[*] Delivered on September 9, 2009, at Washington, D.C.

Barack Obama's speeech: When I spoke here last winter, this nation was facing the worst economic crisis since the Great Depression. We were losing an average of 700,000 jobs per month. Credit was frozen. And our financial system was on the verge of collapse.

As any American who is still looking for work or a way to pay their bills will tell you, we are by no means out of the woods. A full and vibrant recovery is many months away. And I will not let up until those Americans who seek jobs can find them; until those businesses that seek capital and credit can thrive; until all responsible homeowners can stay in their homes. That is our ultimate goal. But thanks to the bold and decisive action we have taken since January, I can stand here with confidence and say that we have pulled this economy back from the brink.

I want to thank the members of this body for your efforts and your support in these last several months, and especially those who have taken the difficult votes that have put us on a path to recovery. I also want to thank the American people for their patience and resolve during this trying time for our nation.

But we did not come here just to clean up crises. We came to build a future. So tonight, I return to speak to all of you about an issue that is central to that future— and that is the issue of health care.

I am not the first President to take up this cause, but I am determined to be the last. It has now been nearly a century since Theodore Roosevelt first called for health care reform. And ever since, nearly every President and Congress, whether Democrat or Republican, has attempted to meet this challenge in some way. A bill for comprehensive health reform was first introduced by John Dingell Sr. in 1943. Sixty-five years later, his son continues to introduce that same bill at the beginning of each session.

Our collective failure to meet this challenge—year after year, decade after decade—has led us to a breaking point. Everyone understands the extraordinary hardships that are placed on the uninsured, who live every day just one accident or illness away from bankruptcy. These are not primarily people on welfare. These are middle-class Americans. Some can't get insurance on the job. Others are self-employed, and can't afford it, since buying insurance on your own costs you three times as much as the coverage you get from your employer. Many other Americans who are willing and able to pay are still denied insurance due to previous illnesses or conditions that insurance companies decide are too risky or expensive to cover.

We are the only advanced democracy on Earth—the only wealthy nation—that allows such hardships for millions of its people. There are now more than thirty million American citizens who cannot get coverage. In just a two year period, one in every three Americans goes without health care coverage at some point. And every day, 14,000 Americans lose their coverage. In other words, it can happen to anyone.

But the problem that plagues the health care system is not just a problem of the uninsured. Those who do have insurance have never had less security and stability than they do today. More and more Americans worry that if you move, lose your job, or change your job, you'll lose your health insurance too. More and more

Americans pay their premiums, only to discover that their insurance company has dropped their coverage when they get sick, or won't pay the full cost of care. It happens every day.

One man from Illinois lost his coverage in the middle of chemotherapy because his insurer found that he hadn't reported gallstones that he didn't even know about. They delayed his treatment, and he died because of it. Another woman from Texas was about to get a double mastectomy when her insurance company canceled her policy because she forgot to declare a case of acne. By the time she had her insurance reinstated, her breast cancer more than doubled in size. That is heartbreaking, it is wrong, and no one should be treated that way in the United States of America.

Then there's the problem of rising costs. We spend one-and-a-half times more per person on health care than any other country, but we aren't any healthier for it. This is one of the reasons that insurance premiums have gone up three times faster than wages. It's why so many employers—especially small businesses—are forcing their employees to pay more for insurance, or are dropping their coverage entirely. It's why so many aspiring entrepreneurs cannot afford to open a business in the first place, and why American businesses that compete internationally—like our automakers—are at a huge disadvantage. And it's why those of us with health insurance are also paying a hidden and growing tax for those without it—about $1000 per year that pays for somebody else's emergency room and charitable care.

Finally, our health care system is placing an unsustainable burden on taxpayers. When health care costs grow at the rate they have, it puts greater pressure on programs like Medicare and Medicaid. If we do nothing to slow these skyrocketing costs, we will eventually be spending more on Medicare and Medicaid than every other government program combined. Put simply, our health care problem is our deficit problem. Nothing else even comes close.

These are the facts. Nobody disputes them. We know we must reform this system. The question is how.

There are those on the left who believe that the only way to fix the system is through a single-payer system like Canada's, where we would severely restrict the private insurance market and have the government provide coverage for everyone. On the right, there are those who argue that we should end the employer-based system and leave individuals to buy health insurance on their own.

I have to say that there are arguments to be made for both approaches. But either one would represent a radical shift that would disrupt the health care most people currently have. Since health care represents one-sixth of our economy, I believe it makes more sense to build on what works and fix what doesn't, rather than try to build an entirely new system from scratch. And that is precisely what those of you in Congress have tried to do over the past several months.

During that time, we have seen Washington at its best and its worst.

We have seen many in this chamber work tirelessly for the better part of this year to offer thoughtful ideas about how to achieve reform. Of the five committees asked to develop bills, four have completed their work, and the Senate Finance

Committee announced today that it will move forward next week. That has never happened before. Our overall efforts have been supported by an unprecedented coalition of doctors and nurses; hospitals, seniors' groups and even drug companies—many of whom opposed reform in the past. And there is agreement in this chamber on about eighty percent of what needs to be done, putting us closer to the goal of reform than we have ever been.

But what we have also seen in these last months is the same partisan spectacle that only hardens the disdain many Americans have toward their own government. Instead of honest debate, we have seen scare tactics. Some have dug into unyielding ideological camps that offer no hope of compromise. Too many have used this as an opportunity to score short-term political points, even if it robs the country of our opportunity to solve a long-term challenge. And out of this blizzard of charges and counter-charges, confusion has reigned.

Well the time for bickering is over. The time for games has passed. Now is the season for action. Now is when we must bring the best ideas of both parties together, and show the American people that we can still do what we were sent here to do. Now is the time to deliver on health care.

The plan I'm announcing tonight would meet three basic goals:

It will provide more security and stability to those who have health insurance. It will provide insurance to those who don't. And it will slow the growth of health care costs for our families, our businesses, and our government. It's a plan that asks everyone to take responsibility for meeting this challenge—not just government and insurance companies, but employers and individuals. And it's a plan that incorporates ideas from senators and congressmen; from Democrats and Republicans—and yes, from some of my opponents in both the primary and general election.

Here are the details that every American needs to know about this plan:

First, if you are among the hundreds of millions of Americans who already have health insurance through your job, Medicare, Medicaid, or the VA, nothing in this plan will require you or your employer to change the coverage or the doctor you have. Let me repeat this: nothing in our plan requires you to change what you have.

What this plan will do is to make the insurance you have work better for you. Under this plan, it will be against the law for insurance companies to deny you coverage because of a pre-existing condition. As soon as I sign this bill, it will be against the law for insurance companies to drop your coverage when you get sick or water it down when you need it most. They will no longer be able to place some arbitrary cap on the amount of coverage you can receive in a given year or a lifetime. We will place a limit on how much you can be charged for out-of-pocket expenses, because in the United States of America, no one should go broke because they get sick. And insurance companies will be required to cover, with no extra charge, routine check-ups and preventive care, like mammograms and colonoscopies—because there's no reason we shouldn't be catching diseases like breast cancer and colon cancer before they get worse. That makes sense, it saves money, and it saves lives.

That's what Americans who have health insurance can expect from this plan—more security and stability.

Now, if you're one of the tens of millions of Americans who don't currently have health insurance, the second part of this plan will finally offer you quality, affordable choices. If you lose your job or change your job, you will be able to get coverage. If you strike out on your own and start a small business, you will be able to get coverage. We will do this by creating a new insurance exchange—a marketplace where individuals and small businesses will be able to shop for health insurance at competitive prices. Insurance companies will have an incentive to participate in this exchange because it lets them compete for millions of new customers. As one big group, these customers will have greater leverage to bargain with the insurance companies for better prices and quality coverage. This is how large companies and government employees get affordable insurance. It's how everyone in this Congress gets affordable insurance. And it's time to give every American the same opportunity that we've given ourselves.

For those individuals and small businesses who still cannot afford the lower-priced insurance available in the exchange, we will provide tax credits, the size of which will be based on your need. And all insurance companies that want access to this new marketplace will have to abide by the consumer protections I already mentioned. This exchange will take effect in four years, which will give us time to do it right. In the meantime, for those Americans who can't get insurance today because they have pre-existing medical conditions, we will immediately offer low-cost coverage that will protect you against financial ruin if you become seriously ill. This was a good idea when Senator John McCain proposed it in the campaign, it's a good idea now, and we should embrace it.

Now, even if we provide these affordable options, there may be those—particularly the young and healthy—who still want to take the risk and go without coverage. There may still be companies that refuse to do right by their workers. The problem is, such irresponsible behavior costs all the rest of us money. If there are affordable options and people still don't sign up for health insurance, it means we pay for those people's expensive emergency room visits. If some businesses don't provide workers health care, it forces the rest of us to pick up the tab when their workers get sick, and gives those businesses an unfair advantage over their competitors. And unless everybody does their part, many of the insurance reforms we seek—especially requiring insurance companies to cover pre-existing conditions—just can't be achieved.

That's why under my plan, individuals will be required to carry basic health insurance—just as most states require you to carry auto insurance. Likewise, businesses will be required to either offer their workers health care, or chip in to help cover the cost of their workers. There will be a hardship waiver for those individuals who still cannot afford coverage, and 95% of all small businesses, because of their size and narrow profit margin, would be exempt from these requirements. But we cannot have large businesses and individuals who can afford coverage game the system by avoiding responsibility to themselves or their employees. Improving our health care system only works if everybody does their part.

While there remain some significant details to be ironed out, I believe a broad consensus exists for the aspects of the plan I just outlined: consumer protections for those with insurance, an exchange that allows individuals and small businesses to purchase affordable coverage, and a requirement that people who can afford insurance get insurance.

And I have no doubt that these reforms would greatly benefit Americans from all walks of life, as well as the economy as a whole. Still, given all the misinformation that's been spread over the past few months, I realize that many Americans have grown nervous about reform. So tonight I'd like to address some of the key controversies that are still out there.

Some of people's concerns have grown out of bogus claims spread by those whose only agenda is to kill reform at any cost. The best example is the claim, made not just by radio and cable talk show hosts, but prominent politicians, that we plan to set up panels of bureaucrats with the power to kill off senior citizens. Such a charge would be laughable if it weren't so cynical and irresponsible. It is a lie, plain and simple.

There are also those who claim that our reform effort will insure illegal immigrants. This, too, is false—the reforms I'm proposing would not apply to those who are here illegally. And one more misunderstanding I want to clear up—under our plan, no federal dollars will be used to fund abortions, and federal conscience laws will remain in place.

My health care proposal has also been attacked by some who oppose reform as a "government takeover" of the entire health care system. As proof, critics point to a provision in our plan that allows the uninsured and small businesses to choose a publicly sponsored insurance option, administered by the government just like Medicaid or Medicare.

So let me set the record straight. My guiding principle is, and always has been, that consumers do better when there is choice and competition. Unfortunately, in 34 states, 75% of the insurance market is controlled by five or fewer companies. In Alabama, almost 90% is controlled by just one company. Without competition, the price of insurance goes up and the quality goes down. And it makes it easier for insurance companies to treat their customers badly—by cherry-picking the healthiest individuals and trying to drop the sickest; by overcharging small businesses who have no leverage; and by jacking up rates.

Insurance executives don't do this because they are bad people. They do it because it's profitable. As one former insurance executive testified before Congress, insurance companies are not only encouraged to find reasons to drop the seriously ill; they are rewarded for it. All of this is in service of meeting what this former executive called "Wall Street's relentless profit expectations."

Now, I have no interest in putting insurance companies out of business. They provide a legitimate service and employ a lot of our friends and neighbors. I just want to hold them accountable. The insurance reforms that I've already mentioned would do just that. But an additional step we can take to keep insurance companies honest is by making a not-for-profit public option available in the insurance exchange. Let me be clear—it would only be an option for those who don't have insurance. No one would be forced to choose it, and it would not impact those of you who already have insurance. In fact, based on Congressional Budget Office estimates, we believe that less than 5% of Americans would sign up.

Despite all this, the insurance companies and their allies don't like this idea. They argue that these private companies can't fairly compete with the government. And they'd be right if taxpayers were subsidizing this public insurance option. But they won't be. I have insisted that like any private insurance company, the public insurance option would have to be self-sufficient and rely on the premiums it collects. But by avoiding some of the overhead that gets eaten up at private companies by profits, excessive administrative costs and executive salaries, it could provide a good deal for consumers. It would also keep pressure on private insurers to keep their policies affordable and treat their customers better, the same way public colleges and universities provide additional choice and competition to students without in any way inhibiting a vibrant system of private colleges and universities.

It's worth noting that a strong majority of Americans still favor a public insurance option of the sort I've proposed tonight. But its impact shouldn't be exaggerated—by the left, the right, or the media. It is only one part of my plan, and should not be used as a handy excuse for the usual Washington ideological battles. To my progressive friends, I would remind you that for decades, the driving idea behind reform has been to end insurance company abuses and make coverage affordable for those without it. The public option is only a means to that end—and we should remain open to other ideas that accomplish our ultimate goal. And to my Republican friends, I say that rather than making wild claims about a government takeover of health care, we should work together to address any legitimate concerns you may have.

For example, some have suggested that that the public option go into effect only in those markets where insurance companies are not providing affordable policies. Others propose a co-op or another non-profit entity to administer the plan. These are all constructive ideas worth exploring. But I will not back down on the basic principle that if Americans can't find affordable coverage, we will provide you with a choice. And I will make sure that no government bureaucrat or insurance company bureaucrat gets between you and the care that you need.

Finally, let me discuss an issue that is a great concern to me, to members of this chamber, and to the public—and that is how we pay for this plan.

Here's what you need to know. First, I will not sign a plan that adds one dime to our deficits—either now or in the future. Period. And to prove that I'm serious, there will be a provision in this plan that requires us to come forward with more spending cuts if the savings we promised don't materialize. Part of the reason I faced a trillion dollar deficit when I walked in the door of the White House is because too many initiatives over the last decade were not paid for—from the Iraq

War to tax breaks for the wealthy. I will not make that same mistake with health care.

Second, we've estimated that most of this plan can be paid for by finding savings within the existing health care system—a system that is currently full of waste and abuse. Right now, too much of the hard-earned savings and tax dollars we spend on health care doesn't make us healthier. That's not my judgment—it's the judgment of medical professionals across this country. And this is also true when it comes to Medicare and Medicaid.

In fact, I want to speak directly to America's seniors for a moment, because Medicare is another issue that's been subjected to demagoguery and distortion during the course of this debate.

More than four decades ago, this nation stood up for the principle that after a lifetime of hard work, our seniors should not be left to struggle with a pile of medical bills in their later years. That is how Medicare was born. And it remains a sacred trust that must be passed down from one generation to the next. That is why not a dollar of the Medicare trust fund will be used to pay for this plan.

The only thing this plan would eliminate is the hundreds of billions of dollars in waste and fraud, as well as unwarranted subsidies in Medicare that go to insurance companies—subsidies that do everything to pad their profits and nothing to improve your care. And we will also create an independent commission of doctors and medical experts charged with identifying more waste in the years ahead.

These steps will ensure that you—America's seniors—get the benefits you've been promised. They will ensure that Medicare is there for future generations. And we can use some of the savings to fill the gap in coverage that forces too many seniors to pay thousands of dollars a year out of their own pocket for prescription drugs. That's what this plan will do for you. So don't pay attention to those scary stories about how your benefits will be cut—especially since some of the same folks who are spreading these tall tales have fought against Medicare in the past, and just this year supported a budget that would have essentially turned Medicare into a privatized voucher program. That will never happen on my watch. I will protect Medicare.

Now, because Medicare is such a big part of the health care system, making the program more efficient can help usher in changes in the way we deliver health care that can reduce costs for everybody. We have long known that some places, like the Intermountain Health care in Utah or the Geisinger Health System in rural Pennsylvania, offer high-quality care at costs below average. The commission can help encourage the adoption of these common-sense best practices by doctors and medical professionals throughout the system—everything from reducing hospital infection rates to encouraging better coordination between teams of doctors.

Reducing the waste and inefficiency in Medicare and Medicaid will pay for most of this plan. Much of the rest would be paid for with revenues from the very same drug and insurance companies that stand to benefit from tens of millions of new customers. This reform will charge insurance companies a fee for their most expensive policies, which will encourage them to provide greater value for the money—an idea which has the support of Democratic and Republican experts. And according to these same experts, this modest change could help hold down the cost of health care for all of us in the long-run.

Finally, many in this chamber—particularly on the Republican side of the aisle—have long insisted that reforming our medical malpractice laws can help bring down the cost of health care. I don't believe malpractice reform is a silver bullet, but I have talked to enough doctors to know that defensive medicine may be contributing to unnecessary costs. So I am proposing that we move forward on a range of ideas about how to put patient safety first and let doctors focus on practicing medicine. I know that the Bush Administration considered authorizing demonstration projects in individual states to test these issues. It's a good idea, and I am directing my Secretary of Health and Human Services to move forward on this initiative today.

Add it all up, and the plan I'm proposing will cost around $900 billion over ten years—less than we have spent on the Iraq and Afghanistan wars, and less than the tax cuts for the wealthiest few Americans that Congress passed at the beginning of the previous administration. Most of these costs will be paid for with money already being spent—but spent badly—in the existing health care system. The plan will not add to our deficit. The middle-class will realize greater security, not higher taxes. And if we are able to slow the growth of health care costs by just one-tenth of one percent each year, it will actually reduce the deficit by $4 trillion over the long term.

This is the plan I'm proposing. It's a plan that incorporates ideas from many of the people in this room tonight—Democrats and Republicans. And I will continue to seek common ground in the weeks ahead. If you come to me with a serious set of proposals, I will be there to listen. My door is always open.

But know this: I will not waste time with those who have made the calculation that it's better politics to kill this plan than improve it. I will not stand by while the special interests use the same old tactics to keep things exactly the way they are. If you misrepresent what's in the plan, we will call you out. And I will not accept the status quo as a solution. Not this time. Not now.

Everyone in this room knows what will happen if we do nothing. Our deficit will grow. More families will go bankrupt. More businesses will close. More Americans will lose their coverage when they are sick and need it most. And more will die as a result. We know these things to be true.

That is why we cannot fail. Because there are too many Americans counting on us to succeed—the ones who suffer silently, and the ones who shared their stories with us at town hall meetings, in emails, and in letters.

I received one of those letters a few days ago. It was from our beloved friend and colleague, Ted Kennedy. He had written it back in May, shortly after he was told that his illness was terminal. He asked that it be delivered upon his death.

In it, he spoke about what a happy time his last months were, thanks to the love and support of family and friends, his wife, Vicki, and his children, who are here tonight. And he expressed confidence that this would be the year that health care reform—"that great unfinished business of our society," he called it—would finally pass. He repeated the truth that health care is decisive for our future prosperity, but he also reminded me that "it concerns more than material things." "What we face," he wrote, "is above all a moral issue; at stake are not just the details of policy, but fundamental principles of social justice and the character of our country."

I've thought about that phrase quite a bit in recent days—the character of our country. One of the unique and wonderful things about America has always been our self-reliance, our rugged individualism, our fierce defense of freedom and our healthy skepticism of government. And figuring out the appropriate size and role of government has always been a source of rigorous and sometimes angry debate.

For some of Ted Kennedy's critics, his brand of liberalism represented an affront to American liberty. In their mind, his passion for universal health care was nothing more than a passion for big government.

But those of us who knew Teddy and worked with him here—people of both parties—know that what drove him was something more. His friend, Orrin Hatch, knows that. They worked together to provide children with health insurance. His friend John McCain knows that. They worked together on a Patient's Bill of Rights. His friend Chuck Grassley knows that. They worked together to provide health care to children with disabilities.

On issues like these, Ted Kennedy's passion was born not of some rigid ideology, but of his own experience. It was the experience of having two children stricken with cancer. He never forgot the sheer terror and helplessness that any parent feels when a child is badly sick; and he was able to imagine what it must be like for those without insurance; what it would be like to have to say to a wife or a child or an aging parent—there is something that could make you better, but I just can't afford it.

That large-heartedness—that concern and regard for the plight of others—is not a partisan feeling. It is not a Republican or a Democratic feeling. It, too, is part of the American character. Our ability to stand in other people's shoes. A recognition that we are all in this together; that when fortune turns against one of us, others are there to lend a helping hand. A belief that in this country, hard work and responsibility should be rewarded by some measure of security and fair play; and an acknowledgement that sometimes government has to step in to help deliver on that promise.

This has always been the history of our progress. In 1933, when over half of our seniors could not support themselves and millions had seen their savings wiped away, there were those who argued that Social Security would lead to socialism. But the men and women of Congress stood fast, and we are all the better for it. In 1965, when some argued that Medicare represented a government takeover of health care, members of Congress, Democrats and Republicans, did not back down. They joined together so that all of us could enter our golden years with some basic peace of mind.

You see, our predecessors understood that government could not, and should not, solve every problem. They understood that there are instances when the gains in security from government action are not worth the added constraints on our freedom. But they also understood that the danger of too much government is matched by the perils of too little; that without the leavening hand of wise policy, markets can crash, monopolies can stifle competition, and the vulnerable can be exploited. And they knew that when any government measure, no matter how carefully crafted or beneficial, is subject to scorn; when any efforts to help people in need are attacked as un-American; when facts and reason are thrown overboard and only timidity passes for wisdom, and we can no longer even engage in a civil conversation with each other over the things that truly matter—that at that point we don't merely lose our capacity to solve big challenges. We lose something essential about ourselves.

What was true then remains true today. I understand how difficult this health care debate has been. I know that many in this country are deeply skeptical that government is looking out for them. I understand that the politically safe move would be to kick the can further down the road—to defer reform one more year, or one more election, or one more term.

But that's not what the moment calls for. That's not what we came here to do. We did not come to fear the future. We came here to shape it. I still believe we can act even when it's hard. I still believe we can replace acrimony with civility, and gridlock with progress. I still believe we can do great things, and that here and now we will meet history's test.

Because that is who we are. That is our calling. That is our character. Thank you, God bless you, and may God bless the United States of America.

Take Health Care Off the Mainframe[*]

Eric Dishman

Intel Fellow, Digital Health Group, general manager and global director of product research and innovation, 1999– ; born Charlotte, NC, March 2, 1968; B.A.s in English, speech communication, and drama, University of North Carolina, Chapel Hill, 1991; M.S., speech communication, Southern Illinois University, 1992; founding member, social science research team, Interval Research, 1993–99.

Editor's introduction: In this speech, presented as part of the TEDMED 2009 conference, Intel Fellow Eric Dishman contends that in its present state health care delivery is too strictly based on a "mainframe" model, in which care occurs in the hospital, doctor's office, or other institutional setting. Dishman proposes that just as technological innovation transformed computers from remote mainframes to PCs and cell phones, so must it move health care from an institutional delivery model to a home-based one. The key to this evolution, he argues, will be better preventive care. People are living longer than at any time in history, and caring for an aging population, especially in institutions, places a heavy financial burden on the rest of society. As the Baby Boom generation retires, this crisis will become the equivalent of, in Dishman's words, "50 tsunamis." So we must make radical changes in how we deliver health care. Dishman concludes by saying that current health care reform legislation will be ineffective if it does not address the flaws in the delivery model.

Eric Dishman's speech: If you think about the phone, and Intel has tested a lot of the things I'm going to show you over the last 10 years in about 600 elderly households—300 in Ireland, and 300 in Portland—trying to understand how do we measure and monitor behavior in a medically meaningful way.

And if you think about the phone, right, it's something that we can use for some incredible ways to help people actually take the right medication at the right time. We're testing these kinds of simple sensor network technologies in the home so that any phone that a senior is already comfortable with can help them deal with

---

[*] Delivered on October 28, 2009, at San Diego, CA. Reprinted with permission.

their medications. And a lot of what they do is they pick up the phone, and it's our system whispering to them which pill they need to take, and they fake like they're having a conversation with a friend. And they're not embarrassed by a meds caddy that's ugly that sits on their kitchen table and says, "I'm old. I'm frail." It's surreptitious technology that's helping them do a simple task of taking the right pill at the right time.

Now, we also do some pretty amazing things with these phones. Because that moment when you answer the phone is a cognitive test every time that you do it. Think about it, all right? I'm going to answer the phone three different times. "Hello? Hey." All right? That's the first time. "Hello? Uh, hey." "Hello? Uh, who? Oh, hey." All right? Very big differences between the way I answered the phone the three times. And as we monitor phone usage by seniors over a long period of time, down to the tenths of a microsecond, that recognition moment of whether they can figure out that person on the other end is a friend and they start talking to them immediately, or they do a lot of what's called trouble talk, where they're like, "Wait, who is this? Oh." Right? Waiting for that recognition moment may be the best early indicator of the onset of dementia than anything that shows up clinically today.

We call these behavioral markers. There's lots of others. Is the person going to the phone as quickly, when it rings, as they used to? Is it a hearing problem or is it a physicality problem? Has their voice gotten more quiet? We're doing a lot of work with people with Alzheimer's and particularly with Parkinson's where that quiet voice that sometimes shows up with Parkinson's patients may be the best early indicator of Parkinson's five to 10 years before it shows up clinically. But those subtle changes in your voice over a long period of time are hard for you or your spouse to notice until it becomes so extreme and your voice has become so quiet.

So, sensors are looking at that kind of voice. When you pick up the phone how much tremor are you having, and how is that like, and what is that trend like over a period of time? Are you having more trouble dialing the phone than you used to? Is is a dexterity problem? Is is the onset of arthritis? Are you using the phone? Are you socializing less than you used to? And looking at that pattern. And what [does] that decline in social health mean, as a kind of a vital sign of the future? And then wow, what a radical idea, we, except in the United States, might be able to use this newfangled technology to actually interact with a nurse or a doctor on the other end of the line. What a great day that will be once we're allowed to actually do those kinds of things.

So, these are what I would call behavioral markers. And it's the whole field that we've been trying to work on for the last 10 years at Intel. How do you put simple disruptive technologies in the first of five phrases that I'm going to talk about in this talk? Behavioral markers matter. How do we change behavior? How do we measure changes in behavior in a meaningful way that's going to help us with prevention of disease, early onset of disease, and tracking the progression of disease over a long period of time?

Now, why would Intel let me spend a lot of time and money, over the last 10 years, trying to understand the needs of seniors and start thinking about these kinds of behavioral markers? This is some of the field work that we've done. We have now lived with 1,000 elderly households in 20 countries over the last 10 years. We study people in Rochester, New York. We go live with them in the winter because what they do in the winter, and their access to health care, and how much they socialize is very different than in the summer. If they have a hip fracture we go with them and we study their entire discharge experience. If they have a family member who is a key part of their care network we fly and study them as well.

So, we study the holistic health experience of 1,000 seniors over the last 10 years in 20 different countries. Why is Intel willing to fund that? It's because of the second slogan I want to talk about. 10 years ago, when I started trying to convince Intel to let me go start looking at disruptive technologies that could help with independent living, this is what I called it: "Y2K + 10."

You know, back in 2000 we were all so obsessed with paying attention to the aging of our computers, and whether or not they were going to survive the tick of the clock from 1999 to 2000 that we missed a moment that only demographers were paying attention to. It was right around New Year's. And that switchover, when we had the larger number of older people on the planet for the first time than younger people. For the first time in human history, and barring aliens landing or some major other pandemic, that's the expectation from demographers, going forward.

And 10 years ago it seemed like I had a lot of time to convince Intel to work on this. Right? Y2K + 10 was coming, the baby boomers starting to retire. Well folks, it's like we know these demographics here. This is a map of the entire world. It's like the lights are on, but nobody is home on this demographic Y2K + 10 problem. Right? I mean we sort of get it here, but we don't get it here. And we're not doing anything about it.

The health reform bill is largely ignoring the realities of the age wave that's coming, and the implications for what we need to do to change not only how we pay for care, but deliver care in some radically different ways. And in fact, it's upon us. I mean you probably saw these headlines. This is Catherine Casey [slide omitted] who is the first boomer to actually get Social Security. That actually occurred this year. She took early retirement. She was born one second after midnight in 1946. A retired school teacher. There she is with [a] Social Security administrator. The first boomer actually, we didn't even wait till 2011, next year. We're already starting to see early retirement occur this year.

Alright, so it's here. This Y2K + 10 problem is at our door. This is 50 tsunamis scheduled on the calendar. But somehow we can't sort of marshal our government and innovative forces to sort of get out in front of it and do something about it. We'll wait until it's more of a catastrophe, and react, as opposed to prepare for it. So, one of the reasons it's so challenging to prepare for this Y2K problem is, I want to argue, we have what I would call mainframe poisoning.

Andy Grove, about six or seven years ago, he doesn't even know or remember this, in a *Fortune Magazine* article he used the phrase "mainframe health care," and I've been extending and expanding this. He saw it written down somewhere. He's like, "Eric that's a really cool concept." I was like, "Actually it was your idea. You said it in a *Fortune Magazine* article. I just extended it." You know, this is the mainframe.

This mentality of traveling to and timesharing large expensive health care systems actually began in 1787. This is the first general hospital in Vienna. And actually the second general hospital in Vienna in about 1850, was where we started to build [. . . an] entire curriculum for teaching med students specialties. And it's a place in which we started developing architecture that literally divided the body, and divided care into departments and compartments. And it was reflected in our architecture. It was reflected in the way that we taught students. And this mainframe mentality persists today.

Now, I'm not anti-hospital. With my own health care problems I've taken drug therapies, I've traveled to this hospital and others, many many times. But we worship the high hospital on a hill. Right? And this is mainframe health care. And just as 30 years ago we couldn't conceive that we would have the power of a mainframe computer that took up a room this size in our purses and on our belts, that we're carrying around in our cellphone today. And suddenly, computing, that used to be an expert driven system, it was a personal system that we all owned as part of our daily lives. That shift from mainframe to personal computing is what we have to do for health care. We have to shift from this mainframe mentality of health care to a personal model of health care.

We are obsessed with this way of thinking. When Intel does surveys all around the world and we say, "Quick response, health care." The first word that comes up is doctor. The second that comes up is hospital. And the third is illness or sickness. Right? We are wired, in our imagination, to think about health care and health care innovation as something that goes into that place. Our entire health reform discussion right now, health I.T., when we talk with policy makers equals how are we going to get doctors using electronic medical records in the mainframe? We're not thinking about how do we shift from the mainframe to the home. And the problem with this is the way we conceive health care. Right?

This is a very reactive, crisis-driven system. We're doing 15-minute exams with patients. It's population-based. We collect a bunch of biological information in this artificial setting. And we fix them up, like Humpty-Dumpty all over again, and send them home, and hope, we might hand them a brochure, maybe an interactive website, that they do as asked and don't come back into the mainframe.

And the problem is, we can't afford it today, folks. We can't afford mainframe health care today to include the uninsured. And now we want to do a double double of the age wave coming through? Business as usual in health care is broken and we've got to do something different. We've got to focus on the home.

We've got to focus on a personal health care paradigm that moves care to the home. How do we be more proactive, prevention-driven? How do we collect vital signs and other kinds of information 24x7? How do we get a personal baseline about what's going to work for you? How do we collect not just biological data but behavioral data, psychological data, relational data, in and on and around the home? And how do we drive compliance to be a customized care plan that uses all this great technology that's around us to change our behavior? That's what we need to do for our personal health model.

I want to give you a couple of examples. This is Mimi from one of our studies —in her 90s, had to move out of her home because her family was worried about falls. Raise your hand if you had a serious fall in your household, or any of your loved ones, your parents or so forth. Right? Classic. Hip fracture often leads to institutionalization of a senior. This is what was happening to Mimi, the family was worried about it, moved her out of her own home, into an assisted living facility. She tripped over her oxygen tank.

Many people in this generation won't press the button, even if they have an alert call system, because they don't want to bother anybody, even though they've been paying $30 dollars a month. Boomers will press the button. Trust me. They're going to be pressing that button non-stop. Right?

Mimi broke her pelvis, lay all night, all morning, finally somebody came in and found her, sent her to the hospital. They fixed her back up. She was never going to be able to move back into the assisted living. They put her into the nursing home unit. First night in the nursing home unit where she had been in the same assisted living facility, moved her from one bed to another, kind of threw her, rebroke her pelvis. sent her back to the hospital that she had just come from, no one read the chart, put her on Tylenol, which she is allergic to, broke out, got bedsores, basically, had heart problems, and died from the fall and the complications and the errors that were there.

Now, the most frightening thing about this is, this is my wife's grandmother. Now, I'm Eric Dishman. I speak English. I work for Intel. I make a good salary. I'm smart about falls and fall-related injuries. It's an area of research that I work on. I have access to senators and CEOs. I can't stop this from happening. What happens if you don't have money, you don't speak English, or don't have the kind of access to deal with these kinds of problems that inevitably occur? How do we actually prevent the vast majority of falls from ever occurring in the first place?

Let me give you a quick example of work that we're doing to try to do exactly that. I've been wearing a little technology that we call Shimmer. It's a research platform. It has accelerometry. You can plug in a three-lead ECG. There is all kinds of sort of plug and play kind of Legos that you can do to capture, in the wild, in the real world, things like tremor, gait, stride length, and those kinds of things.

The problem is, our understanding of falls, today, like Mimi, is get a survey in the mail, three months after you fell, from the state, saying "What were you doing when you fell?" That's sort of the state of the art. But with something like Shimmer, or we have something called the Magic Carpet, embedded sensors in carpet, or camera based systems that we borrowed from sports medicine, we're starting for the first time in those 600 elderly households to collect actual kinematic motion data to understand what are the subtle changes that are occurring that can show us that mom has become [a risk for falls].

And most often we can do two interventions, fix the meds mix. I'm a qualitative researcher, but when I look at these data streams coming in from these homes, I can look at the data and tell you the day that some doctor prescribed them something that nobody else knew that they were on. Because we see the changes in their patterns in the household. Right? These discoveries of behavioral markers, and behavioral changes are game-changing, and like the discovery of the microscope because of our collecting data streams that we've actually never done before.

This is an example in our Trill Clinic in Ireland of . . . actually what you're seeing is, she's looking at data in this picture, from the magic carpet. So, we have a little carpet that you can look at your amount of postural sway, and look at the changes in your postural sway over many months. Here's what some of this data might look like. This is actually sensor firings.

These are two different subjects in our study. It's about a year's worth of data. The color represents different rooms they are in the the house. This person on the left is living in their own home. This person on the right is actually living in an assisted living facility. I know this because look at how punctuated meal time is when they are no longer in their particular rooms here. Right? Now, this doesn't mean that much to you. But when we look at these cycles of data over a longer period of time, and we're looking at everything from motion around different rooms in the house, to sort of micro motions that Shimmer picks up, about gait and stride length, these streams of data are starting to tell us things about behavioral patterns that we've never understood before.

You can go to ORCATech.org—it has nothing to to with whales, it's the Oregon Center for Aging and Technology—to see more about that. The problem is, Intel is still one of the largest funders in world of independent living technology research. I'm not bragging about how much we fund, it's how little anyone else actually pays attention to aging and funds innovation on aging, chronic disease management, and independent living in the home.

So, my mantra here, my fourth slogan is: 10,000 households or bust. We need to drive a national, if not international, Framingham-type heart study of independent living technologies, where we have 10,000 elderly connected households with broadband, full medical characterization, and a platform by which we can start to experiment and turn these from 20 household anecdotal studies that the universities fund, to large clinical trials that prove out the value of these technologies. So, 10,000 households or bust. These are just some of the households that we've done in the Intel studies.

My fifth and final phrase: I have tried for two years, and there were moments when we were quite close, to make this health care reform bill be about reform from something and to something. From a mainframe model to a personal health model, or to mean something more than just a debate about the public option and how we're going to finance. It doesn't matter how we finance health care. We're going to figure something out for the next 10 years, and try it. No matter who pays for it, we better start doing care in a fundamentally different way and treating the home and the patient and the family member, and the caregivers as part of these coordinated care teams and using disruptive technologies that are already here to do care in some pretty fundamental different ways.

The president needs to stand up and say, at the end of a health care reform debate, "Our goal as a country is to move 50 percent of care out of institutions, clinics, hospitals, and nursing homes, to the home, in 10 years." It's achievable. We should do it economically. We should do it morally. And we should do it for quality of life. But there is no goal within this health reform. It's just a mess today.

So, you know, that's my last message to you. How do we set a going-to-the-moon goal of dealing with the Y2K +10 problem that's coming? It's not that innovation and technology is going to be the magic pill that cures all, but it's going to be part of the solution. And if we don't create a personal health movement, something that we're all aiming towards in reform, then we're going to move nowhere. So, I hope you'll turn this conference into that kind of movement [going] forward.

Thanks very much.

"Today, We Have the Opportunity to Complete the Great Unfinished Business of Our Society"*

Nancy Pelosi

Speaker of the House, 2007– ; born Baltimore, MD, March 26, 1940; B.A., Trinity College, Washington, D.C., 1962; northern chair, 1977–1981, state chair, 1981–83, California Democratic Party,; chair, Democratic National Convention Host Committee, 1984; finance chair, Democratic Senatorial Campaign Committee, 1985–86; U.S. representative (D), California, 1987– ; House Minority Whip, 2001–02; House Minority Leader, 2002–07.

Editor's introduction: The first woman in American history to serve as Speaker of the House, Nancy Pelosi was born into a political family in Baltimore, Maryland. Her father, Thomas D'Alesandro, Jr., was a congressman and the city's mayor; her brother, Thomas III, also enjoyed a term as Baltimore's chief executive. The early education she received in the turbulent world of big-city ethnic politics no doubt helped prepare Pelosi for her role in Congress and in shepherding the president's health care bill through that often fractious assembly. In this speech, delivered to her House colleagues just hours before what may be her crowning political achievement, Pelosi calls for the passage of historic national health care legislation. To rally her caucus, she invokes the words of such Democratic stalwarts as Congressman John Lewis and the late Senator Edward Kennedy. In the end, in the face of Republican intransigence and a divided public, and after generations of false starts, Congress passed the bill later that day and health care reform was soon signed into law by President Obama.

Nancy Pelosi's speech: Thank you, my colleagues. Thank you, Mr. Speaker. I thank the gentleman for yielding. I thank all of you for bringing us to this moment.

It is with great humility and with great pride that we tonight will make history for our country and progress for the American people. Just think—we will be joining those who established Social Security, Medicare, and now tonight health care for all Americans.

---

* Delivered on March 21, 2009, at Washington, D.C.

In doing so, we will honor the vows of our founders, who in the Declaration of Independence said that we are "endowed by our Creator with certain unalienable rights, that among these are life, liberty and the pursuit of happiness." This legislation will lead to healthier lives, more liberty to pursue hopes and dreams and happiness for the American people. This is an American proposal that honors the traditions of our country.

We would not be here tonight, for sure, without the extraordinary leadership and vision of President Barack Obama. We thank him for his unwavering commitment to health care for all Americans.

And this began over a year ago under his leadership in the American Recovery and Reinvestment Act, where we had very significant investments in science, technology, and innovation for health care reform. It continued in the president's budget a few months later, a budget which was a statement of our national values, which allocated resources that were part of our value system. And in a way that stabilized our economy, created jobs, lowered taxes for the middle class and did so, and reduced the deficit, and did so in a way that had pillars of investment, including education and health care reform—health care reform and education, equal opportunity for the American people.

And this legislation tonight, if I had one word to describe it [it] would be "opportunity," with its investments in education and health care as a continuation of the President's budget. We all know, and it has been said over and over again, that our economy needs something new, a jolt. And I believe that this legislation will unleash tremendous entrepreneurial power into our economy. Imagine a society and an economy where a person could change jobs without losing health insurance, where they could be self-employed or start a small business. Imagine an economy where people could follow their passions and their talent without having to worry that their children would not have health insurance, that if they had a child with diabetes who was bipolar or pre-existing medical condition in their family, that they would be job-locked. Under this bill, their entrepreneurial spirit will be unleashed.

We all know, we all know that the present health care system and insurance system, health insurance system in our country is unsustainable. We simply cannot afford it. It simply does not work for enough people in terms of delivery of service and it is bankrupting the country with the upward spiral of increasing medical costs.

The best action that we can take on behalf of America's family budgets and on behalf of the federal budget, is to pass health care reform.

The best action we can take to strengthen Medicare and improve care and benefits for our seniors is to pass this legislation tonight, pass health care reform.

The best action we can do to create jobs and strengthen our economic security is pass health care reform.

The best action we can take to keep America competitive, ignite innovation, again unleash entrepreneurial spirit is to pass health care reform.

With this action tonight, with this health care reform, 32 million more Americans will have health care insurance. And those who have insurance now will be spared being at the mercy of the health insurance industry with their obscene increases in premiums, their rescinding of policies at the time of illness, their cutting off of policies even if you have been fully paying but become sick. The list goes on and on about the health care reforms that are in this legislation: insure 32 million more people, make it more affordable for the middle class, end insurance company discrimination based on preexisting conditions, improve care and benefits under Medicare, and extending Medicare's solvency for almost a decade, creating a healthier America through prevention, through wellness and innovation, create 4 million jobs in the life of the bill, and doing all of that by saving the taxpayer $1.3 trillion dollars.

Another Speaker, Tip O'Neill, once said: "All politics is local." And I say to you tonight that when it comes to health care for all Americans, "All politics is personal."

It's personal for the family that wrote to me who had to choose between buying groceries and seeing a doctor. It's personal to the family who was refused coverage because their child had a pre-existing condition—no coverage, the child got worse, sicker. It's personal for women—after we pass this bill, being a woman will no longer be a pre-existing medical condition.

It's personal for a senior gentleman whom I met in Michigan, who told me about his wife who had been bedridden for 16 years. He told me he didn't know how he was going to be able to pay his medical bills. As I said to you before, I saw a grown man cry. He was worried that he might lose his home—that they might lose their home because of his medical bills and he didn't know how he was going to pay them. And most of all, he was too embarrassed to tell his children and ask them for help. How many times have you heard a story like that?

And it's personal for millions of families who've gone into bankruptcy under the weight of rising health care costs. In fact, many, many, many—a high percentage of bankruptcies in our country are caused by medical bills that people cannot pay. And it's personal for 45,000 Americans and their families who have lost a loved one each year because they didn't and couldn't get health insurance.

That is why we're proud and also humbled today to act with the support of millions of Americans who recognize the urgency of passing health care reform. And more than 350 organizations, representing Americans of every age, every background, every part of the country, who have endorsed this legislation. Our coalition ranges from the AARP, who said that our legislation "improves efforts to crack down on fraud and waste in Medicare, strengthening Medicare for today's seniors and future generations." I repeat: "Improves efforts to crack down on fraud and waste in Medicare, strengthening the program for today's and future generations of seniors." To the American Medical Association, the Catholic Health Association, the United Medical—the United Methodist Church, and Voices of America's Children. From A to Z—they are sending a clear message to Members of Congress: Say yes to health care reform.

We have also reached this historic moment because of the extraordinary leadership and hard work and dedication of all the members of Congress, but I want to especially recognize our esteemed Chairs—Mr. Waxman, Mr. Rangel, Mr. Levin, Mr. Miller, Mr. Spratt, Ms. Slaughter—for bringing this bill to the floor today. Let us acknowledge them.

And I want to acknowledge the staff of the committees and of the leadership—they have done a remarkable job—dazzling us with their knowledge and their know-how. I would like to thank on my own staff: Amy Rosenbaum, Wendell Primus, and Arshi Siddiqui.

And now, I want to just close by saying this. It would not be possible to talk about health care without acknowledging the great leadership of Senator Edward Kennedy, who made health care his life's work.

In a letter to President Obama before he passed away—he left the letter to be read after he died. Senator Kennedy wrote that: "Access to health care is the great unfinished business of our society." That is until today.

After more than a year of debate, and by the way, the legislation that will go forth from here has over 200 Republican amendments, and while it may not get Republican votes and be bipartisan in that respect, it is bipartisan in having over 200 Republican amendments.

After a year of debate and hearing the calls of millions of Americans, we have come to this historic moment. Today, we have the opportunity to complete the great unfinished business of our society and pass health insurance reform for all Americans that is a right and not a privilege.

In that same letter to the president, Senator Kennedy wrote, what is "at stake" he said, "At stake are not just the details of policy but . . . the character of our country."

Americans will look back on this day as one which we honored the character of our country and honored our commitment to our nation's founders for a commitment to "life, liberty, and the pursuit of happiness."

As our colleague John Lewis has said, "We may not have chosen the time, but the time has chosen us." We have been given this opportunity. [. . .] I urge my colleagues in joining together in passing health insurance reform—making history, making progress, and restoring the American dream.

I urge an aye vote. Thank you.

"Hell No, You Can't!"*

John Boehner

House Minority Leader, 2007– ; born Reading, Ohio, November 17, 1949; bachelor's degree in business, Xavier University, 1977; various positions including president, Nucite Sales, 1977–1982; trustee, Union Township, Butler County, 1982–84; Ohio state representative, 1985–1990; U.S. representative (R), Ohio, 1990– ; chairman, House Republican Conference, 1995–99; chairman, House Education and the Workforce Committee, 2001–06; House Majority Leader, 2006.

Editor's introduction: After a year of rancorous debate over health care reform legislation, on March 21, 2010, the House of Representatives prepared to vote on the final bill. John Boehner, the Republican leader in Congress, took to the floor to passionately denounce the legislation and to cast shame on his colleagues for ignoring the will of the people. With a striking parody of the "Yes, We Can" slogan popularized by Barack Obama in the 2008 presidential race, Boehner structures part of his speech around rhetorical questions to his fellow representatives about whether they could assert that the pending legislation was crafted openly and transparently. His reply: "Hell no, you can't!" In many ways, Boehner's speech channeled the anger and suspicion generated by the president's proposed health care initiatives and which had been on display at townhall meetings and Tea Party rallies across the country. Not long after Boehner's speech, Congress passed the bill largely on a party-line vote, with not a single Republican supporting it.

John Boehner's speech: Mr. Speaker and my colleagues, I rise tonight with a sad and heavy heart.

Today, we should be standing together, reflecting on a year of bipartisanship, and working to answer our country's call and their challenge to address the rising costs of health insurance in our country.

Today, this body, this institution, enshrined in the first article of the Constitution by our Founding Fathers as a sign of the importance they placed on this House, should be looking with pride on this legislation and our work.

---

* Delivered on March 21, 2010, at Washington, D.C.

But it is not so.

No, today we're standing here looking at a health care bill that no one in this body believes is satisfactory.

Today we stand here amidst the wreckage of what was once the respect and honor that this House was held in by our fellow citizens.

And we all know why it is so.

We have failed to listen to America.

And we have failed to reflect the will of our constituents.

And when we fail to reflect that will—we fail ourselves and we fail our country.

Look at this bill.

Ask yourself: do you really believe that if you like the health plan that you have, that you can keep it?

No, you can't.

In this economy, with this unemployment, with our desperate need for jobs and economic growth, is this really the time to raise taxes, to create bureaucracies, and burden every job creator in our land?

The answer is no.

Can you go home and tell your senior citizens that these cuts in Medicare will not limit their access to doctors or further weaken the program instead of strengthening it?

No, you cannot.

Can you go home and tell your constituents with confidence that this bill respects the sanctity of all human life, and that it won't allow for taxpayer funding of abortion for the first time in 30 years?

No, you cannot.

And look at how this bill was written.

Can you say it was done openly, with transparency and accountability? Without backroom deals, and struck behind closed doors, hidden from the people?

Hell no, you can't!

Have you read the bill? Have you read the reconciliation bill? Have you read the manager's amendment?

Hell no, you haven't!

Mr. Speaker, in a few minutes, we will cast some of the most consequential votes that any of us will ever cast in this chamber.

The decision we make will affect every man, woman, and child in this nation for generations to come.

If we're going to vote to defy the will of the American people, then we ought to have the courage to stand before them and announce our votes, one at a time.

I sent a letter to the Speaker this week asking that the "call of the roll" be ordered for this vote.

Madame Speaker, I ask you. Will you, in the interest of this institution, grant my request?

Will you, Mr. Speaker, grant my request that we have a call of the roll?

Mr. Speaker, will you grant my request that we have a call of the roll?

My colleagues, this is the People's House.

When we came here, we each swore an oath to uphold and abide by the Constitution as representatives of the people.

But the process here is broken.

The institution is broken.

And as a result, this bill is not what the American people need, nor what our constituents want.

Americans are out there . . . making sacrifices and struggling to build a better future for their kids.

And over the last year as the damn-the-torpedoes outline of this legislation became more clear, millions lifted their voices, and many for the first time, asking us to slow down, not try to cram through more than the system could handle.

Not to spend money that we didn't have.

In this time of recession, they wanted us to focus on jobs, not more spending, not more government, certainly not more taxes.

But what they see today frightens them.

They're frightened because they don't know what comes next.

They're disgusted, because they see one political party closing out the other from what should be a national solution.

And they are angry. They are angry that no matter how they engage in this debate, this body moves forward against their will.

Shame on us.

Shame on this body.

Shame on each and every one of you who substitutes your will and your desires above those of your fellow countrymen.

Around this chamber, looking upon us are the lawgivers—from Moses, to Gaius, to Blackstone, to Thomas Jefferson.

By our actions today, we disgrace their values.

We break the ties of history in this chamber.

We break our trust with Americans.

When I handed the Speaker the gavel in 2007, I said: "this is the people's House— and the moment a majority forgets this, it starts writing itself a ticket to minority status."

If we pass this bill, there will be no turning back. It will be the last straw for the American people.

And in a democracy, you can only ignore the will of the people for so long and get away with it.

And if we defy the will of our fellow citizens and pass this bill, we are going to be held to account by those who have placed us in their trust.

We will have shattered those bonds of trust.

I beg you. I beg each and every one of you on both sides of the aisle.

Do not further strike at the heart of this country and this institution with arrogance, for surely you will not strike with impunity.

I ask each of you to vow never to let this happen again—this process, this defiance of our citizens.

It is not too late to begin to restore the bonds of trust with our Nation and return comity to this institution.

And so, join me.

Join me in voting against this bill, so that we may come together anew, and address this challenge of health care in a manner that brings credit to this body, and brings credit to the ideals of this nation, and most importantly, it reflects the will our people.

Federalism Under Attack[*]

How Obamacare Turns Citizens into Government Minions

Thomas Feeney

Senior Visiting Fellow, The Heritage Foundation, 2009– ; born Abington, PA, May 21, 1958; bachelor's degree, Penn State University, 1980; J.D., University of Pittsburgh School of Law, 1983; private practice, Oviedo, Florida, 1983–1990; member (R), Florida House of Representatives, 1991–94; director, James Madison Institute, 1994–96; member (R), 1997–2003, speaker, 2000–03, Florida House of Representatives; U.S. representative (R), Florida, 2003–09.

Editor's introduction: In this speech, presented at a conference on state health insurance reform at the conservative Heritage Foundation, Thomas Feeney argues that the recently passed health care bill represents an encroachment on federalism and individual liberties. Citing the Constitution's Commerce Clause, which assigns powers not explicitly granted to the federal government to the states, he posits that the legislation's requirement that all citizens have health insurance is not supported by the Constitution.

Thomas Feeney's speech: At the time of the 2008 presidential election, a majority of American voters were desperate for virtually any political program that could be sold as "Hope and Change." For many of those same voters, their initial optimism has been replaced by reality and frustration over the dramatic expansion of federal control over decisions that, in America, have historically been made at the individual, community, local, or state levels.

For some, the last straw was health care policy. Indeed, a majority of Americans have expressed concern, skepticism, or downright outrage at the recent health care bill passed by Democrats in Congress and signed by President Barack Obama.

It is easy for advocates of limited constitutional government to get discouraged these days, considering the near-daily national encroachments on individual liberty and the federalist balance in American government. It was Winston Churchill

---

[*] Delivered on April 12, 2010, at Washington, D.C. Reprinted with permission.

who said: "The American people will always do the right thing, after they have tried everything else."

Until American government runs out of bad policies to attempt, citizens' fear of their own government will continue to grow. There are many reasons for this. An important one is a traditional and cultural American suspicion of nationalist encroachment into state, local, or individual decisions. Indeed, Amendment I of the Bill of Rights begins with the declaration that "Congress shall make no law respecting" the following matters: religion, speech, press, assembly, and petitions to government.

On its face, the First Amendment does not restrain state or local governments from doing anything. This country's Founders were concerned with limits not on the states, but on the national government. The last of the Bill of Rights is, of course, the Tenth Amendment, which states that "The powers not delegated to the United States by the Constitution, nor prohibited by it to the States, are reserved to the States respectively, or to the people."

As Alexis de Tocqueville wrote in his masterpiece *Democracy in America*, "The most favorable form of government ever created to promote the prosperity and freedom of man was the federalist system." Writing more than half a century after the adoption of the U.S. Constitution, Tocqueville recognized the inherent beauty and benefits of our form of government.

Tocqueville also warned that undermining our Founders' federalist design and allowing nationalist micromanagement of local and individual decisions would turn all Americans into "minions of an omnipotent government."

THE COMMERCE CLAUSE

America's Founders had Tocqueville's concerns decades earlier: The Founders confined federal control of trade and commercial dealings to activity with foreign sovereigns or "between" different states.

Shortly after the Revolution but before ratification of the Constitution, several states had imposed taxes or regulations on goods imported from sister states, which often retaliated. Some states had begun to punish sister states at such a level that many political leaders feared that economic warfare between the states would lead to dissolution of the Union.

To promote commerce and stop trade wars among the states, Congress included the Commerce Clause in Article I, Section 8 of the Constitution, which describes the powers of Congress. The Commerce Clause provides in full that Congress has the power "To regulate Commerce with foreign Nations, and among the several States, and with the Indian tribes." Intrastate dealings were left to the states to manage.

The Obama health care law exceeds any Commerce Clause power by mandating fines for American citizens who do not purchase federally approved health insurance. But a decision not to purchase a specific good or service is not activity "among the several States," nor is it "Commerce." It is not a legitimate constitutional power of the federal government.

Preserving federalism is good for prosperity, Tocqueville pointed out. In fact, this was the Founders' design. Both individual freedom and personal wealth are protected by constitutional limits on the federal government. As Thomas Jefferson said, "If we were told what to reap and what to [sow] by a federal government, we should soon want for food."

Or, as my favorite economist of our lifetime, Milton Friedman, put it, "If we put the federal government in charge of the Sahara Desert, there would soon be a shortage of sand."

As James Madison described it, "The powers delegated by the . . . Constitution to the federal government are few and defined," while "[t]hose which are to remain in the State governments are numerous and indefinite." The Commerce Clause was a key component of limiting national government.

Unfortunately, in response to the New Deal, the U.S. Supreme Court has incrementally misinterpreted the Commerce Clause to allow Congress to micromanage virtually any behavior. For example, sales of milk by a farmer to a neighbor within the same state were found constitutionally unacceptable on the tenuous theory that local wheat sales by a single farmer impacted wheat prices nationally.

In 1942, the Supreme Court decided in *Wickard v. Filburn* to uphold a federal quota on sales against a farmer who grew a small amount of wheat, most of which was consumed on his own farm. Even though the farmer sold just a minute amount of wheat to his local neighbors, any wheat grown increased the total national supply. A farmer taking excess crops to market a few miles away was now engaged in "interstate commerce"!

RESTORING PROPER PERSPECTIVE

Recently, for the first time in 50 years, the majority of the Supreme Court has begun to put the Commerce Clause in proper perspective—allowing Congress to intervene in sales only if a state law adversely impacts commerce between citizens of different states.

In *United States v. Lopez* in 1995, in a revolutionary restoration of traditional jurisprudence, the Supreme Court struck down a congressional act as violating the long-dormant Commerce Clause. The court held that a "federal" law criminalizing possession of a firearm on school property trampled on the "general police power of the sort retained by the states."

No Supreme Court has ever ruled that Congress could mandate that individuals purchase a particular good or service. Many state attorneys general and governors have brought suit to challenge this and other aspects of nationalized health care law passed in April 2010.

State legislators have the right and obligation to fight for the preservation of federalism and state government prerogatives. If the federal government can micromanage personal health care decisions, state legislatures may as well be dissolved, as our nationalized government has turned them into administrators and tax collectors for a nationalized welfare state. And we, the citizens, have become "minions of omnipotent government."

Nationalization of decisions historically made by individuals, communities, and states is not just confined to health care. The traditional balance of limited federal control is increasingly being undermined by Congress and the executive branch in education policy, water use and environmental regulations, banking, and insurance.

A WATERSHED IN THE FIGHT FOR LIBERTY

Nationalization of health care is a watershed in the fight for American liberty. The Congress has attempted to undermine a fundamental constitutional principle. Citizens and state leaders across the nation are rebelling against usurpation of powers rightfully left to state governments.

Instead of acquiescence in this unprecedented power grab, legislatures, governors, and other policymakers should continue to reject the federal mandates and push for repeal and reform of the new health care legislation. Legislators take the same oath to uphold the U.S. Constitution as do members of Congress, Supreme Court justices, and presidents. As the great Senator Daniel Webster famously said:

> Hold on, my friends, to the Constitution of the United States of America and the republic for which it stands. Miracles do not cluster, and what has happened once in 6,000 years may never happen again. Hold on to your Constitution, for if the American Constitution should fail, there will be anarchy throughout the world.

Why the Health Reform Wars Have Only Just Begun[*]

Stuart M. Butler

Vice President for Domestic and Economic Policy Studies, The Heritage Foundation, 1980–2010; born Shrewsbury, England, July 21, 1947; B.S., 1968, M.A., 1971, Ph.D., 1978, University of St. Andrews, Scotland; author, Enterprise Zones: Greenlining the Inner City *(1981),* Privatizing Federal Spending: A Strategy to Eliminate the Deficit *(1985),* .

Editor's introduction: In this address, delivered to the Cancer Quality Alliance, Stuart Butler predicts major unanticipated changes to the health care system resulting from the reform legislation passed by Congress and signed by the president. Among the vital issues he describes are the question of whether the state or federal government will control the new health care exchanges and how much power such centralized bodies as the Office of Personnel Management (OPM) will exert over health care. In contrast to what proponents of the legislation have pledged, Butler contends that subsidies provided for by the new system could end employer-sponsored insurance by encouraging migration to exchange plans. He argues that many of the predicted reductions in costs are illusory and will not survive congressional meddling. Finally, he proposes three true cost-cutting measures: increasing regulation, granting centralized bodies greater power to allocate and restrict spending, and placing limits on total public health care spending.

Stuart M. Butler's speech: Whenever major bills are enacted, they create a dynamic that causes the programs or system they reform to evolve in often unanticipated ways, frequently requiring important additional decisions down the road. The recent health legislation is a classic example. If it does indeed go into effect as scheduled over the next several years, it will trigger profound changes that will force big decisions over the next several years, implying huge changes for insured Americans.

With a bill this large, and with so many of its provisions intertwined, it is impossible to predict its effects with certainty. As Henry Aaron and Robert Reischauer

---

* Delivered on May 6, 2010, at Washington, D.C. Reprinted with permission.

explained in a recent article, just the timetable for implementation is a political and technical minefield fraught with uncertainty.[1] As the authors point out, the long phase-in of provisions means that there will be many opportunities for Congress to alter or reverse some of the key provisions. Moreover, the administrative changes and ambiguities in the legislation mean that controversial aspects of the legislation will have to be revisited. Thus, many obstacles still confront this legislation, and many Americans believe strongly that the legislation should be substantially changed, cut back, or repealed entirely.

As Americans begin to digest the legislation, they will indeed find many aspects of the law that surprise them and discover also that major decisions have yet to be made.

A FLAWED STRATEGY: AVOID DISCUSSING DETAILS WITH THE PUBLIC

To be sure, the scale of the bill itself made it very difficult during passage for anybody, including those who wrote it, to be fully aware of all its features and implications. But proponents of the legislation generally decided as a strategy not to conduct a detailed conversation with Americans about the long-term changes the legislation would trigger.

Why? Because that strategy was the conventional wisdom among health reformers in the years running up to the reform effort. After the demise of President Bill Clinton's reform effort, a theory took hold that major health reform could be enacted only if proponents avoided a detailed conversation with the public about its likely impacts. The line of argument was that health care is so complex that people would necessarily be confused by the conversation. That confusion would lead to anxiety and then to opposition stoked up by health industry interest groups.

So, the theory went, health reform must be portrayed to Americans in positive generalities. Furthermore, the legislative action must be conducted quickly in order to avoid the public getting lost in the weeds and then becoming confused and anxious and increasingly resistant to change.

The flaws with this operational theory quickly began to appear when President Barack Obama started to advocate health reform. We live in the age of the Internet, Twitter, and blogs, so details of each phase of the legislation leaked out of Washington in seconds and within days were featured in rowdy town hall meetings. The new media rendered the "Keep it simple, stupid" theory impractical. Worse still, once Americans discovered specific items in the legislation that they had not been told about or that seemed to contradict rosy assurances that little would change for the insured, they became increasingly distrustful and angry, and opposition became more intense.

This public reaction does not augur well for the future stages of the reform legislation's rollout. The distrust and anger that built up during the legislative phase will have new targets as decision points are reached in the timetable for implementation. It increases the probability that strong opposition will develop against core elements of the reform measure, perhaps even the entire legislation, as the public focuses on them and when important decisions have to be made—such as when Congress has to decide on future recommendations for savings by the new Medicare commission. This strong undertow of public distrust and anger may be sufficient to block, delay, or transform major features of the statute that have yet to go into effect.

FOUR CRITICAL AREAS OF CONTENTION

Consider just four aspects that will mean profound changes and critical decisions in the years to come. Each underscores both the degree of change that the public will encounter and likely future battles.

1. Who will control the health exchanges?

The concept of a health exchange is to provide the equivalent of a farmers market or shopping mall through which individuals and families can choose the health plan that is best for them and retain it from job to job. In principle, such exchanges are a very welcome improvement on the current employer-based system because they make it possible for families to exercise choice and effective ownership of their health coverage. They also facilitate portability. So the generic idea of an exchange has had broad support among analysts and lawmakers.

Unfortunately, the version enacted by Congress is not generic. It places sweeping requirements on plans that can offer coverage through an exchange. The legislation will also ignite a struggle between the federal government and the states over who will have effective control of the exchanges.

On the face of it, the states "won" the initial skirmish because Congress chose to go with the state-led exchange approach of the Senate version rather than the House's much more centralized national exchange approach. That decision might seem to open the way for a variety of state exchanges, which would encourage innovation and exchanges that more closely reflect the circumstances and political decisions of individual states.

This is the case today, with wide diversity in the exchanges already implemented or being considered. For example, the Massachusetts "Connector" is a highly regulated exchange with considerable additional powers given to the exchange management so that it is one integral component of the state's entire strategy for health coverage and budgeting. Meanwhile, Utah has opted instead for a far more "hands-off" approach—in effect a lightly regulated Expedia.com for health insurance.

Under the new legislation, however, states like Utah will face considerable federal intrusion into their exchange structure when this part of the legislation goes fully into effect in 2014. Health plans in the exchange will have to conform to very tight federal requirements. Moreover, this could be just the beginning of increasing federal control. In all probability, some of the committees in Congress that are responsible for the federal components of the exchange will seek to strengthen the federal role. Also, the Obama Administration's preference for a more uniform ex-change system means the rulemaking and administrative decisions accompanying the legislation will seek to push the envelope on federal control.

There was a similar pattern after the State Children's Health Insurance Program (SCHIP) was enacted in 1997. The legislation gave states wide flexibility to choose methods of covering children, but states needed to obtain federal approval for their method, and the Clinton Administration used the approval process to push states to use its preferred methods of coverage. It seems likely that the Obama Adminis-tration will adopt a similar strategy.

So the design and control of health exchanges is likely to become one of the federal–state battlegrounds that will play out over the next months and years. And right now, given the language in the legislation, the federal government has the upper hand. If indeed the federal government succeeds in molding the exchanges to the full extent that would be possible under the legislation, the result will be a system that differs little from a national exchange with strong federal control. That, in turn, will mean that health plans will evolve into a more standardized industry with tight premium regulation and benefit design. If that proves to be the case, health insurance in the future will look much more like a regulated public utility than a variety of products offered through a farmers market for insurance.[2]

2. Why the "OPM alternative" could develop into a strong public plan.

Proponents of a public option were said to have suffered a severe setback when Congress dropped the House's proposal and instead chose a Senate proposal to create a selection of private national plans to be managed by the Office of Person-nel Management (OPM), the agency that currently runs the Federal Employees Health Benefits Program (FEHBP). However, in reality, this decision by Congress may actually open up the path to a much tougher public plan option than even House advocates imagined.[3]

The first reason for this is that OPM already has considerable powers to regulate FEHBP's private plans, including national plans through Blue Cross and other carriers. But today, OPM does not choose to use these powers fully. In part, this is because the culture of OPM is to be a fairly traditional benefits manager for employees. This contrasts strongly with the regulatory culture at the Centers for Medicare and Medicaid Services (CMS) and the current White House.

However, if a bureau is set up within OPM to operate the new private national plans and this is staffed by officials who share the CMS perspective, the private national plans that are offered are likely to operate as private entities in name only. In fact, the OPM bureau running the new program could so regulate the plans un-der OPM's current rules that they would effectively be administrators of a public option.

Second, the legislation would give even more powers to the new government managers housed at OPM.[4] The act requires OPM to negotiate medical-loss ratios, minimum benefits, premiums, profit margins, and "such other terms and condi-tions of coverage as are in the interests of enrollees in such plans." So the provision in the legislation to create a network of national private plans is likely to become another battleground as it becomes clearer that the "private" national plans will be so regulated and administered that they are virtually indistinguishable from a public option—and arguably an option managed with more executive branch discretion than even the House's version.

3. How reform could mean the end of employer-sponsored insurance.

Despite all the talk of avoiding any disruption of the current system of employer-sponsored insurance, the legislation actually seems destined to accelerate the steady decline of that form of coverage. To be sure, there are many good reasons to move away from the current employer-based system, but that is plainly not what Americans have been told the legislation will accomplish.

The reason for this prognosis is that the statute creates several new incentives for employers to move away from providing coverage. For instance, mandates and "pay or play" provisions might seem to be a tool to prop up the current system in the short term. But over time, the combination of regulations, new taxes on insurance products, and limitations on employers' flexibility to design benefits will induce many firms to drop coverage and most new firms to decide not to offer it.

Moreover, the erosion is likely to increase sharply once employers and their employees focus on the huge subsidy differential for families between exchange-based plans and employer-based plans. Modest-income families who obtain their coverage through the exchange will be able to receive subsidies in the range of $10,000 or more to offset the cost of their coverage—which will be portable from job to job. On the other hand, families with roughly the same income who obtain coverage through their place of work will receive a subsidy in the form of tax relief (from income and payroll taxes) for the employer's contribution to the health plan—in the range of $1,000 for non-portable coverage. In addition, certain employers will face "fines" of $3,000 for any low-income employee who exercises a new legal right to drop the employer's coverage in order to enroll in a subsidized exchange plan.

These numbers mean that many employers who currently provide coverage—and their employees—will have an enormous financial incentive to cash out their existing health benefits and distribute the value as extra cash income, after which the employees can obtain heavily subsidized coverage through the exchange and essentially receive thousands of dollars in additional compensation. Congressional staff were aware of this potential problem and sought to avoid this potential trend by creating various "firewalls" designed to make it very difficult for individual employees to move from employer-sponsored insurance to coverage provided through the exchange.

But the huge inequity in subsidy levels between the two sectors is likely to spark great anger when it becomes evident to Americans. Some lawmakers may try to "fix" the problem by adding new subsidies to employer-sponsored coverage so that the differential is not so great. Doing that was considered in the early days of the legislation. However, creating large new subsidies for employer-sponsored insurance to try to limit the erosion would be extremely expensive, which is why it was rejected when the legislation was formulated. There are modest and temporary subsidies to smaller employers in the legislation to encourage them to offer insurance, but these are unlikely to have much impact.

Alternatively, the differential could in principle be reduced by paring down the subsidies for families within the exchange, but that would encounter resistance since it would reduce the coverage levels in the exchanges and increase family costs. Or lawmakers presumably could stand back and allow the erosion of employer-sponsored coverage to accelerate.

Given these stark and controversial choices, it is likely that this feature of the new health system will become another major battleground.

4. Tackling the inevitable rise in government health spending.

The sponsors of the health legislation have promised a future in which coverage and quality will improve while the total spending "cost curve" will trend down. "Bending the cost curve" downwards was a dubious proposition at the outset.

The common argument was that improving the efficiency of delivery and services at the "street" level would inevitably lead to a reduction in total health spending, but this line of economic reasoning is fallacious. As we see in many sectors of the economy, from cell phones and computers to automobiles, there is no direct connection between greater efficiency and better pricing of individual goods and services and the total expenditure on these good and services in the economy: It depends. As the unit price of computers has declined sharply, for instance, total expenditures have climbed rapidly. Total spending on a product or service is related to how people value it compared with other potential uses of their money.

In health care, economists point out that most people are insulated from the direct costs of health services through insurance or public plans, such as Medicare, so the demand for health care is far less limited by underlying prices than, say, the demand for computers and automobiles—where most people face the full cost of the product. So if we continue to insulate patients from prices at the point of consumption, improved efficiency, quality, and availability of health care most likely will increase the trend-line of total spending over time, not reduce it.

That underlying economic reality about health care is likely to be exacerbated by the health legislation. Indeed, most authorities, including the Congressional Budget Office (CBO), have forecast that the spending trend-line will go up rather than go down. Even then, the CBO's forecast is likely to prove overly optimistic regarding future spending. There are several reasons for that. Among them:

- Limiting the tax exclusions has been seen by economists as a critical incentive to discourage excess demand for health care at the workplace, but the limits on the tax exclusion for employer-sponsored coverage, dubbed the "Cadillac tax," were watered down in the legislation and delayed until 2018. While the CBO adjusted its forecast accordingly, most Washington insiders are skeptical that a controversial tax delayed for that long will ever actually be implemented.

- The CBO projection assumes that physicians' fees in the Medicare program will be cut by about one-fifth this year and then kept on a lower trajectory, as the law prescribes. This fee cut is a major part of the savings to be achieved in Medicare spending. But this approach to reducing Medicare costs has been in place since 1997 and in recent years has been routinely "fixed" (i.e., reversed by Congress) each year. The ink was barely dry on the legislation before a major effort was mounted to "fix" the fee savings (i.e., repeal them) permanently. If, as seems probable, the fee cut is routinely postponed or permanently eliminated, this will add substantially to health spending in the future.

- The legislation creates a commission that will propose major savings in the Medicare program in the form of payment reductions—savings that were considered too controversial for lawmakers to specify in the legislation—and future Congresses will implement the commission's proposals or change them to achieve the equivalent cuts. But if Congresses in the future prove to be no more courageous than the current one, these projected savings will prove illusory.

- The legislation includes a major new program for disability and long-term care services. Given that it is CBO practice only to provide estimates for legislation over the next 10 years, this new program, the Community Living Assistance Services and Support (CLASS) Act, is actually what one might call a "profit center." That's because it is projected, on net, to bring in revenue to the federal government over the next decade, because premium revenue precedes the large benefit payments in future years. While the law gives the Secretary of Health and Human Services (HHS) the power to raise premiums to keep up with benefit outlays, one would have to be an optimist to believe that Congress will go along with that. Indeed, after the first decade, expenditures will increase to such a degree that the chief actuary of HHS has declared the program unsustainable.

Given these features of the legislation and the lack of downward pressure on spending in the health system, the problem of ever-rising health expenditures as a proportion of the economy is likely to become acute within the next decade. The resulting strains on the federal budget and rising concerns from foreign lenders about America's soaring debt are likely to increase demands for new steps to try to slow down total health spending.

But while there will no doubt be much wishful thinking on how to do this painlessly, basically only three broad strategies have been advanced over the years as possible ways to keep the public cost of health spending within bounds. We can expect a vigorous debate in the years to come between proponents of each one, and whichever strategy prevails, Americans are going to experience significant changes in their access to health care services.

Strategy #1: Increase the direct regulation of prices and payments in the health care system.

This strategy would mean even tighter price and payment controls in the public programs, and many lawmakers would likely urge extending such controls throughout private health care in an effort to slow down general health cost. A problem with this approach is that the many centuries of world experience with price controls is hardly encouraging, including their attendant shortages, gaming, and inequities and poor results in controlling spending.

The political advantage is that, at the outset, direct price controls tend to be popular, as they probably would seem to be when applied to such areas as pharmaceutical prices and insurance premiums. But once the effects of the controls start to work through the system, leading to such things as restricted formularies, longer waiting lines, physicians withdrawing from Medicare, etc., public support is likely to ebb. Nonetheless, if health spending soars above the trajectory promised in the legislation, tighter price and payment controls are very likely to be proposed, and if they are implemented, there will be new limits on access to care.

Strategy #2: Give greater powers to bodies like the new Medicare commission to make decisions about the allocation and volume of health care resources and to place limits on access to those services.

An alternative to trying to limit spending levels by controlling prices is to directly allocate and restrict spending on services. This is a strategy undertaken in many other countries, most notably through the National Institute for Health and Clinical Excellence (NICE) in the United Kingdom. It involves giving considerable powers to an administrative agency while reducing the powers of the public or the legislature to circumvent or block the agency's decisions.

The U.S. reform legislation takes a step in this direction by creating an Independent Payment Advisory Board (IPAB) to propose changes in Medicare to reach spending targets (though the board can only alter payments, not change such things as eligibility). Significantly, the board's proposal will be given "fast track" consideration by Congress and will go into effect unless Congress enacts alternative steps to achieve the same savings.

If spending is not curbed under the new law, there will likely be calls to strengthen the IPAB and widen the policy tools it can use. Some proponents of the commission strategy will probably also propose similar bodies for other aspects of the health system beyond Medicare in the same way that Britain's NICE is able to do. Indeed, Donald Berwick, nominated to be administrator of CMS, is a declared fan of NICE, describing it as a "global treasure."

If Americans were to pursue that approach, it would mean a shift in the locus of health decision-making power over access to care to an appointed board, with less ability for Americans directly or through their elected representatives to alter those decisions. It is worth noting that in the debate over the reform legislation, Americans appeared quite resistant to the idea of boards preempting decisions by their health providers or Congress.

Strategy #3: Place a direct limit on total public spending for health care.

A more direct way of controlling the growth of government spending on health care is to end the open-ended entitlement commitment to publicly supported health spending (in which the "budget" is really just a projection) and replace it with a real budget that limits the government's financial exposure. In effect, it would make the federal health budget a "defined contribution" rather than a "defined benefit."

Fixed budgets of this kind are quite familiar to managers of "discretionary" programs, such as defense, education, or highways, as they are to health program managers in most other countries. In addition to a budget for public funds, there could also be a budget for tax subsidies—principally the individual tax exclusion for employer-sponsored insurance—which would imply an adjustable cap on tax relief.

A bipartisan group of budget analysts (including this author) have proposed applying long-term (perhaps 30-year) budgets to entitlement programs such as Social Security, Medicare, and Medicaid.[5] Their proposal would allow the budget for these programs to be reassessed every five years, but it would end the "auto-pilot" status of public funds for major health care programs and make the 30-year budget the default.

If public funds for health care were subject to a real budget in this way, it would clearly have a direct impact on the future spending trend-line. It would also raise critical issues that would have to be settled in the future. For one thing, the long-term budget would have to be designed in such a way that it balanced the reduced taxpayer financial risk associated with a defined contribution budget and the increased financial risk for Medicare enrollees and other beneficiaries of programs. That said, one of the key objectives of a defined contribution budget is to use greater cost-consciousness to encourage beneficiaries to seek better value for money and so temper the growth in health care costs and hence the future cost of the programs.

If such a limited budget were put into place, it could be allocated using two approaches, or a combination of the two.

A budget for service providers. One approach would be for the government to allocate funds directed to facilities and institutions (as, say, Canada and Britain do). The major decisions over the availability and type of resources would lie with the government and providers.

In this case, the beneficiary's services would depend on those decision-makers. So Americans would have to ponder whether the agency, board, or legislature would distribute budgeted funds in a manner they believed to be fair and effective, and whether their particular needs or concerns would be appropriately considered.

An "individual" budget, or voucher. The other approach would be to distribute the budget to program beneficiaries for them to use to choose the plans or services that they thought would best meet their needs. This could be accomplished though some form of income- and risk-adjusted "voucher" for purchasing coverage—

sometimes called "premium-support." Federal employees have a version of this system, since the government pays a percentage of their premiums up to a limit, and they are responsible for the remainder of the plan they choose.

In this case, the beneficiaries' own decisions would determine how the budget was distributed. So Americans would have to consider whether the formula for calculating their voucher properly reflected their income and medical needs and whether they had the information to make good choices.

CONCLUSION: BIG DECISIONS STILL LIE AHEAD

The health care legislation passed in 2010 will have profound implications well beyond the high-profile elements that attracted most public attention during the debate. Attention will turn to each of these less obvious features if the legislation is fully implemented on schedule.

For example, a struggle will ensue over who ultimately controls the new health exchanges—the states or the federal government. How that is resolved could determine the nature of health insurance in this country. The so-called OPM alternative to the seemingly deep-sixed public option will soon be seen to be an end-run for that option. If that remains on the statute book, we could see a far stronger public option than anyone thought possible. Employers and employees will wake up to the fact—indeed, many already are doing so—that the legislation will speed up the erosion of employer-based insurance. Will that be allowed to happen? And rosy projections that health spending will taper down will most likely quickly prove to be an illusion. If—and however—Congress responds to all this, it will mean big changes in access to services and control over the system. As these and other features become clearer to more and more Americans, they will have a lot to say about what should happen. The health reform battle is far from over.

FOOTNOTES

1. Henry Aaron and Robert Reischauer, "The War Isn't Over," *New England Journal of Medicine*, Vol. 362, No. 14 (April 8, 2010), pp. 1259–1261, at http://content.nejm.org/cgi/content/full/362/14/1259 (June 25, 2010).

2. See Stuart M. Butler, "Risking Big Changes with Small Reforms," *New England Journal of Medicine*, Vol. 362, No. 8 (February 25, 2010), pp. 673–675, at http://content.nejm.org/cgi/content/full/362/8/673 (June 25, 2010).

3. Ibid.

4. Ibid.

5. See, for example, Joseph Antos, Robert Bixby, Stuart Butler, Paul Cullinan, Alison Fraser, William Galston, Ron Haskins, Julia Isaacs, Maya MacGuineas, Will Marshall, Pietro Nivola, Rudolph Penner, Robert Reischauer, Alice M. Rivlin, Isabel Sawhill, and C. Eugene Steuerle, "Taking Back Our Fiscal Future," The Brookings Institution and The Heritage Foundation, April 2008, at http://s3.amazonaws.com/thf_media/2008/pdf/wp0408.pdf (June 25, 2010).

2

Financial and Regulatory Reform

Speech at the National Press Club[*]

Barney Frank

U.S. representative (D), Massachusetts, 1981– ; born Bayonne, NJ, March 31, 1940; bachelor's degree, Harvard University, 1962; graduate studies toward Ph.D., 1962–68; J.D., Harvard Law School, 1977; chief assistant to Boston mayor Kevin White, 1968–1971; administrative assistant to Congressman Michael J. Harrington, 1971–72; representative, Massachusetts House of Representatives, 1973–1981.

Editor's introduction: In this address, presented before the National Press Club, Congressman Barney Frank asserts that what led to the recent economic crisis was non-regulation, which he distinguishes from deregulation. He characterizes the current situation as reminiscent of that in the late 19th century, when new industries outstripped the measures in place to regulate them, and of that during the Great Depression, pointing out that these two periods resulted in, in the former case, the Federal Trade Commission (FTC) and the Federal Reserve, and in the latter, the Securities Exchange Commission (SEC) and the Federal Deposit Insurance Corporation (FDIC). In recent years, he argues, financial activity and profit-making have served as ends in themselves rather than as means to a greater societal end. He also describes the problems that have resulted from securitization. Frank contends that new regulatory legislation must include measures to put ailing financial institutions out of business, contain derivatives, and deal with the issue of executive pay, preferably by letting shareholders rather than boards decide on compensation.

Barney Frank's speech: Thank you. I very much appreciate the forum that the Press Club offers for these kinds of discussions and let me reinforce what may have been an entirely unnecessary admonition. No one who has been familiar with the media in America could ever think hearing applause that it came from members of the media.

I want to first address an issue about financial reform that puts it in context. One question that has been raised about President Obama is whether or not he

* Delivered on July 27, 2009 at Washington, D.C.

is asking Congress to do too much—a refreshing change, I think, from the past. And the answer is no. And in particular, there is no validity to any suggestion that because many of my colleagues are so deeply engaged now in trying to deal with health care or were earlier dealing with cap and trade, or are dealing with other very important issues, like labor law reform, to make real the right of men and women to bargain collectively about their own job situation, which they have lost, unfortunately, or to improve education. These are not conflicting, and nothing in what is being done elsewhere is in any way retarding our efforts to deal with the financial system.

Those efforts are essential. We are in the midst of a debate about who is responsible for what in the past, and I will touch on that because having some sense of that is important in deciding what to do in the future. But our primary goal is not to try to undo the past, but to prevent its recurrence. The goal of the Congress today, with our committee having a major piece of it, is to try to prevent things from recurring, the financial crisis that we have had.

Our general view, and by that I mean the members of our committee and the people who work with me on the staff, and members of the House in general and our Senate counterparts, is that the problem was non-regulation. And it's very important to stress that it's non-regulation, not deregulation. There was some deregulation; there was the passage of the Graham-Leach-Bliley Act in 2000, a bipartisan product of the Clinton Administration and a Republican Congress. I voted against it. But I do not think that was the major cause of our problem. Our problem was, rather, that of non-regulation. We have a very healthy phenomenon in this free enterprise country in which the private sector innovates, and the innovation is very important. And by definition, only those innovations which provide value added are going to survive because it's voluntary. If someone comes up with a new idea that doesn't work, it doesn't work, it goes away. The only innovations that thrive are those that attract people's money in a free enterprise society. And that's a constant process.

But there are periods when innovation reaches critical mass, when there is such a combination of new things, it often means that with new technology combined with new ideas, that the existing regulatory framework is left behind. And the role of the public sector is to come up with regulations that allow society the benefit of those innovations in the private sector while curtailing some of the abuses. The problem with the current situation, I believe, is that we had for too long a dominant ideological viewpoint that rejected that—which rejected the notion that innovation of a very, very substantial sort, innovation that just was turning around a whole lot of previous assumptions and that very much changed existing patterns, that that did not require new regulation.

One of the arguments we have today is, from some people, "Well, was the cause of the problem"—assuming that there were things that should have been regulated that weren't—"was the cause of the problem regulators who are ideologically opposed to regulating, or an inadequacy of regulatory structures?" And the answer is very clear: yes. It was both. It was both people who did not believe in regulating, and a regulatory structure that facilitated their ability not to regulate.

And it's true, there were two extreme cases. You can have the most complete regulatory powers given to individuals who simply do not believe regulation is ever useful, and it won't work. And frankly, Alan Greenspan, as he has acknowledged, came close to that by flatly refusing to use many of the regulatory powers given to the Federal Reserve. That was in the old days. The Federal Reserve led other bank regulators into becoming born-again consumer advocates. It's been one of the most interesting conversions we have seen recently in the United States.

But, it is made easier for those who believe firmly in never regulating, never to regulate, when no responsibility is fixed on who should do it. The more you disperse responsibility, the harder it is to overcome that aversion. On the other hand, it is true, if you had wonderful regulators firmly committed to trying to propose rules that would stop the bad things, or minimize the bad and let the good go, they could overcome regulatory inefficiency. But, we can't legislate on the assumption that we're going to either have people totally opposed or wonderful super-regulators. We need to regulate for normal human beings, and that's what we hope to do because we think it is important, both that there be regulatory structures that provide focused responsibility for the right side of regulation, and the appointment of individuals to do it. It's best to have both, but it is better to have at least one than to have neither. And we think we can structure it so you do get both, at least for the near term.

Because it is very important when you get new regulations, and this is something that we shouldn't lose sight of, by definition in the political process, the new regulation is going to come under the aegis of people who believe in it and the first set of regulators will be good ones. And that's very important.

Franklin Roosevelt led the United States into a new set of regulations for finance capitalism, and then appointed people who would run it. By the way, for those who have criticized the Obama Administration because there are people in the administration who had participated in the financial system we are now trying to change and improve and regulate. Think of the example that was set by Franklin Roosevelt, when having established the Securities and Exchange Commission, he appointed as its first chair someone who knew what he had to regulate, Joseph P. Kennedy. And Joseph P. Kennedy was a very effective Chair of the SEC precisely because he knew what had been legal, what was no longer legal, what was no longer approved. So, we will be going forward with setting up that kind of a structure.

Now, I mentioned the New Deal. To me, we are in the third iteration of this phenomenon of innovation that is qualitatively different than what had been before in terms of a system, and the need for regulation to catch up. The first example came in the late 19th century when American business created the large industrial enterprises, far outstripping what had been before. If we hadn't had that, we never would have had the wealth created and spread the way it was. So the late 19th century was a time of large enterprises. People did it in the financial and manufacturing area, in finance and steel and railroads, et cetera.

And then came Theodore Roosevelt and Woodrow Wilson, who spent their time coming up with regulation not to cancel out the innovation, but to try to contain its excesses. And you got the antitrust laws, you got the establishment of the Federal Trade Commission, you got the establishment of the Federal Reserve. And I think that was a very good system.

Then years later, decades later, Franklin Roosevelt confronts the need to do that again and creates a framework for mutual funds, a Securities and Exchange Commission, the Federal Deposit Insurance Corporation. By the way, for those who want to combine history and current events, if you want to read predictions that efforts to regulate innovation, efforts to rein in abuse are foredoomed and will, in fact, deny us the benefits of the innovation and curtail the ability of the financial system to provide benefits, you could either read today's Congressional Record, come to my markup session tomorrow when we will hear my conservative colleagues say that. Or, you could read what they said about Theodore Roosevelt and Woodrow Wilson, or what they said about Franklin Roosevelt. There is a pattern in which some people argue that any attempt seriously to set rules for these innovations will destroy the economy. We reject that. We think that, in fact, the most pro-market thing Franklin Roosevelt could have done is what he did do; setting up the SEC and setting up rules for mutual funds and setting up the FDIC, in fact, saved capitalism and allowed it to go forward. And we plan to do the same thing if we are successful, to set rules which provide a framework in which this wonderful, vigorous, capitalist system can go forward.

We have several things that we need to do. And by the way, in that, we do reject one argument, and it comes from many conservatives. And by the way, there's an element of partisanship here. Can I say I do not understand why partisan is always a bad word, or at least it's always been a bad word since the end of World War II when the partisans in Yugoslavia fought the Nazis. But in every other context, if you Google partisan, it's a bad thing. Political parties are necessary for democracy. They have not, in my view, been successful self-governing polities where you don't have parties. Partisanship becomes a problem if it is excessive because there are issues in any democracy which are going to be legitimately partisan where two different parties have two different viewpoints. Remember, the parties are not, particularly in America today, sides randomly picked for a color war at camp. They are not one ones and twos. They are people who have different viewpoints.

And in particular on this central issue of whether or not there should be an appropriate regulatory intervention not to cancel out innovation, but to channel it, there are different viewpoints. There were those who thought that Theodore Roosevelt and Woodrow Wilson got it wrong, that Franklin Roosevelt got it wrong, and that we're getting it wrong today, that the best thing to do is to simply leave it at free enterprise with all of the goods and bads. And others of us think that if you do this right, it's tough and it's difficult and you have to be careful and you have to have humility about how you do it and fully listen to everybody, but you can make the system better by reducing the bad while not in any way diminishing the good things that happen.

And the parties differ on that. The Republican Party in the House has a very different view, and the Democratic Party has a different view. And that's called democracy. And we had an election. Look, we had elections in 2002 and 2004 in which the people who did not believe in regulation won, and they did not give any regulation. Nothing was done in that general area. And then we had elections in 2006 and in 2008 which were different.

And I say that because I want to raise the stakes for myself and my colleagues. We now have for the first time since 1993, a Democratic president, a Democratic House, and a Democratic Senate. We have the responsibility as Democrats to come up with a system of rules that allow the free enterprise system to flourish and provide all the benefits it can provide while diminishing the abuses, while protecting consumers, while encouraging investors to feel safe about investing, and basically to give us the benefits of the function of the financial system. And it's up to us.

I will tell you that I believe that my Republican colleagues had that responsibility and failed. They had four years, 2003, '04, '05 and '06, when they had the Presidency and both houses of Congress, and nothing was done in the regulatory area. Now, I understand there was a theory that says that was my fault, and Chris Dodd's and some others. Apparently, that view is that I had a secret hold on Tom DeLay that I wish I knew about. If I were to have made a list of things I would have deterred him from doing, it would have been a lot larger than simply derivatives.

But in fact, we had a difference of viewpoint. There were some who thought the problem was that we had been too good to poor people, that the problem was a Democratic approach that said, "Let's try to help low income people." Let me be very clear, and measured and balanced. Utter nonsense. The Community Reinvestment Act is what they blame. And in fact, talk to the community bankers, the people who run the smaller, locally based banks who justifiably object when people denounce banks and they get swept in, getting blamed for things that they were not guilty of doing.

If only financial institutions subject to the Community Reinvestment Act had made mortgage loans, we would not be in the crisis we are in today. The overwhelming majority of those loans were made by institutions not covered by the Community Reinvestment Act, and there was not a regulator who served under the Bush Administration, or the Clinton Administration who will tell you that the CRA—well, you never know, could be one—but there's this consensus, it clearly didn't happen. Again, look at the loans. What happened was an explosion of loans being made outside of the regular banking system. And by the way, that ties in with my thesis because the banks covered by the Community Reinvestment Act who did not cause the subprime crisis were the regulated ones. It was largely the unregulated sector of the lending industry and the under-regulated and the lightly regulated that did that.

We now have our responsibility, and here's what we believe needs to be done. We want to make it very clear that the financial sector is an essential intermediary in our economy. The phrase intermediary is an important one. In fact, in periods when cash has disappeared from the system, or credit has disappeared from the system, it's called, when it happens to the banks, disintermediation. Disintermediation means that the financial sector no longer performs its important intermediary function. What's that function? To gather up money in fairly small amounts from large numbers of people, bundle it (a good word, bundling in this context) and making it available to people who will use it for productive purposes. That's the financial function.

Financial activity is not an end in itself; it is a means to an end. It is a means by which we gather up the savings of individuals and their need to invest and provide for their own personal income and make it available to those who will invest it in large amounts and productive activities. And frankly, I believe one of the problems is that over the past 20 years in particular, a certain amount of financial activity became the end rather than the means. Let me be very clear. I do not expect anybody in this society to do very important work for nothing. Obviously, enterprises have to make a profit. Financial activity has to have a profit. But the purpose of that profit is to enable them to be the intermediary. So, I have had people come to us and complain, "Well, if you do that, I can't make any money." The answer is, "That's not our job. We're not here to help you make money." We are here to help have a system in which you will make money as an incident of your providing funds to those who would use it productively.

And to some extent, there's been financial activity that was an end in itself. That's what's behind the denunciation of speculation. Sure, risk-taking is there, and people can call anything that they don't like speculation, but there is an element in which people have been doing things solely to make money on them. And to the extent that is curtailed, the society is no worse off other than for the handful of people there who were doing it, and they can go out and get real jobs and it won't be any loss to anybody else.

We believe, first of all, a large part of this came from innovation, a good thing. Securitization—thirty years ago, most loans were made by people who expected to be paid back by the borrower. And that meant you had to wait until the borrower paid you back to re-lend that money. Securitization comes, and it means money that's outside the deposit-taking system because there are new sources of liquidity, and it means that you don't wait to be paid back. You sell the right to be paid back by other people. And we then had a whole range of instruments involved that took those rights to be paid back and magnified them and cut them up into a whole range of very innovative financial devices.

Now, basically this securitization is a good thing because it means the money turns over more quickly. If I have to wait for everybody to pay me back, I can't make as many loans. So if they're good loans, let's put it this way, the more good loans that are made, the better. The problem is, securitization had two impacts: it allowed more good loans to be made, and it allowed more bad loans to be made. It turns out a very simple human truth got lost. If I lend you money and I expect to be paid back, I'm going to be more careful than if I lend you money and you're going to pay back somebody else. And securitization has weakened that borrower/lender relationship and the discipline.

And while I think the rating agencies have done, on the whole, a rather poor job, and today it seems to me the rating agencies are trying to overcompensate for weakness by excess. And let me say on behalf of the working press, they may enjoy this phrase, but I'm reminded of a great phrase by one of the great editorial writers of all time, Murray Kempton, who said as an editorial writer, his job was to come down from the hills after the battle was over and shoot the wounded. I think you see some of that with the rating agencies. But in fact, rating agencies, when millions of loans are made by people who don't have the discipline of expecting to be paid back, I don't know how anybody could rate those.

Anyway, here's the lineup we think you need to do. We think you need to put some limits on securitization. People should not be able to lend money without having any risk retention. We think that there needs to be somewhere in the system an ability to limit leverage, to put maximum leverage rules in place so that people do not wind up owing not only much more money than they have, sometimes I think we have in this society as a whole people owing much more money than there is. You have to limit leverage.

You have to come up with a way to put ailing financial entities out of our misery. It's called the resolving power, which is a strange word; it means dissolving. We have a way to do that with banks. We did not have a decent way to do that with AIG or Lehman Brothers or Merrill Lynch, and all of them caused problems as the Bush Administration legitimately, people of good will, Ben Bernanke and Hank Paulson, tried to avoid terrible financial harm from what would happen.

We need to contain derivatives. Yes, they play a very important role, but they have gotten out of hand and we need to do something about it. We need to protect consumers because protection of consumers now has dissipated in ways that result in a lack of activity because there is no way to focus responsibility.

And we need to deal with executive compensation. The problem with executive compensation is essentially from the systemic standpoint, that it gives perverse incentives. That if you are a top decision maker, or maybe even somebody else down the chain, you may have a system in which you are incentivized to take a risk because if the risk pays off, you make money. And if the risk doesn't pay off, you suffer no penalty. Heads you win, tails you break even. It's like selling lottery tickets that only cost you money if they pay off. We'd sell a lot of tickets, we wouldn't raise much money. That's part of it.

Now, there's also a problem with salaries being excessive. Our view is, and we will be working on this tomorrow, that the regulators, the Securities and Exchange Commission, should prevent there from being systems that give perverse incentives. As to the amounts, we think that's up to the shareholders. We have the radical notion on the Democratic side that the shareholders who own the company ought to be able to set outer limits on pay. Because the notion that it will be done by the board of directors, I think, is fruitless because boards of directors and CEOs are inevitably the closest of collaborators. There is not, and should not be an adversarial relationship between the CEO and the boards of directors. I think it's impossible to structure one in a well functioning organization. But given that it's a mistake to think that one day a year, they'll go to arm's length and be labor and management. So we want the shareholders to be involved in setting the pay. That's our package.

Now, I have a challenge to make. And let me tell you, that package has broad support in the Congress, I believe. And I accepted a challenge. I believe as Democrats we have the responsibility to put a systemic risk regulation regime in place that will limit the kind of leverage that got us into trouble with people being overextended. That will allow us in the future to deal with an AIG or Lehman Brothers and put them out of business in an orderly way without either shocking the system or having enormous public funds have to go into them as went into AIG.

I believe we can curtail speculation in derivatives that is excessive without reducing the real economic function that they provide in society. I think we can impose risk retention rules on originators of loans so that we still get the benefit of the higher turnover, but don't lose the lender/borrower discipline. I believe we can protect consumers from abuses without endangering the system. Indeed, if we had protected consumers better from subprime mortgages they shouldn't have gotten, we'd have a sounder system, not a less sound system.

We're going to do those. There is a commitment, as I've said. It's a responsibility for us as Democrats to do them. We are convinced that this is the way to prevent these abuses. And I invite the judgment of failure if we are not able to deliver that. And I will tell you, I am not politically inclined to take on responsibility I don't think I can handle. I am giving us this responsibility because I am confident we are going to meet it. I believe you are going to see during this Congress, I believe by the end of this year, a package that does it.

One last point I want to make, and I want to offer advice, unpaid, to my friends in the financial community, and to the rest of the financial community because that first category—that first category, it's actually—it's kind of cyclical, maybe. I think I didn't have that many a few years ago. Then I became chairman of the committee, I made a lot of new friends without getting any nicer. And, we've worked together. We worked together last year. When Ben Bernanke and Hank Paulson came to us on behalf of the Bush Administration and said, "We face serious financial collapse if you can't collaborate," none of us thought this was going to be the most popular thing to do, but we did it in a very bipartisan way. The Democrats in the House and Republicans and Democrats in the Senate worked very closely with the Bush Administration. And yes, there were many in the financial community who were grateful for our help.

But I think some of them have forgotten that. Not everybody, but there are some in the financial community who call to mind what was said of the Bourbons, the restored monarchy in France after Napoleon. "They have forgotten nothing because they learned nothing." And I do think, and let me go back to my youth and to the days when radio had a function other than the spewing of venom, and when fiction on the radio was labeled as fiction, and there were people who in the financial community want, some of the older people here will catch the reference, they want to revert, return, they want to return, to the thrilling days of yesteryear.

And let me make one amendment. They want to return to the thrilling days of yesteryear when the "Loan Arrangers" will ride again. And in this view, the loan arrangers will be accompanied by their faithful and submissive companion, government.

And that's not going to happen. We are going to put these rules into effect. And in fact, if they want to stick with that analogy—they don't, I do, but let me just say for the sake of my own metaphorical consistency—there was an old unpleasant joke when I was a kid, and it may be relevant now. We may have to give them a new definition in that context of Kemo Sabe. Older people will explain to younger people what I mean by that.

I am making this response to the financial community. I want them to work with us. They need to understand, what I talked about, restricting leverage, having a systemic risk regulator, curtailing the excesses in derivatives, some risk retention, protection of consumers in a single, effective agency—those are all going to happen. I can guarantee you that the votes are there, not because I want them to be, but because I have had a series of conversations with people and I know that is what is going to happen. And I know if the financial community or people who believe in total deregulation, if they want to make that a national debate, I welcome it. They will lose that debate. It's a good debate to have. I believe just as we had that debate in the early part of the 20th century and in the New Deal, we will have it again and we will win it. We will prove that the best thing you can do for capitalism is to have rules that give investors the confidence to get back into the system, that protect the great majority of decent people from abuses.

That doesn't mean that there's no role for them. I believe we should be containing derivatives. There are a couple of ways to do it. On the table is banning naked credit default swaps; there are alternatives to that, a much tighter regime of openness and price discovery that comes from putting them on exchanges. We will talk to them—we hope to talk to them about that.

But there are some tests they have to meet. One, tomorrow there will be a meeting called by Secretaries Donovan and Geithner about one of the great failings of my friends in the financial community today: their unwillingness to help us reduce mortgage foreclosures. It's not in their own interest. The cascade of foreclosures—and to make it worse, by the way, because I'm glad we did unemployment compensation as part of the Economic Recovery Bill and I was very pleased when Ben Bernanke said in testimony last week, in response to a Republican question, that if it had not been for that bill, unemployment would be higher today. But, you cannot pay your mortgage in many cases out of unemployment compensation. So, we face a potential of more foreclosures with disastrous effects for individuals and communities and the whole economy.

The financial community was successful with the community banks and the credit unions in the lead in defeating a bankruptcy reform. Their argument was that we didn't need that to reduce mortgage foreclosures; but so far, that's not been proven right. We need much better cooperation in reducing foreclosures. We need people in the major financial institutions to understand how angry the American people are, that people who were in many cases collectively the causes of a crisis and the beneficiaries of serious economic activity on the part of the government to help them get out of the crisis. . . . Look, we didn't do the rescue plan or the TARP, and I long for the good old days when I thought that tarp is what you used to cover the infield when it was raining. But we're not there anymore.

We didn't do that to help the banks, but helping the banks was the inevitable byproduct of it. You could not restore the credit system of the United States from imminent danger of collapse, as Hank Paulson and Ben Bernanke, I think, accurately said. You could not have done that without helping some of the institutions there. You can't get a whole new set of institutions.

Having done that, though, for them to return to those thrilling days of yesteryear with the level of compensation is a great mistake. And by the way, I do have to say to my friends in the financial community, think about what you say about your character when you tell us that you have to have enormous bonuses to align your interests with those of the people who pay your salary. In other words, you get hired for this very prestigious job and you get a salary, and now we have to give you extra money for you to do your job right? I must say, that does not speak well of the character of the people there. I think they're unfair to themselves. To be honest with you, I'll be their compensation consultant. I think if you cut their bonuses by 90 percent, they'd work just as hard. But, that's not what they've done, so we will have to deal with this in legislation. Not to curtail the overall amount, but to restructure them.

But I am asking the financial community to cooperate with us. Help us figure out the best way to do derivatives. Follow Joseph Kennedy and accept the reality of this regulation and work with us. And that applies to the community banks. The community banks were not the ones who did subprime mortgages; they are not the ones who did credit card abuses.

By the way, another example in the financial sector is salary increases, compensation increases going up, not helping in mortgages. And, we passed a credit card bill and we were told, "Oh, we need more time to work it out so we can do the pricing right." Well, that was the reason for the delay; not so they could jack things up in the interim. And they are inviting a much harsher response if they are not willing to cooperate with us on these. Again, TARP recipients who now tell us that we should not curtail the excessive use of derivatives because it might reduce their profits, they are putting themselves outside of the debate we're going to have. And I would much rather they be in it, because they need to understand they can't stop it.

And to the community banks, yes they have been unfairly traduced because they weren't the problem. But, they have to be careful not to allow themselves to be used by some of their big, big brothers who would like to have them shelter them. We can set up a consumer protection agency that will respect all of the community banks. They were not the perpetrators of the abuses; they will not be the subjects of the corrections. And they need to work with us to help us do that. So, we are ready to go forward with a set of regulations that respond to these innovations that we believe will give us the benefit of the innovations and diminish the abuses. And our models are Theodore Roosevelt, Woodrow Wilson, and Franklin Roosevelt.

We invite the financial community to participate with us given what we believe is necessary and how we do it. But it's going to happen one way or the other, and the debate will be, I believe, in terms of history, as important as the one in the early 20th century, as important as the New Deal, and I believe will end just as beneficially for the American economy. Thank you.

Financial Reform Must Not Lead to More Taxpayer-Funded Bailouts[*]

Mitch McConnell

Minority Leader (R), U.S. Senate, 2006– ; born Tuscumbia, AL, February 20, 1942; B.A., University of Louisville, 1964; J.D., University of Kentucky College of Law, 1967; intern under Senator John Sherman Cooper, then an assistant to Senator Marlow Cook, 1967–1974; U.S. Deputy Assistant Attorney General, 1974–77; judge-executive, Jefferson County, AL, 1978–1984; U.S. senator (R), Kentucky, 1985– ; Majority Whip, 2003–05.

Editor's introduction: In this speech, delivered from the Senate floor, Mitch McConnell argues against the financial reform bill under consideration. Pointing to provisions that further empower the FDIC and the Treasury Department and criticizing the size of the emergency fund, he maintains that the bill would actually worsen the problems that led to the 2008 financial crisis.

Mitch McConnell's speech: A lot of smart people have thought about how to prevent a repeat of the kind of financial crisis we saw in the fall of 2008. We've heard plenty of ideas. But if there's one thing Americans agree on when it comes to financial reform, it's this: never again should taxpayers be expected to bail out Wall Street from its own mistakes. We cannot allow endless taxpayer-funded bailouts for big Wall Street banks. And that's why we must not pass the financial reform bill that's about to hit the floor. The fact is, this bill wouldn't solve the problems that led to the financial crisis. It would make them worse.

The American people have been telling us for nearly two years that any solution must do one thing—it must put an end to taxpayer-funded bailouts for Wall Street banks. This bill not only allows for taxpayer-funded bailouts of Wall Street banks; it institutionalizes them.

The bill gives the Federal Reserve enhanced emergency lending authority that is far too open to abuse. It also gives the Federal Deposit Insurance Corp and the Treasury Department broad authority over troubled financial institutions without

* Delivered on April 13, 2010, at Washington, D.C.

requiring them to assume real responsibility for their mistakes. In other words, it gives the government a new backdoor mechanism for propping up failing or failed institutions.

A new $50 billion fund would also be set up as a backstop for financial emergencies. But no one honestly thinks $50 billion would be enough to cover the kind of crises we're talking about. During the last crisis, AIG alone received more than three times that from the taxpayers. Moreover, the mere existence of this fund will ensure that it gets used. And once it's used up, taxpayers will be asked to cover the balance. This is precisely the wrong approach.

Far from protecting consumers from Wall Street excess, this bill would provide endless protection for the biggest banks on Wall Street. It also directs the Fed to oversee 35 to 50 of the biggest firms, replicating on an even larger scale the same distortions that plagued the housing market and helped trigger a massive bubble we'll be suffering from for years. If you thought Fannie and Freddie were dangerous, how about 35 to 50 of them?

Everybody agrees on the need to protect taxpayers from being on the hook for future Wall Street bailouts. This bill would all but guarantee that the pattern continues. We need to end the worst abuses on Wall Street without forcing the taxpayer to pick up the tab. That's what Republicans are fighting for in this debate. The taxpayers have paid a high enough price already. We're not going to expose them to even more pain down the road.

The way to solve this problem is to let the people who make the mistakes pay for them. We won't solve this problem until the biggest banks are allowed to fail.

Remarks by the President on Wall Street Reform[*]

Barack Obama

Editor's introduction: In this speech, presented at the Cooper Union in New York City, the president observes that despite some encouraging signs, much work remains to be accomplished to achieve a full economic recovery. Stating that "a free market was never a free license," he calls for better regulation and improved consumer protections, including a process for winding down failing financial institutions in a way that would obviate costly taxpayer-funded bailouts. The proposal the president outlines consists of four central components: the Volcker Rule, that would place limits on the size of banks and the kinds of risks financial institutions can take; greater transparency in financial markets to prevent the opaque instruments that had contributed to the financial crisis; consumer protections to ensure that everyday people are not bilked; and a "say on pay" for shareholders of financial institutions.

Barack Obama's speech: Thank you very much. Everybody, please have a seat. Thank you very much. Well, thank you. It is good to be back. It is good to be back in New York, it is good to be back in the Great Hall at Cooper Union.

We've got some special guests here that I want to acknowledge. Congresswoman Carolyn Maloney is here in the house. Governor David Paterson is here. Attorney General Andrew Cuomo. State Comptroller Thomas DiNapoli is here. The Mayor of New York City, Michael Bloomberg. Dr. George Campbell, Jr., president of Cooper Union. And all the citywide elected officials who are here. Thank you very much for your attendance.

It is wonderful to be back in Cooper Union, where generations of leaders and citizens have come to defend their ideas and contest their differences. It's also good to be back in Lower Manhattan, a few blocks from Wall Street. It really is good to be back, because Wall Street is the heart of our nation's financial sector.

Now, since I last spoke here two years ago, our country has been through a terrible trial. More than 8 million people have lost their jobs. Countless small businesses have had to shut their doors. Trillions of dollars in savings have been

---

* Delivered on April 22, 2010, at New York, NY.

lost—forcing seniors to put off retirement, young people to postpone college, entrepreneurs to give up on the dream of starting a company. And as a nation we were forced to take unprecedented steps to rescue the financial system and the broader economy.

And as a result of the decisions we made—some of which, let's face it, were very unpopular—we are seeing hopeful signs. A little more than one year ago we were losing an average of 750,000 jobs each month. Today, America is adding jobs again. One year ago the economy was shrinking rapidly. Today the economy is growing. In fact, we've seen the fastest turnaround in growth in nearly three decades.

But you're here and I'm here because we've got more work to do. Until this progress is felt not just on Wall Street but on Main Street we cannot be satisfied. Until the millions of our neighbors who are looking for work can find a job, and wages are growing at a meaningful pace, we may be able to claim a technical recovery—but we will not have truly recovered. And even as we seek to revive this economy, it's also incumbent on us to rebuild it stronger than before. We don't want an economy that has the same weaknesses that led to this crisis. And that means addressing some of the underlying problems that led to this turmoil and devastation in the first place.

Now, one of the most significant contributors to this recession was a financial crisis as dire as any we've known in generations—at least since the '30s. And that crisis was born of a failure of responsibility—from Wall Street all the way to Washington—that brought down many of the world's largest financial firms and nearly dragged our economy into a second Great Depression.

It was that failure of responsibility that I spoke about when I came to New York more than two years ago—before the worst of the crisis had unfolded. It was back in 2007. And I take no satisfaction in noting that my comments then have largely been borne out by the events that followed. But I repeat what I said then because it is essential that we learn the lessons from this crisis so we don't doom ourselves to repeat it. And make no mistake, that is exactly what will happen if we allow this moment to pass—and that's an outcome that is unacceptable to me and it's unacceptable to you, the American people.

As I said on this stage two years ago, I believe in the power of the free market. I believe in a strong financial sector that helps people to raise capital and get loans and invest their savings. That's part of what has made America what it is. But a free market was never meant to be a free license to take whatever you can get, however you can get it. That's what happened too often in the years leading up to this crisis. Some—and let me be clear, not all—but some on Wall Street forgot that behind every dollar traded or leveraged there's [a] family looking to buy a house, or pay for an education, open a business, save for retirement. What happens on Wall Street has real consequences across the country, across our economy.

I've spoken before about the need to build a new foundation for economic growth in the 21st century. And given the importance of the financial sector, Wall Street reform is an absolutely essential part of that foundation. Without it, our house will continue to sit on shifting sands, and our families, businesses, and the global economy will be vulnerable to future crises. That's why I feel so strongly that we need to enact a set of updated, commonsense rules to ensure accountability on Wall Street and to protect consumers in our financial system

Now, here's the good news: A comprehensive plan to achieve these reforms has already passed the House of Representatives. A Senate version is currently being debated, drawing on ideas from Democrats and Republicans. Both bills represent significant improvement on the flawed rules that we have in place today, despite the furious effort of industry lobbyists to shape this legislation to their special interests.

And for those of you in the financial sector I'm sure that some of these lobbyists work for you and they're doing what they are being paid to do. But I'm here today specifically—when I speak to the titans of industry here—because I want to urge you to join us, instead of fighting us in this effort. I'm here because I believe that these reforms are, in the end, not only in the best interest of our country, but in the best interest of the financial sector. And I'm here to explain what reform will look like, and why it matters.

Now, first, the bill being considered in the Senate would create what we did not have before, and that is a way to protect the financial system and the broader economy and American taxpayers in the event that a large financial firm begins to fail. If there's a Lehmans or an AIG, how can we respond in a way that doesn't force taxpayers to pick up the tab or, alternatively, could bring down the whole system?

In an ordinary local bank when it approaches insolvency, we've got a process, an orderly process through the FDIC, that ensures that depositors are protected, maintains confidence in the banking system, and it works. Customers and taxpayers are protected and owners and management lose their equity. But we don't have that kind of process designed to contain the failure of a Lehman Brothers or any of the largest and most interconnected financial firms in our country.

That's why, when this crisis began, crucial decisions about what would happen to some of the world's biggest companies—companies employing tens of thousands of people and holding hundreds of billions of dollars in assets—had to take place in hurried discussions in the middle of the night. And that's why, to save the entire economy from an even worse catastrophe, we had to deploy taxpayer dollars. Now, much of that money has now been paid back and my administration has proposed a fee to be paid by large financial firms to recover all the money, every dime, because the American people should never have been put in that position in the first place.

But this is why we need a system to shut these firms down with the least amount of collateral damage to innocent people and innocent businesses. And from the start, I've insisted that the financial industry, not taxpayers, shoulder the costs in the event that a large financial company should falter. The goal is to make certain that taxpayers are never again on the hook because a firm is deemed "too big to fail."

Now, there's a legitimate debate taking place about how best to ensure taxpayers are held harmless in this process. And that's a legitimate debate, and I encourage that debate. But what's not legitimate is to suggest that somehow the legislation being proposed is going to encourage future taxpayer bailouts, as some have claimed. That makes for a good sound bite, but it's not factually accurate. It is not true. In fact, the system as it stands—the system as it stands is what led to a series of massive, costly taxpayer bailouts. And it's only with reform that we can avoid a similar outcome in the future. In other words, a vote for reform is a vote to put a stop to taxpayer-funded bailouts. That's the truth. End of story. And nobody should be fooled in this debate.

By the way, these changes have the added benefit of creating incentives within the industry to ensure that no one company can ever threaten to bring down the whole economy.

To that end, the bill would also enact what's known as the Volcker Rule—and there's a tall guy sitting in the front row here, Paul Volcker, who we named it after. And it does something very simple: It places some limits on the size of banks and the kinds of risks that banking institutions can take. This will not only safeguard our system against crises, this will also make our system stronger and more competitive by instilling confidence here at home and across the globe. Markets depend on that confidence. Part of what led to the turmoil of the past two years was that in the absence of clear rules and sound practices, people didn't trust that our system was one in which it was safe to invest or lend. As we've seen, that harms all of us.

So by enacting these reforms, we'll help ensure that our financial system—and our economy—continues to be the envy of the world. That's the first thing, making sure that we can wind down one firm if it gets into trouble without bringing the whole system down or forcing taxpayers to fund a bailout.

Number two, reform would bring new transparency to many financial markets. As you know, part of what led to this crisis was firms like AIG and others who were making huge and risky bets, using derivatives and other complicated financial instruments, in ways that defied accountability, or even common sense. In fact, many practices were so opaque, so confusing, so complex that the people inside the firms didn't understand them, much less those who were charged with overseeing them. They weren't fully aware of the massive bets that were being placed. That's what led Warren Buffett to describe derivatives that were bought and sold with little oversight as "financial weapons of mass destruction." That's what he called them. And that's why reform will rein in excess and help ensure that these kinds of transactions take place in the light of day.

Now, there's been a great deal of concern about these changes. So I want to reiterate: There is a legitimate role for these financial instruments in our economy. They can help allay risk and spur investment. And there are a lot of companies that use these instruments to that legitimate end—they are managing exposure to fluctuating prices or currencies, fluctuating markets. For example, a business might hedge against rising oil prices by buying a financial product to secure stable fuel costs, so an airlines might have an interest in locking in a decent price. That's how markets are supposed to work. The problem is these markets operated in the shadows of our economy, invisible to regulators, invisible to the public. So reckless practices were rampant. Risks accrued until they threatened our entire financial system.

And that's why these reforms are designed to respect legitimate activities but prevent reckless risk taking. That's why we want to ensure that financial products like standardized derivatives are traded out in the open, in the full view of businesses, investors, and those charged with oversight.

And I was encouraged to see a Republican senator join with Democrats this week in moving forward on this issue. That's a good sign. That's a good sign. For without action, we'll continue to see what amounts to highly-leveraged, loosely-monitored gambling in our financial system, putting taxpayers and the economy in jeopardy. And the only people who ought to fear the kind of oversight and transparency that we're proposing are those whose conduct will fail this scrutiny.

Third, this plan would enact the strongest consumer financial protections ever. And that's absolutely necessary because this financial crisis wasn't just the result of decisions made in the executive suites on Wall Street; it was also the result of decisions made around kitchen tables across America, by folks who took on mortgages and credit cards and auto loans. And while it's true that many Americans took on financial obligations that they knew or should have known they could not have afforded, millions of others were, frankly, duped. They were misled by deceptive terms and conditions, buried deep in the fine print.

And while a few companies made out like bandits by exploiting their customers, our entire economy was made more vulnerable. Millions of people have now lost their homes. Tens of millions more have lost value in their homes. Just about every sector of our economy has felt the pain, whether you're paving driveways in Arizona, or selling houses in Ohio, or you're doing home repairs in California, or you're using your home equity to start a small business in Florida.

That's why we need to give consumers more protection and more power in our financial system. This is not about stifling competition, stifling innovation; it's just the opposite. With a dedicated agency setting ground rules and looking out for ordinary people in our financial system, we will empower consumers with clear and concise information when they're making financial decisions. So instead of competing to offer confusing products, companies will compete the old-fashioned way, by offering better products. And that will mean more choices for consumers, more opportunities for businesses, and more stability in our financial system. And unless your business model depends on bilking people, there is little to fear from these new rules.

Number four, the last key component of reform. These Wall Street reforms will give shareholders new power in the financial system. They will get what we call a say on pay, a voice with respect to the salaries and bonuses awarded to top executives. And the SEC will have the authority to give shareholders more say in corporate elections, so that investors and pension holders have a stronger role in determining who manages the company in which they've placed their savings.

Now, Americans don't begrudge anybody for success when that success is earned. But when we read in the past, and sometimes in the present, about enormous executive bonuses at firms—even as they're relying on assistance from taxpayers or they're taking huge risks that threaten the system as a whole or their company is doing badly—it offends our fundamental values.

Not only that, some of the salaries and bonuses that we've seen creates perverse incentives to take reckless risks that contributed to the crisis. It's what helped lead to a relentless focus on a company's next quarter, to the detriment of its next year or its next decade. And it led to a situation in which folks with the most to lose—stock and pension holders—had the least to say in the process. And that has to change.

Let me close by saying this. I have laid out a set of Wall Street reforms. These are reforms that would put an end to taxpayer bailouts; that would bring complex financial dealings out of the shadows; that would protect consumers; and that would give shareholders more power in the financial system. But let's face it, we also need reform in Washington. And the debate—the debate over these changes is a perfect example.

I mean, we have seen battalions of financial industry lobbyists descending on Capitol Hill, firms spending millions to influence the outcome of this debate. We've seen misleading arguments and attacks that are designed not to improve the bill but to weaken or to kill it. We've seen a bipartisan process buckle under the weight of these withering forces, even as we've produced a proposal that by all accounts is a commonsense, reasonable, non-ideological approach to target the root problems that led to the turmoil in our financial sector and ultimately in our entire economy.

So we've seen business as usual in Washington, but I believe we can and must put this kind of cynical politics aside. We've got to put an end to it. That's why I'm here today. That's why I'm here today.

And to those of you who are in the financial sector, let me say this, we will not always see eye to eye. We will not always agree. But that doesn't mean that we've got to choose between two extremes. We do not have to choose between markets that are unfettered by even modest protections against crisis, or markets that are stymied by onerous rules that suppress enterprise and innovation. That is a false choice. And we need no more proof than the crisis that we've just been through.

You see, there has always been a tension between the desire to allow markets to function without interference and the absolute necessity of rules to prevent markets from falling out of kilter. But managing that tension, one that we've debated since the founding of this nation, is what has allowed our country to keep up with a changing world. For in taking up this debate, in figuring out how to apply well-worn principles with each new age, we ensure that we don't tip too far one way or the other—that our democracy remains as dynamic and our economy remains as dynamic as it has in the past. So, yes, this debate can be contentious. It can be heated. But in the end it serves only to make our country stronger. It has allowed us to adapt and to thrive.

And I read a report recently that I think fairly illustrates this point. It's from *Time Magazine.* I'm going to quote: "Through the great banking houses of Manhattan last week ran wild-eyed alarm. Big bankers stared at one another in anger and astonishment. A bill just passed . . . would rivet upon their institutions what they considered a monstrous system . . . such a system, they felt, would not only rob them of their pride of profession but would reduce all U.S. banking to its lowest level." That appeared in *Time Magazine* in June of 1933. The system that caused so much consternation, so much concern was the Federal Deposit Insurance Corporation, also known as the FDIC, an institution that has successfully secured the deposits of generations of Americans.

In the end, our system only works—our markets are only free—when there are basic safeguards that prevent abuse, that check excesses, that ensure that it is more profitable to play by the rules than to game the system. And that is what the reforms we've been proposing are designed to achieve—no more, no less. And because that is how we will ensure that our economy works for consumers, that it works for investors, and that it works for financial institutions—in other words, that it works for all of us—that's why we're working so hard to get this stuff passed.

This is the central lesson not only of this crisis but of our history. It's what I said when I spoke here two years ago. Because ultimately, there is no dividing line between Main Street and Wall Street. We will rise or we will fall together as one nation. And that is why I urge all of you to join me. I urge all of you to join me, to join those who are seeking to pass these common sense reforms. And for those of you in the financial industry, I urge you to join me not only because it is in the interest of your industry, but also because it's in the interest of your country.

Thank you so much. God bless you, and God bless the United States of America. Thank you.

Statement on Financial Regulatory
Reform Legislation*

Russell "Russ" Feingold

U.S. senator (D), Wisconsin, 1993– ; born Janesville, WI, March 2, 1953; B.A., University of Wisconsin-Madison, 1975; Rhodes Scholar, 1977; B.A., Magdalen College, University of Oxford, U.K., 1977; J.D., Harvard Law School, 1979; attorney in private practice, 1979–1985; state senator, Wisconsin State Senate, 1983–1993.

Editor's introduction: In this presentation, delivered from the floor of the Senate, Russ Feingold argues that proposed legislation must do much more than previous congressional initiatives to reform the financial system. Among the central issues, he declares, is how to deal with financial institutions that have grown "too big to fail." Feingold discusses several provisions that he believes need to be included for the financial regulation bill under consideration to be worthy of his vote. In the end, Feingold did not support the measure that passed into law.

Russ Feingold's speech: Mr. President, I am glad the Senate is finally considering the critically important issue of financial regulatory reform. Few things are as important as ensuring we never again suffer the kind of meltdown in the financial markets that shoved our economy into the worst recession since the Great Depression.

It remains to be seen if this bill will do that. While it includes some good reforms, more needs to be done, and the track record of Congress in this area is at best checkered.

For the last thirty years, presidents and congresses have consistently given in to Wall Street lobbyists and weakened essential safeguards. And as has been the case in so many areas, members of both political parties are to blame. Legislation that paved the way for the creation of massive Wall Street entities and removed essential protections for our economy passed with overwhelming bipartisan support.

From the Savings and Loan crisis in the late 1980s to the more recent financial crisis that triggered the horrible economic downturn from which we are still re-

---

* Delivered on May 6, 2010, at Washington, D.C.

covering, those three decades of bipartisan blunders have been devastating for our nation. And the price of those blunders has been paid by homeowners, Main Street businesses, retirees, and millions of families facing an uncertain economic future.

The impact of the recent financial crisis on the nation's economy has been enormous. Millions have lost their job, and millions more lucky enough to have a job are forced to work fewer hours than they want and need to work. According to a study done by the Pew Trust, the financial crisis cost American households an average of nearly $5,800 in lost income.

And, of course, families lost a significant amount of personal savings. As a nation, we lost $7.4 trillion in stock wealth between July 2008 and March 2009, and another $3.4 trillion in real estate wealth during that same time.

We simply cannot afford to continue down the path policymakers have set over the last thirty years.

The test for this legislation is a simple one—whether or not it will prevent another financial crisis. And central to that test will be how this bill will address "too big to fail."

This is a critical issue that has been growing for some time now as increased economic concentration in the financial services sector has put more and more financial assets under the control of fewer and fewer decision-makers.

Mr. President, years ago, a former senator from Wisconsin, William Proxmire, noted that as banking assets become more concentrated, the banking system itself becomes less stable as there is greater potential for system-wide failures. Sadly, Senator Proxmire was absolutely right as recent events have proven.

Even beyond the issue of systemic stability, the trend toward further concentration of economic power and economic decision-making, especially in the financial sector, is not healthy for the nation's economy.

Banks have a very special role in our free market system; they are rationers of capital. When fewer and fewer banks are making more and more of the critical decisions about where capital is allocated, there is an increased risk that many worthy enterprises will not receive the capital needed to grow and flourish.

For years, a strength of the American banking system was the strong community and local nature of that system. Locally made decisions made by locally owned financial institutions—institutions whose economic prospects are tied to the financial health of the community they serve—played a critical role in the economic development of our nation, and especially for our smaller communities and rural areas.

But we have moved away from that system. Directly as a result of policy changes made by Congress and regulators, banking assets are controlled by fewer and fewer institutions, and the diminishment of that locally owned and controlled capital has not benefited either businesses or consumers.

And of course most dramatically, taxpayers across the country must now realize that Senator Proxmire's warning about the concentration of banking assets proved to be all too prescient when President Bush and Congress decided to bail out those mammoth financial institutions rather than allowing them to fail, a bailout I strongly opposed.

The trend toward increased concentration of capital was greatly accelerated in 1994 by the enactment of the Riegle-Neal Interstate Banking and Branching Act and especially in 1999 by the enactment of the Gramm-Leach-Bliley Act, which tore down the protective firewalls between commercial banking and Wall Street investment firms. Those firewalls had been established in the wake of the country's last great financial crisis 80 years ago by the Banking Act of 1933, the famous reform measure also known as the Glass-Steagall Act.

Prior to Glass-Steagall, devastating financial panics had been a regular feature of our economy. But that changed with the enactment of that momentous legislation, which stabilized our banking system by implementing two key reforms. First, it established an insurance system for deposits, reassuring bank customers that their deposits were safe and thus forestalling bank runs. And second, it erected a firewall between securities underwriting and commercial banking. Financial firms had to choose which business to be in.

That firewall was a crucial part of establishing another protection, deposit insurance, because it prevented banks that accepted FDIC insured deposits from making speculative investment bets with that money.

The Gramm-Leach-Bliley Act tore down that firewall, as well as the firewall that separated insurance from Wall Street banks, and we have seen the disastrous results of that policy. I voted against tearing down the firewall that separated Main Street from the Wall Street banks, and I did it for the same reason I voted against the Wall Street bailout—because I listened to the people of Wisconsin, who didn't want to give Wall Street more and more power. Wall Street was gambling with the money of hardworking families, and too many members of Congress voted to let them do it. Well, I didn't support it before, and I won't support it now. We've got to get this legislation right, and protect the people of Wisconsin, and every state, from something like this happening ever again.

I was pleased to join the senator from Washington (Ms. Cantwell) and the senator from Arizona (Mr. McCain) in introducing legislation to correct that enormous mistake Congress made in passing Gramm-Leach Bliley. And I look forward to supporting an amendment to this measure based on the Cantwell-McCain-Feingold bill.

The measure before us seeks to make up for the lack of a protective firewall between the speculative investment bets made by Wall Street firms and the safety net-backed activities of commercial banking by imposing greater regulatory oversight. But we have seen just how creative financial firms can be at eluding regulation when so much profit is at stake. No amount of regulatory oversight can take the place of the legal firewall established by Glass-Steagall. When it is offered, I urge my colleagues to support Senator Cantwell's amendment to restore that sensible protection. Rebuilding the Glass-Steagall firewall is essential in preventing another financial crisis.

But even if we restore Glass-Steagall, there are additional steps we should take to address "too big to fail" in this bill. I am pleased to be joining the senator from North Dakota (Mr. Dorgan) in offering his amendment to address the problem directly by requiring that no financial entity be permitted to become so large that its failure threatens the financial stability of the United States.

And I also look forward to supporting an amendment that will be offered by the senator from Ohio (Mr. Brown) and the senator from Delaware (Mr. Kaufman) that proposes bright line limits on the size of financial institutions.

The disposition of those three proposals will go a long way in determining my vote for the final version of this measure. I very much want this body to craft a bill that can prevent the kind of crisis we experienced in the future. But the bill before us needs some work before we can make that claim.

Dodd-Frank Not Real Reform, Just More of the Same*

Richard Shelby

U.S. senator (R), Alabama, 1994– ; born Birmingham, AL, May 6, 1934; bachelor's degree, University of Alabama, 1957; J.D., University of Alabama School of Law, 1963; city prosecutor, Tuscaloosa, AL, 1963–1971; state senator, Alabama State Senate, 1970–78; U.S. representative (D), 1979–1987; U.S. senator (D), Alabama, 1987–1994.

Editor's introduction: In this address, presented on the floor of the Senate, Richard Shelby, the ranking Republican on the Banking, Housing, and Urban Affairs Committee, delivers an indictment of the process that lead to the financial reform legislation then under consideration. He contends that there was insufficient consultation and analysis in drawing up the bill, which in the end fails to address many of the root causes of the global financial panic. He accuses the majority of using legislation to do favors for their own special interests rather than shoring up the financial system.

Richard Shelby's speech: Mr. President, I rise today to offer remarks on the Dodd-Frank regulation conference report.

Nearly two years ago, the financial crisis exposed massive deficiencies in the structure and culture of our financial regulatory system. Years of technological advances, product development, and the advent of global capital markets rendered the system ill-suited to achieve its mission in the modern economy.

Decades of insulation from accountability distracted regulators from focusing on that mission.

Instead of acting to ensure safe and sound markets, they primarily became focused on expanding the scope of their bureaucratic reach.

After the crisis, which cost of trillions of dollars and millions of jobs, it was clear that significant reform was necessary.

Despite broad agreement on the need for reform, however, the majority decided that it would rather move forward with a partisan bill.

---

* Delivered on July 15, 2010, at Washington, D.C.

The result is a 2,300 page legislative monster that expands the scope and power of ineffective bureaucracies, creates vast new bureaucracies with little accountability, and seriously undermines the competitiveness of the American economy.

Unfortunately, the bill does very little to make our financial system safer. Therefore, I will oppose the Dodd-Frank bill and urge my colleagues to do the same.

Mr. President, this was not a preordained outcome. It is the direct result of the decisions made by the Obama Administration.

Had they sincerely wanted to produce a bipartisan bill, I have no doubt that we could have crafted a strong bill that would have garnered 80 or more votes in the Senate. If the American people haven't noticed by now, that is not how things work under Democrat rule.

Unfortunately, the partisan manner in which this bill was constructed is not its greatest shortcoming. One would have assumed that the scope of the crisis—trillions of dollars lost and millions of jobs eliminated—would have compelled the Banking Committee to spend the time necessary to thoroughly examine the crisis and develop the best possible legislation in response.

Unfortunately, such an assumption would be entirely unfounded.

The Banking Committee never produced a single report on or conducted an investigation into any aspect of the financial crisis.

In contrast, during the Great Depression, the Banking Committee set up an entire subcommittee to examine what regulatory reforms were needed. The Pecora Commission, as it came to be known, interviewed, under oath, the big actors on Wall Street, and produced a multi volume report.

Unfortunately, this time around, the Democrat-run committee gave Wall Street executives a pass. There were no investigations, no depositions, and no subpoenas.

In fact, Mr. President, Chairman Dodd never called on the likes of Robert Rubin, Lloyd Blankfein, or Angelo Mozilo, just to name a few, to testify before the committee.

Not a single individual from AIG's Financial Products division was questioned by the committee or its staff.

Although Congress did establish the Financial Crisis Inquiry Commission to do the work that the majority party refused to do, the commission's work will not be completed until the end of this year.

Most amazingly, the Banking Committee did not hold even a single hearing on the final bill before its mark up.

The committee never took the time to receive public testimony or survey experts about the likely outcomes that the legislation would produce.

We know that the majority heard from Wall Street lobbyists, government regulators, and liberal activists, but they clearly decided that they did not want the American people to have a chance to understand and comment on their bill before it was enacted. Why? The majority knows that this bill is a job killer and will saddle Americans with billions of dollars in hidden taxes and fees. Allowing the public to weigh in on this bill could have spelled the end of the Democrat version of reform.

Mr. President, we owed more to those who lost their jobs, their homes, and their life savings. This truly was a missed opportunity.

The difference between what we needed to do, what we could have done, and what the majority has chosen to do, is considerable.

Congress could have focused this legislation on financial stability. It could have utilized the findings of the Financial Crisis Inquiry Commission. Instead, the Democrat majority chose to adopt legislative language penned by federal regulators in search of expanded turf.

They chose to legislate for the political favor of community organizer groups and liberal activists seeking expansive new bureaucracies that they could leverage for their own political advantage.

The result is an activist bill that has little to do with the recent or any crisis and a lot to do with expanding government to satisfy special interests.

Congress could have written a bill to address the problem of too big to fail once and for all. In fact, the Shelby-Dodd amendment began to address this problem.

Unfortunately, the Democrats, once again, overreached at the eleventh hour and undermined the seriousness of our efforts by emphasizing social activism over financial stability.

Democrats insisted that the overall financial stability mission of the Financial Stability Oversight Council was less important than the political needs of certain preferred constituencies.

This dangerous mixing of social activism and financial stability follows the exact same model that led us to the crisis in the first place: private enterprise co-opted through political mandates to achieve social goals. Fannie and Freddie proved that this combination can be highly destructive.

Congress could have written legislation to address key issues known to have played a role in the recent crisis.

On the Government Sponsored Enterprises, Fannie and Freddie, the bill is silent, aside from a mere study.

- On the tri party repo market, the bill is silent.
- On runs in money markets, the bill is silent.
- On the reliance of market participants on short-term commercial paper funding, the bill is silent.
- On maturity transformations that allowed the shadow banking system to effectively create money out of AAA-rated securities, thereby making the system much more vulnerable, the bill is silent.
- On the financial system's overall vulnerability to liquidity crises, the bill is silent.

Mr. President, we know with certainty that all of these factors—none of which are addressed in the bill—were integral to the recent crisis.

While we do not want to write legislation that only deals with the last crisis, we do want to enact a law that addresses what we know were systemic problems. This bill fails to do so.

Congress could have written a bill to streamline regulation and eliminate the gaps that firms exploit in a race to the regulatory bottom.

This bill does the opposite by making our financial regulatory system even more complex. We will still have the Fed, the FDIC, the SEC, the CFTC, the OCC, and the remainder of the regulatory alphabet soup.

In fact, most of the existing regulators that so recently failed us have been given expanded power and scope. This bill also will add new letters to the already confused soup, such as the CFPB and the OFR. In addition to increased regulatory complexity, there will be new special activist offices within each regulator for almost every imaginable special interest.

Congress could have set up reasonable new research capabilities in its new Stability Oversight Council to complement financial research performed by the Federal Reserve and others.

Instead, Democrats decided to establish the Office of Financial Research with an unconstrained director and a focus on broad information collection and processing.

I believe that this office will not only fail to detect systemic threats and asset price bubbles in the future, it will threaten civil liberties and the privacy of Americans, waste billions of dollars of taxpayer resources, and lull markets into the false belief that this new government power will protect the financial system from risky trades.

Congress could have been transparent in identifying the bill's fiscal effects and costs.

Instead, Democrats wrote a bill that hijacks taxpayer resources but hides that fact from public view. Just as the administration refuses to acknowledge trillions of dollars of contingent taxpayer liabilities residing with Fannie and Freddie, this bill refuses to provide Americans with a transparent view of the costs of the new multibillion dollar consumer protection bureaucracy.

According to the report on the bill offered by the majority, the consumer bureaucracy's budget is—and I quote—"paid for by the Federal Reserve system." Mr. President, make no mistake, "paid for by the Fed" means paid for by the taxpayers.

Taxpayers will be on the hook for billions of dollars of unchecked, unencumbered, and unappropriated spending financed by the inflationary money printing authority of the Fed which will be hidden from the American people in the arcane Federal budget.

Congress could have also used this legislative opportunity to begin the process of reforming the failed mortgage giants Fannie and Freddie, whose ever-growing bailouts have no upper limit. When it became clear that this was not the intention of the Democrats, Republicans sought to address the current and worsening condition of the GSEs.

We suggested establishing taxpayer protections, such as portfolio caps, on the mortgage giants. We recommended making the cost of the Fannie and Freddie bailouts transparent to the public. We offered initial steps toward the inevitable unwinding of these failed institutions. Yet, at every turn, the Democrat majority blocked Republican efforts to establish at least a foundation for reform.

The Democrat preferred approach in this bill to reforming the mortgage giants is—a study.

Let me repeat that notion: in order to address a bailout that has cost American taxpayers roughly $150 billion to date, with unlimited future taxpayer exposure, the Democrats propose a study. It does not take a study to determine that $150 billion and unlimited loss exposure needs to be addressed immediately.

Congress could have focused on securities market practices that were known to have contributed to systemic risks in our financial system. Instead, Democrats overreached once again.

For example, this bill gives the Securities and Exchange Commission, which has failed to carry out its existing mandates, a new systemic risk mandate to oversee advisors to hedge funds and private equity funds. Yet, no one contends that private funds were a cause of the recent crisis, or that the demise of any private fund during the crisis resulted in a systemwide shock.

Congress could have acted to curtail Wall Street's speculative excesses and enhance Main Street's access to credit.

Instead, large financial firms on Wall Street seem to have benefitted, judging by the behavior of their stock prices, while the legislation almost surely will increase uncertainties and costs for Main Street and America's job creators.

The actual provisions in the bill will benefit big Wall Street institutions because they substantially increase the amount and cost of financial regulation. Only large financial institutions will have the resources to navigate all of the new laws and regulations that this legislation will generate. As a result, this bill disproportionately will hurt small and medium-sized banks which had nothing to do with the crisis.

While the largest financial institutions will get special regulation under this bill, the unintended result will be lower funding costs for these firms. That will benefit the big banks and hurt the small banks. Therefore, this bill will result in higher fees, less choice, and fewer opportunities to responsibly obtain credit for blameless consumers.

Moreover, the bill raises taxes, which, as we all know, ultimately are born by consumers. Make no mistake, when Wall Street writes a check to pay its higher taxes, the ones who end up paying those taxes are American consumers and workers.

Congress could have written legislation for consumer protection that respects both American consumers and the need for safety and soundness in our financial system.

Instead, the Dodd-Frank bill was constructed by architects in the Treasury Department who have a certain condescension for American consumers and their choices.

Their ultimate goal is to substitute the judgment of a benevolent bureaucrat for that of the American consumer, thereby controlling consumer behavior without regard for the safety and soundness of our banks.

The American people are being told not to worry, however, because it is all being done for their own good.

While a consumer protection agency may sound like a good idea, the way it is constructed in this bill will slow economic growth and kill jobs by imposing massive new regulatory burdens on businesses—small and large.

It will stifle innovation in consumer financial products and reduce small business activity. It will lead to reduced consumer credit and higher costs for available credit.

Less credit at a higher price will dampen the very small-business engines of job creation that our economy desperately needs right now. That is a price that I am not willing to pay.

Congress could have implemented reforms to improve derivatives market activities. Instead, this bill's derivative title seems to have been inspired by a desire to be punitive or to provide short-term political support during an election, or both. Instead of imposing a rational and effective regulatory framework on the OTC derivatives market, the bill runs roughshod over the Main Street businesses that use derivatives to protect themselves.

Mr. President, the Dodd-Frank bill will increase companies' costs and limit their access to risk-mitigating derivatives without making our financial system safer in the process. As a result, there will be fewer opportunities for businesses to grow, fewer jobs for the unemployed, and higher prices for consumers.

Congress could have written a bill to put an end to the over reliance on credit rating agencies and under reliance on their own due diligence. Instead, the Dodd-Frank bill sets up new regulations and liability provisions to give the impression that ratings are "accurate."

It then takes a contradictory direction and instructs regulators to replace references to ratings with other standards of creditworthiness.

To make matters even more confusing, the bill also provides for the establishment of a government-sponsored body that will select a credit rating agency to perform an initial rating of a security issue.

I anticipate that the net effect of these conflicting provisions will be a reduction in competition among credit rating agencies.

Potential competitors either will be deterred by all of the new regulatory requirements or be destroyed by the liability provisions set up in the bill. The lack of competition led to poor quality ratings in the run up to the crisis. This bill perpetuates and, in fact, worsens that problem.

Mr. President, Congress could have eased regulatory burdens on small and medium-sized businesses that were not integral to the recent crisis or any crisis. Instead, Main Street corporations will be subject to a panoply of new corporate governance and executive compensation requirements.

These new requirements will be costly and potentially harmful to shareholders because they empower special interests and encourage short-term thinking by managers. These features were included solely for the purpose of appeasing the unions and other special interest lobbyists, and there is no demonstrated link between these changes and enhanced stability of our financial system or improved investor protection.

Congress could have held hearings or analyzed a number of changes that this bill makes to the securities laws. Instead, dramatic changes in those laws were written into the Dodd-Frank bill with little discussion and no analysis.

The myriad of miscellaneous provisions will certainly generate several unintended consequences.

Mr. President, throughout this process there has been a lot of talk about the influence of Wall Street on this bill. To be sure, in the early stages of the negotiations, Wall Street and the big banks were very engaged.

I think the American people need to know, however, that, in the end, the real influence peddlers on this bill were not Wall Street lobbyists, but rather liberal activists and Washington bureaucrats. Wall Street and the big banks just happened to be the incidental beneficiaries of their success.

When Chairman Dodd and I began this process we agreed that the bureaucratic status quo was unacceptable and that radical change was necessary. With that in mind, we agreed to consolidate all the financial regulators and constrain the Fed to its monetary policy role.

This was not a result the big banks wanted. The last thing a large regulated financial institution wants is a new regulator. After all, they have spent years and millions of dollars developing a relationship with their current regulators.

A major regulatory reorganization would seriously upset the status quo and cost them a great deal of money. Neither Chairman Dodd nor I were persuaded, however. Change was necessary, and change was going to come.

Unfortunately, that vision of reform began to die as the bureaucrats and liberal left began to exercise their influence over the Democrats. When it became apparent that I was not willing to embrace the left's expansive consumer bureaucracy, it also became apparent that actual regulatory reform was not what the majority was seeking.

All other serious reform was scuttled by the Democrats in defense of the new consumer bureaucracy. That was the point at which Chairman Dodd began to seek out a new negotiating partner—ultimately to no avail.

As the Fed and the other regulators began to regain their foothold with the Democrats, and the administration and the activist left consolidated its support around an expansive new bureaucracy, all hope for real reform vanished. Ultimately, all the Democrats will succeed in doing—with the help of a few Republicans—is give the failed bureaucracies more power, more money, and a pat on the back with the hope that they will do a better job next time.

That is not real reform, Mr. President, that is just more of the same.

We had an opportunity to lead the world by creating a modern, efficient and competitive regulatory structure that would serve our economy well for decades to come.

Instead, the Democrats have squandered that opportunity by merely expanding our obsolete, inefficient, and uncompetitive system. To make it even worse, they have added to the bureaucratic morass several more unrestrained and unaccountable agencies.

It became apparent early on that the administration and the Democrat majority were not really interested in regulatory reform. All they were really trying to do is exploit the crisis in order to expand government further and reward special interests, Wall Street, and political activist groups.

The Dodd-Frank bill will not enhance systemic stability. It will not prevent future bailouts of politically favored institutions and groups by the government.

This bill serves only to expand the federal bureaucracy and government control of private sector activities. It will impose large costs on American taxpayers and businesses without creating one new private sector job. It will lower the availability of credit, raise its cost, and hinder economic growth.

For any one of these reasons, I urge my colleagues to reject this bill.

3

Disarmament and Arms Control

Pros and Cons of Multilateral Nonproliferation

Lessons Learned from the Bush Administration[*]

Jackie Wolcott

Executive director, U.S. Commission on International Religious Freedom, 2009– ; born Hicksville, OH, August 25, 1954; B.A., Bowling Green State University, 1976; intern and then staff aide to Senator Robert Taft, Jr., 1975–76; office manager, then executive assistant, then chief of Staff to Congressman Tom Corcoran, 1977–1984; Special Assistant for Congressional Affairs, Bureau of Near Eastern and South Asian Affairs, U.S. State Department, 1984–85; White House liaison, State Department, 1985–1987; Associate Director for National Security, Office of Presidential Personnel, The White House, 1987–89; assistant to the secretary, U.S. Department of Veterans Affairs, 1989–1990; Deputy Assistant Secretary of State, Bureau of International Organization Affairs, 1990–93; independent contractor, 1993–2001; Deputy Assistant Secretary of State, Bureau of International Organization Affairs, 2001–03; Ambassador and United States Permanent Representative to the Conference on Disarmament in Geneva and Special Representative of the President for the Non-Proliferation of Nuclear Weapons, 2003–06; U.S. governor, International Atomic Energy Agency Board of Governors, 2004–05; U.S. Ambassador to the U.N. Security Council, 2006–08; Special Envoy for Nuclear Nonproliferation, State Department, 2008–09.

Editor's introduction: In this address, presented to The Heritage Foundation, Jackie Wolcott asserts that most existing multilateral institutions cannot address today's nuclear proliferation threats. She describes the Conference on Disarmament as mired in the past and discusses the International Atomic Energy Agency's "hallmark failure" on Iranian nuclear initiatives. She goes on to say that the Non-Proliferation Treaty is devoted to form over substance and has no real teeth, and she explains why the United Nations (UN) Security Council's requirement of consensus before votes results in only tepid agreements. She also identifies the Nuclear Suppliers Group, the Proliferation Security Initiative, and the Global Nuclear En-

---

[*] Delivered on February 13, 2009, at Washington, D.C.

ergy Partnership as groups that, in her view, boast better records in fighting illegal trafficking and promoting peaceful nuclear energy.

Jackie Wolcott's speech: It's a great honor to be here at The Heritage Foundation, an institution that for decades has been front and center in promoting policies that advance the cause of freedom and liberty, not just here in the United States, but throughout the world. And it's great to see so many friends here, many of whom I had the pleasure of serving with in government.

First on that list is, of course, Kim Holmes. I had the great honor and fun of working with Kim as his political deputy at State. One of my lasting impressions from that time was working with him as we re-entered the U.N. Human Rights Commission in 2003 after having been voted off it for the first time ever.

The first issue we faced was Libya's candidacy to chair the Commission. With Kim's able leadership—and believe me, not everyone at the State Department wanted to do this—we waged a worldwide campaign against Libya, then under U.N. sanctions as a terrorist state, eventually calling for a vote to decide its fate. It was the first time in the history of the Human Rights Commission that anyone had forced such a vote. Yes, we went down in flames, but we did it for the right reasons and performed what I think was a badly needed reality check on an institution that had grown comfortable with absurdity.

When my friends here at Heritage first invited me to speak, I pondered what best I might offer that is not already well known and obvious to experts who follow U.S. nonproliferation policy. It seemed to me that perhaps my experience over the past several years might provide a somewhat unique view of the various, related multilateral efforts still underway today. Obviously, now that I am outside of government, I am no longer confined by the bureaucratic "clearance" process, so I hope we can have an informal, non-technical discussion of the challenges and opportunities we face with respect to nuclear nonproliferation.

As Kim mentioned, I've had the opportunity to represent the U.S. at a number of multilateral institutions in Geneva, Vienna, and New York. Most recently, I was Special Envoy dealing with nuclear nonproliferation and emerging nuclear energy worldwide.

While I will address several broad themes today, I would be remiss if I did not draw often on my experiences dealing with the case of Iran. For in a very real sense, Iran has shaken the traditional multilateral system—piece by piece—to its core, and despite the machinations of the blame-America-first crowd, its nuclear weapons program remains the greatest common challenge to each of the institutions in which I served.

At the outset, let me be clear that my remarks here today are based on what I consider to be the inconvenient truth some still try to deny. Diplomats and analysts can debate the size, scope, and pace of the program, or the role of hardliners vs. reformers in Tehran, but Iran's actions over the past several decades cannot lead but to one inexorable conclusion: Iran desires and—if left to its own devices—will soon have a nuclear weapons capability. No sane person really thinks Iran continues to test a ballistic missile capability in order to launch satellites, but even the most wishful thinking cannot ignore the reams of internationally acquired evidence regarding Iran's covert uranium enrichment program, its weaponization research, and the involvement of its military in almost every facet of these programs.

THE SHORTCOMINGS OF EXISTING MULTILATERAL INSTITUTIONS

To better understand how we might move forward, let me take a moment to discuss as a baseline where we have been and where we are now. Broadly speaking, I think it is a fair and accurate assessment to state that existing multilateral institutions are ill equipped, unable, or in some cases unwilling to address the most urgent proliferation security-related threats we face. One could even make the case that these institutions, when they fail to act decisively, in effect legitimize illicit programs. While we should not ignore the role these institutions might play, it is naïve—dangerously so—to assume they can resolve the urgent proliferation matters we confront.

Conference on Disarmament. Some might find that a rather sweeping statement, so I hope you will allow me to illustrate through some specific cases. But before I do, I'd like to talk about time travel. No, I haven't been spending too much time with my colleagues from our national labs discussing the folding of space, although that at times sounds easier than convincing certain countries to forgo the fuel cycle. Trust me, though: Time travel is possible.

All you have to do is visit the Conference on Disarmament (CD) in Geneva. The mustaches and sideburns have disappeared, but the crusaders of disarmament are still waging the Cold War in Geneva. And worst of all, they let these people loose several times a year, most notably on the Nuclear Non-Proliferation Treaty (NPT) conference rooms, to argue—no doubt to Iran's and North Korea's great satisfaction—that proliferation threats would simply cease to exist if the U.S. dismantled its nuclear arsenal. Given this time warp, it is no wonder the organization hasn't produced one solitary piece of work since 1996.

I have spent many a meeting listening to its proponents attempt to tug and stretch the disarmament philosophy into relevancy, but when pressed it is difficult for them to argue that a Comprehensive Test Ban Treaty, for example, would address current or emerging threats. They offer no credible assurance that a new Cold War treaty could avoid the now-familiar pitfalls associated with the systematic failure to prosecute existing treaty violations.

And so these proponents of disarmament return to the political path of least resistance and focus their attention on the United States and hand the Iranians and North Koreas of the world an incredibly valuable gift—time and diplomatic cover to continue their illicit work.

It is a shame so much time and effort is wasted at the CD, but most of us here will agree that on balance, in a venue so mired in the past, no work is good work.

Still, the CD illustrates well how outdated, unwilling machinery can infect the workings of the system as a whole.

You really have to hand it to John Bolton. Despite the mustache, he understood the Geneva Mafia—a term that even they use—and he thought it would be useful to speak with one consistent voice wherever they appeared in the world. So when he tapped me as Ambassador to the CD in late 2003, he gave me diplomatic responsibility for the Nuclear Non-Proliferation Treaty as well. The charge was fairly simple: Defend the United States and its interests; utilize each venue as a platform for exposing the true threats to international peace and security; and when in doubt, say no to the CD.

Later, when he and Kim also gave me interim responsibility for the International Atomic Energy Agency, let me tell you, it became very complicated.

International Atomic Energy Agency. In 1957, the International Atomic Energy Agency (IAEA) was created, according to its statute, as "an independent intergovernmental, science and technology-based organization, in the United Nations family, that serves as the global focal point for nuclear cooperation." Put differently, it was largely established as a technical organization to help facilitate the peaceful development of civil nuclear programs. In this regard, it has served the international community reasonably well.

The problem, of course, is in its dealings with countries that are pursuing weapons under the guise of peaceful nuclear programs. In some cases, its technical response has been beneficial, as in the case of the IAEA developing the Additional Protocol in 1997. One can also point to its decision to refer North Korea to the U.N. Security Council in both 1993 and 2003. But a fair cost-benefit analysis also would have to include its track record as the world's so-called nuclear watchdog.

There have been several well-documented instances in which it simply did not detect or adequately judge illicit nuclear programs, but obviously, the hallmark failure of the IAEA has been the case of Iran, most notably in 2003 when it failed its mandate by refusing to formally find Iran in non-compliance with IAEA statutes and refer it to the Security Council. While the Security Council is by no means a panacea, it is quite clear that the international community in the fall of 2003 missed an important opportunity to signal to Iran that its nuclear weapons program was unacceptable. Some board members and IAEA officials alike—for assorted reasons—didn't want to lose jurisdiction over the Iran issue from Vienna. Despite our best efforts at home and abroad, the referral didn't come until early 2006.

While some IAEA officials certainly enabled this delay, responsibility ultimately falls to states and their often tried, often failed policy of negotiation. Many of you here have correctly argued that negotiation is not policy, just one of a number of available tools to *achieve* a policy, and when we fail to recognize the distinction, we end up with nothing or worse. Europe's negotiations with Iran achieved nothing, but what's worse is that they delayed the referral process in Vienna for over two years.

First the Europeans promised negotiations would dismantle Iran's nuclear program, and when the operative negotiating term quickly became "suspend," we were promised that it soon would be changed to "halt." Dismantlement became a wish rather than a goal. At the same time, the Europeans promised Iran that if it agreed to a temporary suspension and some form of verification, the U.S. would eventually accept its program. Though the resulting so-called Treaty of Paris was lauded as bringing the world back from the brink of another Iraq-like U.N. Security Council drama, it was a failure even before it was abrogated. The goalposts weren't just moved; they were disposed of altogether at a very early stage.

The Europeans still like to claim that their negotiations slowed Iran's nuclear progress. Iran, of course, took a different view, with their chief negotiator even boasting later that the ongoing negotiations afforded Iran the necessary time to complete a critical part of the fuel cycle. Iran, like North Korea, has recycled this tactic many times to great success: If they delay, the West will eventually negotiate with itself and back down.

The last several years have also been witness to a rather new phenomenon that has further weakened the ability of the IAEA to do its job. For years, the IAEA had been known as an apolitical technical agency. It was thought that consensus decisions, an unwritten rule known affectionately as the "Spirit of Vienna," would guard against the kind of deadlocking politicization so common in Geneva and other U.N. cities. As the U.S. Representative to the IAEA Board of Governors from 2004–2005, I had a front-row seat as Iran and its Non-Aligned Movement allies quickly turned the "Spirit of Vienna" on its ear. Board meetings now are often highly politicized events, complete with anti-Western tirades, procedural obfuscation, and other tactics used to derail action on cases like Iran.

Nuclear Non-Proliferation Treaty. The Nuclear Non-Proliferation Treaty, broadly speaking, established a bargain where countries have both entitlements and obligations with respect to their acquisition and handling of nuclear materials. Perhaps the NPT's greatest contribution has been to help strengthen the abstract norm that countries outside of the five which already possessed nuclear weapons should forgo such programs. Unfortunately, we don't just deal in abstract norms; we must deal with real-world, empirical cases of countries manipulating the so-called right to peaceful nuclear energy to further their pursuit of a weapons capability.

Rather than confront these serious issues, however, many NPT members devote all of their efforts year after year, conference after conference, to blaming the world's problems on the United States and, to some degree, the other nuclear weapons states. Interestingly, in my experience, China largely gets a pass. Given the incongruity of events inside and outside these conference rooms, I felt little guilt when irritating my colleagues—both foreign and domestic—by reminding them that we were working on the Nuclear Non-Proliferation Treaty, not the Nuclear Peaceful Uses Treaty or the Nuclear Disarmament Treaty.

Form over substance almost uniformly dominates NPT meetings, as evidenced by members' reaction to North Korea's announced withdrawal from the Treaty in 2003. At first, member states appeared to be in denial, even going so far as to argue

that the DPRK was still a Treaty party because it didn't follow the proper technical procedures of withdrawal. At several meetings, organizers even put out a name
placard for the DPRK, knowing there would be an empty seat. This certainly addressed threats to decorum, just as it ensured against what might have been a useful
debate on how to address those who violate and then withdraw from the Treaty.

There is very little within the NPT about how to formally find or address noncompliance. Indeed, as IAEA Chief Mohamed ElBaradei likes to point out, the
IAEA, as a technical agency, only verifies safeguards agreements; it is up to member
states to judge compliance with the NPT itself.

One would think that the mounting evidence and multilateral action to date
would indicate some general agreement regarding Iran's noncompliance with the
NPT. In the world of multilateral diplomacy, however, nothing is agreed until it
is negotiated and printed in a resolution. And once agreed, for better or worse,
a document's content will be repeated and reused in conference rooms and texts
for years and years. Iran fully understands this, so naturally it sought to exploit
ElBaradei's—shall we say—*nuanced* verdicts, its political base, and the West's
penchant for consensus negotiations to influence the content of the various
multilateral resolutions on its nuclear program. The resulting paper trail is a mixed
bag, with a little something for everyone. On balance, Iran might have lost some
battles, but it is still winning the multilateral paper war.

United Nations Security Council. Turning to the U.N. Security Council, I find
it deeply troubling that the only body charged with addressing threats to international peace and security persists in punting the Iran file back to Vienna. I think it
is fair to say that the Security Council's reaction to Iran has been not just ineffective, but tragically counterproductive. The reason is pretty straightforward: A bad
resolution is worse than no resolution.

At the highest levels, the U.S. was well aware that consensus as a precondition
to a vote in the Security Council would weaken the substance of the provisions
aimed at countering Iranian proliferation, but a conscious decision was made to
follow the Europeans and let them put form before substance. In effect, we handed
Russia, China, and even Germany a line-item veto and surrendered our ability to
leverage the harsh public scrutiny associated with formal Security Council vetoes.

This is not to say that we didn't do our damnedest to push the diplomatic envelope—and we did score some, albeit temporary, victories. I have here in my
hand one special memory, a note John Bolton handed me toward the end of a
particularly tough meeting of the P-5, the five permanent members of the Security
Council. It reads, "Headline for this meeting: British-French effort to surrender
thwarted." In the end, however, we were bound by instructions and consensus, and
bearing witness to the evisceration of each draft resolution was like watching a car
crash that you know is about to happen. At one point, the Russian ambassador in
New York quipped that he would not receive instructions to conclude negotiations
in New York until Washington, Paris, and London stopped sending concessions
to Moscow.

Unfortunately, a tepid symbol of consensus in New York does very little to provide countries concrete authority for dealing with real-world proliferation. When we shy away from provoking a clear choice—meaning, pressing to a vote—the Security Council can enable a dangerous status quo. In the case of Iran, this allowed it to gain significant time, space, and negotiating advantage in the process.

John Bolton has referred to a phenomenon he calls the "We Never Fail in New York Syndrome." The consequence of this "impossibility of failure" attitude is that many of the resolutions passed, such as those on Iran, are toothless while others are simply thematic in nature.

These thematic resolutions in the Security Council were a particular pet peeve of mine. No civilized person, for example, supports using children in armed conflict, but it is unclear to me what a generic statement on the subject from the Security Council serves or solves. That's why we have the U.N. General Assembly: to produce statements on every issue known to man. It always seemed suspiciously as if the Council used these debates to deflect the fact that it was incapable of actually resolving true threats to international peace and security.

To be sure, the Security Council does address important regional security threats from time to time, but this occurs only when there is convergence in views of the P-5 members. It is for this reason that the Council spends roughly 70 percent of its time discussing regional peacekeeping conflicts, largely confined to Africa.

Returning to the case of Iran, I believe it is unrealistic to expect the Security Council to play an important role in resolving Iran's illicit nuclear weapons program. Simply, if bluntly, put, Russia and China have divergent interests from ours, and we have handed them the ability to avoid the public outcry that would accompany a veto. Both Russia and China have significant commercial and military interests in Iran which underlie much of their approach on this issue. Let me add that, from my vantage point in the Security Council, there was clearly an understanding between the two that China would back Russia's positions on Iran, and Russia in return would support China on North Korea. This dynamic drove much of our closed-door debate each time we negotiated Security Council resolutions on these two biggest threats to international peace and security.

EFFORTS OUTSIDE OF FORMAL INSTITUTIONS

The point of my remarks is not to disparage all multilateral action—indeed, quite the contrary. But it is important to have a clear-eyed view of the limitations of formal institutions, particularly when we allow our fear of failure or illegitimacy to delay the adoption of more creative, ad hoc arrangements.

The Nuclear Suppliers Group. A first important movement away from formal multilateral mechanisms was promoted in the mid-1970s—interestingly, by the United States and the Soviet Union. Acknowledging that there remained unaddressed proliferation risks involved with the transfer of nuclear material and equipment, a set of 15 like-minded nations, known as the "London Club," began meeting to discuss the creation of a uniform set of nuclear supply standards that did not disrupt the commercial market.

Today, this group, which includes over 40 participating governments, is better known as the Nuclear Suppliers Group, or NSG. While the NSG does not take action *per se*, NSG members seek to strengthen nonproliferation efforts through adherence to a set of nuclear export guidelines. Recently, amid renewed concerns about the transfer of sensitive fuel-cycle technologies, the U.S. has led an effort to further strengthen these guidelines, a campaign that still unfolds today.

The Proliferation Security Initiative. One of the Bush Administration's most creative and ground-breaking efforts in this regard was the Proliferation Security Initiative. It is a stark departure from multilateral business as usual. Rather than waste time on speeches and conference agendas, PSI supporters concentrate their cooperative efforts on interdicting shipments of weapons of mass destruction at sea, in the air, and on land. Today, more than 90 countries around the world support PSI and stand ready to utilize existing authorities and resources to actively prevent the trafficking of the world's worst weapons. Libya is just one success story of PSI.

Another innovative development sought to sever the lines of support proliferators use to finance their activities. The financial measures the Bush Administration pioneered have since become multilateral with the European Union, even the U.N. Security Council, coming on board in select cases. More broadly, the Financial Action Task Force, a coalition of 34 countries, originally focused primarily on money laundering but today is helping banks and financial institutions to avoid becoming unwitting partners in proliferation activities. These types of activities should be strengthened and expanded.

Managing the Fuel Cycle. As I have mentioned earlier, the fundamental flaw in the NPT's grand bargain is that it allows would-be proliferators to develop a weapons capability under the guise of peaceful nuclear energy programs. I would like finally to discuss initiatives that aim to help seal this loophole by stemming the spread of enrichment and reprocessing technologies.

To further extend the benefits of nuclear power to more states, as well as enhance measures of nonproliferation and waste management, the United States initiated the Global Nuclear Energy Partnership, or GNEP, in 2006. GNEP offers a single, informal forum that spans the full spectrum of nuclear energy experience where states speak freely in search of mutually beneficial approaches to the development or further expansion of nuclear energy. Today, 24 other states have joined us as partners in this initiative.

GNEP aims to tackle some of nuclear power's greatest impediments and offers potential for widely acceptable solutions to these challenges, but realization of its objectives will surely take time. This fact was recognized by Presidents George W. Bush and Vladimir Putin, the founders of the GNEP vision.

As a result, a second initiative was the Joint Declaration on Nuclear Energy and Nonproliferation, issued July 3, 2007, in Washington and Moscow. It described a pragmatic course through which the United States, Russia, and other supplier states could assist the responsible development of nuclear energy and, most important, create a viable alternative to uranium enrichment and spent-fuel reprocessing.

Guided by the Joint Declaration, which I was tasked as Special Envoy to implement, the U.S. began building cooperative relationships with key states in the Middle East, Southeast Asia, and North Africa that were willing to pursue nuclear power in a responsible and transparent way and consider alternatives to the development of sensitive fuel technologies. I quickly found that our embassies around the world were quite inconsistent—perhaps not surprisingly so—on reporting what was actually happening in their host countries regarding nuclear energy development plans. Firsthand knowledge of programs and intentions is key to assessing motivations as well as transparency, and it was that that we sought in our travels around the world, meeting with key energy and foreign ministry officials.

You may ask, why promote nuclear power at all? Simply put, nuclear energy development around the world is happening now, with or without us. Other supplier countries are actively courting business, and some do not have the high standards of safety, security, and nonproliferation that we have. In my view, we would be irresponsible not to engage.

In the past year alone, the U.S. signed nuclear cooperation Memoranda of Understanding with Jordan, Bahrain, the United Arab Emirates, and Saudi Arabia. These agreements symbolize our shared political commitments to pursue cooperation consistent with the highest nuclear standards and to pursue deployment of nuclear power without the transfer of the most sensitive technologies. Significantly, in each of these agreements, there is explicit language of our partners' intent to rely on the international market and not pursue enrichment and reprocessing.

The goals of this effort will take some time to accomplish, but my experience over the past year convinced me that we were on the right track. I believe that if we create a groundswell of partners, especially in the Middle East, who are committed to transparency and forgoing these technologies, we can further isolate Iran, expose its activities for what they really are, and convince others who might consider following Iran's approach to make the right strategic choice.

CONCLUSION

So what lessons can we draw from these experiences? I have intentionally avoided a formal road map for the Obama Administration, partly because I will be the first to admit I do not have all the answers. With that said, though, a "new tone in foreign policy," as referred to by Vice President Joseph Biden last week in Germany, will not correct the existing impediments within today's multilateral nonproliferation architecture.

Put differently, I don't think being "nicer" or adopting a different "tone" is going to persuade the Iranians or North Koreans to abandon their nuclear weapons programs. As many Bush Administration critics conveniently forget to point out, the case of Libya reminds us that critical security decisions are based on perceived national interests—not the niceties of diplomacy.

We need to recognize and acknowledge that international institutions sometimes fail. It would better serve our interests and those of the wider nonproliferation community if we realize that it is not really our job to save these organizations from themselves. As our multilateral adventures with Iran clearly demonstrate, when we hold the prestige of an organization itself above its stated purpose, we risk sending a message that unacceptable threats can indeed become tolerable. Failure, on the other hand, could actually force these institutions to adapt to the true challenges confronting the international community or naturally lead the U.S. and other like-minded partners to seek solutions elsewhere.

This does not mean abandoning all multilateral tools. There is room for multilateral cooperation, and it can be effective, but it needs to be sensible and targeted. I often found it deeply ironic that as much as the Bush Administration was accused of being unilateralist, we were the ones who were pushing to make PSI an accepted norm within the international community; who pressed to have the IAEA and the Security Council fulfill their mandates; who organized GNEP and the Joint Declaration as multilateral ways to positively influence the nuclear energy renaissance.

In an increasingly interconnected global economy, we must identify which levers to use to give us maximum strategic advantage; I think targeting proliferation financing, for example, is a good start. The U.S. has demonstrated tremendous leadership in these areas, and when we have led, other countries have come on board.

Let me close by saying that it was a great privilege to work on these issues, and with some terrific people, including some in this room. And I thank The Heritage Foundation again for giving me this forum and opportunity to share these observations.

"Human Destiny Will Be What We Make of It"[*]

Barack Obama

Editor's introduction: In this oration, presented in Prague, the capital city of the Czech Republic, President Barack Obama asserts "America's commitment to seek the peace and security of a world without nuclear weapons." He pledges to work toward this bold—some would say unattainable—goal by reducing arms stockpiles through a new Strategic Arms Reduction Treaty (START) with Russia, pressing for the U.S. ratification of the Comprehensive Test Ban Treaty, and strengthening the Nuclear Non-Proliferation Treaty. He also promises to foster peaceful nuclear power for any nation that plays by international rules, calls for strong international action against such rule-breakers as North Korea and Iran, and announces an international effort to keep fissile materials out of the hands of terrorists.

Barack Obama's speech: Thank you so much. Thank you for this wonderful welcome. Thank you to the people of Prague. Thank you to the people of the Czech Republic. Today, I'm proud to stand here with you in the middle of this great city, in the center of Europe. And, to paraphrase one of my predecessors, I am also proud to be the man who brought Michelle Obama to Prague.

To Mr. President, Mr. Prime Minister, to all the dignitaries who are here, thank you for your extraordinary hospitality. And to the people of the Czech Republic, thank you for your friendship to the United States.

I've learned over many years to appreciate the good company and the good humor of the Czech people in my hometown of Chicago. Behind me is a statue of a hero of the Czech people—Tomas Masaryk. In 1918, after America had pledged its support for Czech independence, Masaryk spoke to a crowd in Chicago that was estimated to be over 100,000. I don't think I can match his record—but I am honored to follow his footsteps from Chicago to Prague.

For over a thousand years, Prague has set itself apart from any other city in any other place. You've known war and peace. You've seen empires rise and fall. You've led revolutions in the arts and science, in politics and in poetry. Through it all,

---

[*] Delivered on April 5, 2009, at Prague, The Czech Republic.

the people of Prague have insisted on pursuing their own path, and defining their own destiny. And this city—this Golden City which is both ancient and youthful—stands as a living monument to your unconquerable spirit.

When I was born, the world was divided, and our nations were faced with very different circumstances. Few people would have predicted that someone like me would one day become the President of the United States. Few people would have predicted that an American President would one day be permitted to speak to an audience like this in Prague. Few would have imagined that the Czech Republic would become a free nation, a member of NATO, a leader of a united Europe. Those ideas would have been dismissed as dreams.

We are here today because enough people ignored the voices who told them that the world could not change.

We're here today because of the courage of those who stood up and took risks to say that freedom is a right for all people, no matter what side of a wall they live on, and no matter what they look like.

We are here today because of the Prague Spring—because the simple and principled pursuit of liberty and opportunity shamed those who relied on the power of tanks and arms to put down the will of a people.

We are here today because 20 years ago, the people of this city took to the streets to claim the promise of a new day, and the fundamental human rights that had been denied them for far too long. Sametová Revoluce . . . the Velvet Revolution taught us many things. It showed us that peaceful protest could shake the foundations of an empire, and expose the emptiness of an ideology. It showed us that small countries can play a pivotal role in world events, and that young people can lead the way in overcoming old conflicts. And it proved that moral leadership is more powerful than any weapon.

That's why I'm speaking to you in the center of a Europe that is peaceful, united and free—because ordinary people believed that divisions could be bridged, even when their leaders did not. They believed that walls could come down; that peace could prevail.

We are here today because Americans and Czechs believed against all odds that today could be possible.

Now, we share this common history. But now this generation—our generation—cannot stand still. We, too, have a choice to make. As the world has become less divided, it has become more interconnected. And we've seen events move faster than our ability to control them—a global economy in crisis, a changing climate, the persistent dangers of old conflicts, new threats and the spread of catastrophic weapons.

None of these challenges can be solved quickly or easily. But all of them demand that we listen to one another and work together; that we focus on our common interests, not on occasional differences; and that we reaffirm our shared values, which are stronger than any force that could drive us apart. That is the work that we must carry on. That is the work that I have come to Europe to begin.

To renew our prosperity, we need action coordinated across borders. That means investments to create new jobs. That means resisting the walls of protectionism that stand in the way of growth. That means a change in our financial system, with new rules to prevent abuse and future crisis.

And we have an obligation to our common prosperity and our common humanity to extend a hand to those emerging markets and impoverished people who are suffering the most, even though they may have had very little to do with financial crises, which is why we set aside over a trillion dollars for the International Monetary Fund earlier this week, to make sure that everybody—everybody—receives some assistance.

Now, to protect our planet, now is the time to change the way that we use energy. Together, we must confront climate change by ending the world's dependence on fossil fuels, by tapping the power of new sources of energy like the wind and sun, and calling upon all nations to do their part. And I pledge to you that in this global effort, the United States is now ready to lead.

To provide for our common security, we must strengthen our alliance. NATO was founded 60 years ago, after Communism took over Czechoslovakia. That was when the free world learned too late that it could not afford division. So we came together to forge the strongest alliance that the world has ever known. And we should—stood shoulder to shoulder—year after year, decade after decade—until an Iron Curtain was lifted, and freedom spread like flowing water.

This marks the 10th year of NATO membership for the Czech Republic. And I know that many times in the 20th century, decisions were made without you at the table. Great powers let you down, or determined your destiny without your voice being heard. I am here to say that the United States will never turn its back on the people of this nation. We are bound by shared values, shared history. . . . We are bound by shared values and shared history and the enduring promise of our alliance. NATO's Article V states it clearly: An attack on one is an attack on all. That is a promise for our time, and for all time.

The people of the Czech Republic kept that promise after America was attacked; thousands were killed on our soil, and NATO responded. NATO's mission in Afghanistan is fundamental to the safety of people on both sides of the Atlantic. We are targeting the same al Qaeda terrorists who have struck from New York to London, and helping the Afghan people take responsibility for their future. We are demonstrating that free nations can make common cause on behalf of our common security. And I want you to know that we honor the sacrifices of the Czech people in this endeavor, and mourn the loss of those you've lost.

But no alliance can afford to stand still. We must work together as NATO members so that we have contingency plans in place to deal with new threats, wherever they may come from. We must strengthen our cooperation with one another, and with other nations and institutions around the world, to confront dangers that recognize no borders. And we must pursue constructive relations with Russia on issues of common concern.

Now, one of those issues that I'll focus on today is fundamental to the security of our nations and to the peace of the world—that's the future of nuclear weapons in the 21st century.

The existence of thousands of nuclear weapons is the most dangerous legacy of the Cold War. No nuclear war was fought between the United States and the Soviet Union, but generations lived with the knowledge that their world could be erased in a single flash of light. Cities like Prague that existed for centuries, that embodied the beauty and the talent of so much of humanity, would have ceased to exist.

Today, the Cold War has disappeared but thousands of those weapons have not. In a strange turn of history, the threat of global nuclear war has gone down, but the risk of a nuclear attack has gone up. More nations have acquired these weapons. Testing has continued. Black market trade in nuclear secrets and nuclear materials abound. The technology to build a bomb has spread. Terrorists are determined to buy, build or steal one. Our efforts to contain these dangers are centered on a global non-proliferation regime, but as more people and nations break the rules, we could reach the point where the center cannot hold.

Now, understand, this matters to people everywhere. One nuclear weapon exploded in one city—be it New York or Moscow, Islamabad or Mumbai, Tokyo or Tel Aviv, Paris or Prague—could kill hundreds of thousands of people. And no matter where it happens, there is no end to what the consequences might be—for our global safety, our security, our society, our economy, to our ultimate survival.

Some argue that the spread of these weapons cannot be stopped, cannot be checked—that we are destined to live in a world where more nations and more people possess the ultimate tools of destruction. Such fatalism is a deadly adversary, for if we believe that the spread of nuclear weapons is inevitable, then in some way we are admitting to ourselves that the use of nuclear weapons is inevitable.

Just as we stood for freedom in the 20th century, we must stand together for the right of people everywhere to live free from fear in the 21st century. And as nuclear power—as a nuclear power, as the only nuclear power to have used a nuclear weapon, the United States has a moral responsibility to act. We cannot succeed in this endeavor alone, but we can lead it, we can start it.

So today, I state clearly and with conviction America's commitment to seek the peace and security of a world without nuclear weapons. I'm not naive. This goal will not be reached quickly—perhaps not in my lifetime. It will take patience and persistence. But now we, too, must ignore the voices who tell us that the world cannot change. We have to insist, "Yes, we can."

Now, let me describe to you the trajectory we need to be on. First, the United States will take concrete steps towards a world without nuclear weapons. To put an end to Cold War thinking, we will reduce the role of nuclear weapons in our national security strategy, and urge others to do the same. Make no mistake: As long as these weapons exist, the United States will maintain a safe, secure and effective arsenal to deter any adversary, and guarantee that defense to our allies—including the Czech Republic. But we will begin the work of reducing our arsenal.

To reduce our warheads and stockpiles, we will negotiate a new Strategic Arms Reduction Treaty with the Russians this year. President Medvedev and I began this process in London, and will seek a new agreement by the end of this year that is legally binding and sufficiently bold. And this will set the stage for further cuts, and we will seek to include all nuclear weapons states in this endeavor.

To achieve a global ban on nuclear testing, my administration will immediately and aggressively pursue U.S. ratification of the Comprehensive Test Ban Treaty. After more than five decades of talks, it is time for the testing of nuclear weapons to finally be banned.

And to cut off the building blocks needed for a bomb, the United States will seek a new treaty that verifiably ends the production of fissile materials intended for use in state nuclear weapons. If we are serious about stopping the spread of these weapons, then we should put an end to the dedicated production of weapons-grade materials that create them. That's the first step.

Second, together we will strengthen the Nuclear Non-Proliferation Treaty as a basis for cooperation.

The basic bargain is sound: Countries with nuclear weapons will move towards disarmament, countries without nuclear weapons will not acquire them, and all countries can access peaceful nuclear energy. To strengthen the treaty, we should embrace several principles. We need more resources and authority to strengthen international inspections. We need real and immediate consequences for countries caught breaking the rules or trying to leave the treaty without cause.

And we should build a new framework for civil nuclear cooperation, including an international fuel bank, so that countries can access peaceful power without increasing the risks of proliferation. That must be the right of every nation that renounces nuclear weapons, especially developing countries embarking on peaceful programs. And no approach will succeed if it's based on the denial of rights to nations that play by the rules. We must harness the power of nuclear energy on behalf of our efforts to combat climate change, and to advance peace opportunity for all people.

But we go forward with no illusions. Some countries will break the rules. That's why we need a structure in place that ensures when any nation does, they will face consequences.

Just this morning, we were reminded again of why we need a new and more rigorous approach to address this threat. North Korea broke the rules once again by testing a rocket that could be used for long range missiles. This provocation underscores the need for action—not just this afternoon at the U.N. Security Council, but in our determination to prevent the spread of these weapons.

Rules must be binding. Violations must be punished. Words must mean something. The world must stand together to prevent the spread of these weapons. Now is the time for a strong international response . . . and North Korea must know that the path to security and respect will never come through threats and illegal weapons. All nations must come together to build a stronger, global regime. And that's why we must stand shoulder to shoulder to pressure the North Koreans to change course.

Iran has yet to build a nuclear weapon. My administration will seek engagement with Iran based on mutual interests and mutual respect. We believe in dialogue. But in that dialogue we will present a clear choice. We want Iran to take its rightful place in the community of nations, politically and economically. We will support Iran's right to peaceful nuclear energy with rigorous inspections. That's a path that the Islamic Republic can take. Or the government can choose increased isolation, international pressure, and a potential nuclear arms race in the region that will increase insecurity for all.

So let me be clear: Iran's nuclear and ballistic missile activity poses a real threat, not just to the United States, but to Iran's neighbors and our allies. The Czech Republic and Poland have been courageous in agreeing to host a defense against these missiles. As long as the threat from Iran persists, we will go forward with a missile defense system that is cost-effective and proven. If the Iranian threat is eliminated, we will have a stronger basis for security, and the driving force for missile defense construction in Europe will be removed.

So, finally, we must ensure that terrorists never acquire a nuclear weapon. This is the most immediate and extreme threat to global security. One terrorist with one nuclear weapon could unleash massive destruction. Al Qaeda has said it seeks a bomb and that it would have no problem with using it. And we know that there is unsecured nuclear material across the globe. To protect our people, we must act with a sense of purpose without delay.

So today I am announcing a new international effort to secure all vulnerable nuclear material around the world within four years. We will set new standards, expand our cooperation with Russia, pursue new partnerships to lock down these sensitive materials.

We must also build on our efforts to break up black markets, detect and intercept materials in transit, and use financial tools to disrupt this dangerous trade. Because this threat will be lasting, we should come together to turn efforts such as the Proliferation Security Initiative and the Global Initiative to Combat Nuclear Terrorism into durable international institutions. And we should start by having a Global Summit on Nuclear Security that the United States will host within the next year.

Now, I know that there are some who will question whether we can act on such a broad agenda. There are those who doubt whether true international cooperation is possible, given inevitable differences among nations. And there are those who hear talk of a world without nuclear weapons and doubt whether it's worth setting a goal that seems impossible to achieve.

But make no mistake: We know where that road leads. When nations and peoples allow themselves to be defined by their differences, the gulf between them widens. When we fail to pursue peace, then it stays forever beyond our grasp. We know the path when we choose fear over hope. To denounce or shrug off a call for cooperation is an easy but also a cowardly thing to do. That's how wars begin. That's where human progress ends.

There is violence and injustice in our world that must be confronted. We must confront it not by splitting apart but by standing together as free nations, as free people. I know that a call to arms can stir the souls of men and women more than a call to lay them down. But that is why the voices for peace and progress must be raised together.

Those are the voices that still echo through the streets of Prague. Those are the ghosts of 1968. Those were the joyful sounds of the Velvet Revolution. Those were the Czechs who helped bring down a nuclear-armed empire without firing a shot.

Human destiny will be what we make of it. And here in Prague, let us honor our past by reaching for a better future. Let us bridge our divisions, build upon our hopes, accept our responsibility to leave this world more prosperous and more peaceful than we found it. Together we can do it.

Thank you very much. Thank you, Prague.

SAIC Nuclear Arms Control Through
Leadership Symposium[*]

Sam Nunn

Co-chairman and CEO of the Nuclear Threat Initiative (NTI), 2001– ; born Macon, GA, September 8, 1938; bachelor's degree, Emory University, 1960; J.D., Emory University School of Law, 1962; U.S. Coast Guard and reserves and private law practice, 1962–68; member (D), Georgia House of Representatives, 1968–1972; U.S. senator (D), Georgia, 1972–1997.

Editor's introduction: In this talk, presented at a symposium at the Science Applications International Corporation (SAIC), former senator Sam Nunn discusses his vision of a world free of nuclear weapons, referencing an SAIC report and several editorials he co-wrote for the *Wall Street Journal*. He also addresses the criticism his proposals have evoked, especially in regards to North Korea and Iran.

Sam Nunn's speech: Two and a half years ago, George Shultz, Bill Perry, Henry Kissinger and I stirred the pot with an op-ed in *The Wall Street Journal* entitled "A World Free of Nuclear Weapons." Prior to that, an SAIC report prepared for the Defense Threat Reduction Agency in 2006 had a significant effect on my thinking and confirmed my own assessment based on discussions around the globe.

The SAIC Report focused on "Foreign Perceptions of U.S. Nuclear Policy and Posture" and was released by Lou Dunn and others on January 8, 2006.

The 2006 Report concluded that there is a widespread perception abroad that:

1. The U.S. is placing an increased emphasis on nuclear weapons .

2. U.S. nuclear policy has shifted from one of nuclear deterrence to one of pre-emption and first use.

3. The U.S. is lowering the nuclear threshold.

---

[*] Delivered on June 23, 2009, at McLean, VA. Reprinted with permission.

4. The difference between nuclear and conventional weapons is being blurred by U.S. policies.

The report did not agree with these perceptions, but did lay them out clearly. The Report observed that:

1. In general, America should do a better job articulating U.S. nuclear policies.

2. We should pursue a sustained strategic dialogue with Russia and China.

3. We are missing opportunities to shape the psychology of proliferation and turn the tables on Iran, to influence tomorrow's potential seekers of nuclear weapons and to help avoid a proliferation chain reaction.

4. The report specifically recommended that the U.S.:

   a. Defend the legitimacy of nuclear deterrence in today's world;

   b. Reaffirm the goal of the ultimate elimination of nuclear weapons;

   c. Join the nuclear disarmament debate and shape it; and

   d. Set out the political, technical and military conditions for contemplating a world without nuclear weapons.

THE 2007 AND 2008 *WALL STREET JOURNAL* COMMENTARIES

In our January 2007 *Wall Street Journal* op-ed, George Shultz, Bill Perry, Henry Kissinger and I examined the gathering nuclear storm—including the potential spread of nuclear weapons to states and terrorists; the proliferation of enrichment and the spread of nuclear technology and know-how; and the residual nuclear threat from the Cold War. We concluded that the world was on the precipice of a new and dangerous nuclear era.

We proposed a number of urgent steps that would reduce risk and lay the groundwork for a safer world. Those steps included:

- Changing nuclear force postures in the United States and Russia to increase warning and decision time and ease our fingers away from the nuclear trigger.

- Reducing substantially nuclear forces in all states that possess them.

- Moving toward developing cooperative multilateral ballistic-missile defense and early warning systems that will reduce tensions over defensive systems and enhance the possibility of progress in other areas.

- Eliminating short-range "tactical" nuclear weapons—beginning with accountability and transparency among the United States, NATO and Russia.

- Working to bring the Comprehensive Test Ban Treaty into force—in the United States and in other key states.

- Securing nuclear weapons and materials around the world to the highest standards.

- Developing a multinational approach to civil nuclear fuel production, phasing out the use of highly enriched uranium in civil commerce, and halting the production of fissile material for weapons.

- Enhancing verification and enforcement capabilities—and our political will to do both.

- Redoubling our efforts to resolve regional confrontations and conflicts that give rise to new nuclear powers.

We concluded that without the bold vision of world free of nuclear weapons, the actions will not be perceived as fair or urgent; and without the actions, the vision will not be perceived as realistic or possible.

Much of the reaction to our op-ed has been positive from statesmen spanning the political spectrum in Britain, Germany, Italy, Norway, and Russia. Gordon Brown and his UK government have specifically endorsed our approach.

Closer to home, during last year's presidential campaign, both then-Senator Barack Obama and Senator John McCain embraced this effort. President Obama in his recent speech in Prague, and Senator McCain earlier this month on the Senate floor, reaffirmed the statements of support they each made during the campaign and linked their views to the vision and steps we had espoused. In April, President Obama and Russian President Medvedev met in London and said: "We committed our two countries to achieving a nuclear [weapons] free world."

QUESTIONS FROM CRITICS

There have also been critics that have challenged the approach we have put forward in the *Wall Street Journal*, in particular, our reaffirmation of the vision of a world free of nuclear weapons.

I am the first to admit that this goal raises a lot of hard questions, and skeptics play an important role. This subject needs study, analysis, debate and action.

Most of the criticism of our *Wall Street Journal* article has centered on the vision, although there are certainly some who oppose some of the steps like ratification of the CTBT or negotiation of a verifiable Fissile Material Cutoff Treaty. Let me discuss a few of these criticisms, all of which I take seriously.

The first criticism comes from two friends I greatly admire and respect—former Defense Secretary Harold Brown and former CIA Director John Deutsch. They both subscribe to most of the steps, but believe that the vision undercuts progress toward achieving those steps.

Harold and John contend that while the U.S. has ratified the Nonproliferation Treaty with its commitment to nuclear disarmament and that "no one suggests abandoning the hope embodied in such a well intentioned statement—hope is not a policy, and, at present, there is no realistic path to a world free of nuclear weapons."

My reply—exactly. That is the fundamental problem with the NPT and exactly why the four of us have laid out a pathway of achievements that we believe are essential to reverse reliance on nuclear weapons globally as a vital contribution to preventing their proliferation into potentially dangerous hands, and ultimately ending them as a threat to the world.

We do not believe it is realistic today to set a date certain for abolishing all nuclear weapons. Instead, we believe that crucial steps are essential to build confidence, and that the world has to build trust, cooperation, and technical capability over many years to have a realistic prospect of ultimately ending nuclear weapons as a threat to the world. Verification and enforcement will be crucial.

I also note that since Harold and John first made this critique, a number of senior statesman and experts around the globe have enthusiastically embraced a renewed commitment to the vision of a nuclear free world. That suggests to me there is strong support abroad for the hypothesis that the vision and the steps are both essential. Of course, the vision of a nuclear-free world without steps or benchmarks has been the heart of the Nuclear Nonproliferation Treaty for many years. That's the problem—the vision has to be tied to the steps, but the steps also have to be tied to the vision.

A second concern—can we preserve stability as we and other nations reduce nuclear weapons toward zero?

My reply—adjusting U.S. and Russian strategic force postures is sure to be a complicated undertaking. But if we were smart enough at the height of the Cold War to be able to begin reducing nuclear weapons in a verifiable way, surely in the second decade after the end of the Cold War, we can find a way to expand decision time and improve stability, two possible avenues for thought.

Is prompt launch capability required for the U.S. and Russia if numbers are being reduced and survivability can be assured?

Can we find ways to increase warning and decision time by mutual steps and reduce the risk of a catastrophic accident or miscalculation as we reduce numbers? The stability question will require a lot of work as long as nuclear weapons exist.

The third critique is that there is no relationship between what the U.S. and Russia do with their nuclear stockpiles and the actions of North Korea, Iran, or, for that matter, al Qaeda.

My response—the four of us are not saying that if Russia and the United States set a shining example that Iran and North Korea will suddenly see the light and immediately abandon their nuclear programs. That is not our point.

But we do believe that if we take this path, many more nations are likely to join us in a tough approach to prevent the proliferation of nuclear weapons and materials and prevent catastrophic terrorism.

The fourth critique is the crucial long-term question of how we manage the issues associated with the "end game" of getting to zero and how we would enforce the maintenance of such a regime and deal with potential violators.

My response—this is a "Catch 22" question, because you cannot have a complete and satisfactory answer to this question until we have taken many of the steps, and until we have proven that the world can deal effectively with both verification technology and enforcement policy and political will.

That said, near-term successes are essential as we move forward. Unless the world demonstrates that we can deal with Iran and North Korea and secure nuclear materials globally, we are not likely to make much progress on the long-term steps required to protect our security.

I do not believe that it is possible or essential to answer all of the "end game" questions with precision or complete confidence until we have real achievements. I do believe we have to acknowledge, however, that this is a question that will require the long-term and continued attention of our "best and brightest."

To effectively deal with the end game, we will need the leadership, experience and skills of our laboratories, as well as our military leaders and policy makers and their counterparts in other nuclear nations.

MY QUESTIONS

Now that I have made it clear that I do not pretend to have complete answers to the questions posed by the critics and skeptics, let me pose a few questions of my own.

First, how can we defend America without taking these essential steps? How can we take these steps without the cooperation of other nations? How can we get the cooperation of other nations without the vision and hope that the world will someday end these weapons as a threat to mankind? The Lou Dunn report made it clear—we can't.

Second, can deterrence work in a world with a growing number of new nuclear weapons states? How do we deal with submarines and cyber attacks?

Throughout the Cold War, the U.S. and the Soviet Union were good, we were diligent, but we were also very lucky. We had more than a few close calls.

Will this skill, dedication, diligence and luck continue for decades to come, and also apply to new nuclear states in the Middle East, Northeast Asia, and South Asia?

Warren Buffett has a sobering statistic: if there is a 10 percent chance of a nuclear catastrophe in a given year, and that threat persists for 50 years, over that time frame, we have only a one-half percent chance of avoidance.

Third, what are our alternatives?

- To rely on nuclear deterrence indefinitely?

- To rely on missile defense as a total answer?

- To rely on luck or divine providence?

President Obama has made it clear that the U.S. will maintain an effective, safe and reliable deterrent as long as any country has nuclear weapons. I agree. To meet this commitment, people with differing views on the end game must work together to assure that:

- We maintain and refresh the talent pool in our laboratories and production facilities on which that deterrent depends.

- We strengthen the proficiency of those we entrust with our deployed nuclear forces.

- We build a sustainable political consensus sufficient to build a fully capable and responsive nuclear infrastructure.

It is essential to remember that the infrastructure investments required will need to be sustained over a minimum of 20 years—a period of ten Congresses and five presidential terms. This will require the broadest possible political support that can only be achieved with presidential leadership and agreement in the Congress.

CONCLUSION

Let me close by leaving you with this thought. Imagine that a man from Mars at some point in the future were to dig into the rubble after a nuclear catastrophe. Would he explain the devastation in the same way we explain the decline of other species: "too slow in adapting to a changing environment?" Mankind must avoid this epitaph.

We need our best minds working on these issues, both in and out of government, in every relevant field—politics and diplomacy—science and technology—and others.

You have my thanks for the work you have done and encouragement to go forward with the daunting task before us.

Verification and the New START Treaty*

Paula DeSutter

Consultant, Tenere' Veritas, LLC, 2009– ; born San Diego, CA, January 3, 1958; B.A., political science, University of Nevada, Las Vegas (UNLV), 1979; M.A., economics, UNLV, 1981; M.A., international relations, University of Southern California (USC), 1984; M.S., national security studies, National War College, 1994; various positions, Verification and Intelligence Bureau, Arms Control and Disarmament Agency (ACDA); Senior Visiting Research Fellow, National Defense University Center for Counter-Proliferation Research, 1993–94; staff member, U.S. Senate Select Committee on Intelligence (SSCI), 1998–2002; professional staff liaison to Senator Jon Kyl; assistant secretary of state, Bureau of Verification, Compliance, and Implementation, 2002–09; author, Denial and Jeopardy: Deterring Iranian Use of NBC Weapons *(1998).*

Editor's introduction: In this speech, delivered as part of The Heritage Foundation panel "A Good or Bad START?" Paula DeSutter refutes the Obama Administration's assertion that the New START arms control treaty with Russia has a robust verification regime to determine whether the Russians are living up to their end of the agreement. DeSutter argues that New START offers fewer verification tools than the original START. Under the new treaty, she claims, the United States would know significantly less about current and future Russian missiles compared to the earlier agreement, thus allowing the Russians to advance and expand their strategic forces without American knowledge.

Paula DeSutter's speech: One downside to what I view as the Bush Administration's more realistic view of arms control—which is that it is only worth pursuing arms control if it serves our national security interests—is that far fewer people are familiar with the intricacies of arms control concepts and jargon, especially when it comes to United States and Soviet, and then Russian, strategic arms control. The American people have not been exposed to these issues for some time. The Moscow

---

* Delivered June 30, 2010, at Washington, D.C. Reprinted with permission.

Treaty doesn't really count, in my view, because there was little public debate prior to ratification.

The lessened familiarity with the terminology and concepts that we arms control geeks talk about means that when discussing these issues, we will lose our audience if we speak the way we speak among ourselves. We really need to focus on commonsense concepts and explaining issues to our great-aunt or our cousin or any of the other fine Americans across America, who care about this great nation, about our security, and about the safety of our generations to come.

The American public—blessedly—are not arms control experts. They will not read the New START treaty and its annexes article by article. But they have common sense and do not want to be spoken over or down to by a bunch of D.C. snobs, which is how they are likely to see those of us from "inside the Beltway." They expect their Senators and Representatives to do due diligence. They expect that their tax dollars are paying them to look this over, explain the issues to them in commonsense terms, and then cast their votes to make sure that their security and their interests are protected.

We are training a new generation of rising experts, of people who are willing to focus on these issues and who care about issues that your friends back home and at high school reunions probably don't want to talk about. It's really important work and it's not always fun. When you become a true certified geek, you will think this is really fun. So when you hit that moment, go for it! May you build on the good things we've done and fix the things we didn't do as well as we thought we had!

BASIC QUESTIONS ON VERIFICATION

Everyone here should have read The Heritage Foundation's recent *Backgrounder*, "New START: Potemkin Village Verification" on New START's verification weaknesses. If you haven't, I strongly recommend it. It hits virtually all of the major points that are wrong with verification of the treaty. I personally think it was a bit optimistic, if that tells you anything.

So what I wanted to do today is to talk about some of the general concepts and hopefully the commonsense evaluations that should guide assessments of verification. We know that there is no perfect verification. We are talking about sovereign nations. We are talking about whether verification is good enough, given the risks. How do we evaluate that? The United States seeks to answer two questions: What is the degree of verifiability, and is verification effective?

The Degree of Verifiability: First, we need to consider the proposed limitations and the clarity of the language by which the limitations are expressed, which must be weighed against our ability to detect noncompliance in a timely fashion, using both our own national means and methods of verification and possible treaty-mandated or agreed-upon cooperative measures. This assessment must include an evaluation of the means verified parties have of denying the United States the ability to detect noncompliance. Language clarity is an often underestimated element of verifiability, because to assess compliance, verifiers must be able to determine if a detected action is permitted or prohibited.

Effectiveness of Verification: Degree of verifiability must be then be weighed against a broader set of criteria to determine whether verification can be considered to be effective. Such "effectiveness" judgments are informed by a broader context, including: the compliance history of the parties to the potential agreement; the risks associated with noncompliance; the difficulty of responding to deny violators the potential benefits of their violations; and the impact of constraints imposed on U.S. freedom of action, particularly given the risk of undetected cheating prior to a "breakout" from a regime.

Why do effectiveness judgments have to be informed by larger context, like the compliance history of the party with whom you are reaching the agreement? It is common sense. If you are reaching an agreement with the Brits, you are not going to be as concerned as if you are reaching an agreement with the North Koreans, the Iranians, or, let's say, the Russians—who have violated every agreement we have ever had with them. Russia is currently not complying by policy, and they've said so, with regard to the Treaty on Conventional Forces in Europe.

You also have to examine the risks associated with noncompliance. There are some agreements where it does not really matter very much if somebody cheats because the agreement is not very important, does not much constrain the United States, and the consequences for national security are limited if there is cheating, although violations can be politically significant. Another part of the assessment should be that if the other side is cheating, how difficult is it to respond either by changing your national programs and policies to redress the imbalance created by noncompliance or to bring that country back into compliance? Iran is the perfect example of why that can be so difficult. It's Fred Iklé's "After Detection—What?" argument.

The best-case scenario from a national security standpoint is an agreement which has a high degree of verifiability, is reached with a good treaty partner with a record of compliance as scrupulous as our own, with clearly understood and readily implementable sanctions for noncompliance, but which does not constrain the United States' freedom of action in pursuing unilateral measures to secure the nation.

The worst-case scenario from a national security standpoint is an agreement with a low degree of verifiability, with parties with a history of intentional non-compliance, that significantly constrains U.S. freedom of action, and with only a low capability to deny a violator the benefits of its violation and restore at least the level of security that existed prior to the agreement.

Such a worst-case scenario would be compounded if the ineffectiveness of verification was poorly understood, since this would inevitably lead to a false sense of security. Other tools and approaches to address the threat thought to be addressed by the agreement are unlikely to be pursued with the rigor and urgency that might be called for. In such situations an agreement can therefore damage, rather than enhance, national security and international stability.

NEW START

Let us ask a question: Is any treaty better than no treaty? Does it matter what the treaty says?

Secretary of State Clinton echoed statements which have been made by others, including former Secretary of Defense James Schlesinger, that having negotiated and signed the treaty, if we don't ratify it, we will: a) have no strategic nuclear agreement with Russia, and b) lose credibility.

Senator Kerry basically said the world would end without it, and that with it proliferation would end and peace would break out. Senator Lugar was more moderate: "In my judgment, the question before us is not whether we should have a strategic nuclear arms agreement with Russia, but, rather, whether the New START Treaty's provisions meet our objectives. . . ."

The Senate can: a) give its advice and consent; b) give advice and consent with reservations and express its concern and interpretation of what it gave its advice and consent to; c) refuse to give its advice and consent.

However, verification is only one of the issues. Does it really matter so long as we are getting *some* data? Should verification be weaker or stronger as numbers go down?

The Administration is asserting that this treaty has a "robust" verification regime, and essentially that it is effectively verifiable. But it is certainly much less verifiable than the original START. The Administration has argued that less verification is needed now. To me, at lower numbers the consequences of circumvention or cheating are more dangerous and destabilizing, particularly in the absence of robust missile defenses.

MONITORING WARHEAD NUMBERS

Secretary of State Clinton said in her testimony on June 17, that "for the first time ever, we will be monitoring the actual numbers of warheads on deployed strategic missiles." Sounds pretty good. Now, remember how to make commonsense arguments, how to explain this, how Senators are going to explain this to their constituents.

The verification measures in the New START treaty add nothing to what was there before in the original START treaty. They are using the original START Reentry Vehicle On-Site Inspection regime, complete with all of the same shrouds and covers that were used during the original START, some of which we found to violate the Treaty because we couldn't confirm the number of Reentry Vehicles (RVs). And those are all still permitted. But they say we are going to use the Radiation Detection Equipment (that was negotiated for the New START) to confirm that an object that appears to be a possible RV is non-nuclear. That, they say, solves the problem. Maybe, maybe not.

I was not a big fan of the attribution regime for missiles because it didn't always take into account the full capacity that we knew Russian and Soviet ICBMs had—but there's nothing in the treaty that says the Russians may have only a certain number of Reentry Vehicles on any particular type of missile or any particular missile. And you can change the number of warheads on any given missile. So you do your RV onsite inspection and you discover that missile X in that silo has six Reentry Vehicles when you thought it had only a couple of warheads. So what? That tells you nothing about *any* other missile in the inventory.

Now, there can be either intentional or unintentional noncompliance. The original START treaty was very complicated, and so we anticipated some unintentional noncompliance. But we also saw significant intentional noncompliance. With the New START treaty, I think it is true that there will be fewer violations. Why? Not because the Russians have changed their compliance approach, but because there is no reason for them to bother cheating. Cheating, especially on any significant scale in the New START treaty, if you find it, it is equivalent to the Russians simply being ill-mannered. So getting back to RV onsite inspection, in my view there is no basis for the Administration's statement that there is something new there.

UNIQUE IDENTIFIERS (UIDS)

But, they say, we have another verification achievement: Unique Identifiers (UIDs). Secretary of Defense Gates said at the May 18 hearing that: "Unique identifiers, for the first time, will be assigned to each ICBM, SLBM, and nuclear-capable heavy bomber, allowing us to track the disposition and patterns of operation of accountable systems throughout their life cycles." That sounds pretty good. Again, with verification the devil is always in the details.

Senator Isakson asked Admiral Mullen about whether the unique identifiers would be visibly or technically detectable: "Is that going to be like a transponder from an airplane?" Admiral Mullen said: "I think some may know. I don't. It is very clear that it was going to be visible and verifiable and every single weapon would have it." He later clarified that "actually, the UIDs are mechanical, they're not technically detectable."

The Inspection annex says that unique identifiers "shall be applied by the inspected Party, using its own technology. . . . Such a unique identifier shall not be changed. Each Party shall determine for itself the size of the unique identifier." Inspectors are supposed to be able to check them. So you can't see them through National Technical Means (NTMs), you have very few inspections, and even though the inspected party is not supposed to change the unique identifier, how would you know? Plus, there will be no way to know if there are duplicates. Has anybody ever painted a room? It is easy to change paint. Maybe I am underestimating the ability of this system to work. So, I think of this as "verification by paint, or in a good case, nail polish." This contributes in this regime, as near as I can tell, virtually nothing.

Numbers of Inspections: The number of inspections, as I mentioned, went down. There are 18 inspections permissible per year (10 are the "Type 1 Inspections" of deployed bases and 8 are "Type 2 Inspections" of non-deployed facilities and items). Secretary of Defense Gates said we can do a data inspection and Reentry Vehicle On-Site Inspections at the same inspection. The Administration, in the Questions and Answers, said that since under the old START "there are 73 facilities that we inspected . . . under this treaty, there are only 27. And, in fact, based on the number of inspections—18—there are almost twice as many inspections per facility per year than under the previous treaty." Maybe. So, we have onsite inspector numbers going down, the rights of the inspectors to go to critical places much less. So, NTM takes on a more important value in this.

ROBUST NATIONAL TECHNICAL MEANS (NTMS)

Secretary of Defense Gates said: "The Treaty provides for noninterference with national technical means of verification, such as reconnaissance satellites, ground stations, and ships. This provides us with an independent method of gathering information that can assist in validating data declarations." Okay, sounds pretty good. What's the problem?

First, the problem is that our NTM infrastructure is, shall we say, broken. We do not have the independent satellite capabilities to be able to achieve the level of contribution to verification that we had in the Intermediate Nuclear Forces (INF) treaty or in the START treaty. Second, the treaty permits concealment activities— you can't interfere with NTM, but you can conceal activities at ICBM bases. After I read that I called people and said, can that be true?

TELEMETRY NOT NECESSARY

The other thing that happened has to do with telemetry. Secretary of Defense Gates said that "while telemetry is not needed to verify the provisions of this Treaty, the terms, nonetheless, call for the exchange of telemetry on up to five launches per year per side." The other side decides which systems they want to give you telemetry for! Admiral Mullen added later: "the telemetry needs of this Treaty are different from the telemetry needs we had in the past. And we really don't need telemetry for the kind of verification that we need for this Treaty that we had before, to include the ability to understand the weight of a missile, when we didn't know what was actually inside it."

These are fundamental misunderstandings of what we use telemetry for! You want to know the throw-weight so you can figure out how many RVs a missile can carry and how many RVs it is being tested to carry. You want to know how many RVs they are putting on the next generation of missiles, and how many on the SS-27. You need to know that. So, since they say they are monitoring the actual number of deployed RVs, they ought to want to know carriage capacity. Since the testing party decides which flights it will broadcast, you can't expect to get telemetry and interpretive data for any flight tests of new systems. It appears that the only telemetry for which data is exchanged is the telemetry that is broadcast. Encapsulated data isn't shared. It also appears that only the data from the first stage will be broadcasted.

Now you can do some monitoring on your own but that is why these telemetry protocols were created. And what the Administration has done by shortening and constricting the telemetry protocol demonstrates a fundamental lack of understanding of the importance of telemetry and the telemetry exchanges for verification.

One interesting side note, I personally fought hard during the Bush Administration to get the full START Telemetry Protocol into the treaty, with a cut-out only for missile defense tests (interceptors and target vehicles). The Pentagon didn't want any of the Protocol in, and the intelligence community didn't want the missile defense exemption. They fought for months against the missile defense exemption because they were concerned they would lose too much data. Eventually the policy, having taken note of the intelligence community's concerns, was that we would insist on the full START Telemetry Protocol with the exception for missile defense. In New START, the Obama Administration has agreed to significantly less, but apparently the intelligence community is going along with it. It does not make much sense to me and is very disturbing.

WHAT THE RUSSIANS, IN THE COURSE OF JUST BEING RUSSIANS, COULD DO TO GET AROUND THE NUMBERS

Article III, Paragraph 6 provides that if all the ICBM or Submarine-launched Ballistic Missile (SLBM) launchers for a certain missile type are eliminated, all those missiles of that type go out of accountability. It means that the Russians could eliminate the launchers for a type of missile, taking it out of treaty accountability, but retain a capability to launch them from a different launcher.

Eliminated systems can only be inspected or observed by NTMs within a certain timeframe. It would be a simple matter to "eliminate" items at several locations, thereby precluding inspection of all "eliminated" systems. If the U.S. inspectors declare an elimination to be inadequate, the Russians can argue it was different from the others.

What is even more disturbing is the fact that the only use of converted launchers or missiles that is precluded by the treaty is the use for missile defense. Anti-satellite weapons, Space Launch, marketing abroad like they did the INF Transporter-Erector-Launchers are not prohibited.

The Protocol, Part 3, Section 1, Paragraph 2, sets the standard for elimination. Items are to be rendered "inoperable, precluding their use for original purpose." A flat tire would come close to making a Transporter-Erector-Launcher inoperable and precluding its use for its original purpose.

Moreover, according to Paragraph 4, if the Russians propose a conversion or elimination procedure the other side believes is inadequate, all the Russians have to do is do a demonstration under the Bilateral Consultative Commission. Whether or not the other party is convinced about adequacy, those procedures can be used to take systems out of accountability.

Last but not least is the issue of heavy bombers. Russian Prime Minister Putin has called for production of two new heavy bombers. Since they only count as one warhead, this is a good deal for the Russians. Moreover, there are no provisions for determining the number of weapons on deployed heavy bombers. Given that the bombers are counted as one nuclear warhead, this makes no sense.

So, we will know significantly less about current and future Russian missiles under New START. We are not going to gain much through identifiers; we are not going to gain much for treaty purposes through the Reentry Vehicle onsite inspections; the telemetry protocol has been gutted. And so what are we left with? Not that much. So it is true that even with a fantastically tight verification regime you are going to have the possibility of violations. We knew in the START treaty—it was very technical and complex and you had to go back and forth—that there would be at least technical violations.

What is true, I believe, of the New START treaty, again on the upside, is that there will be very few violations because we have made it virtually impossible for the United States to collect the type of information and weigh it against a solid treaty with solid language that would permit us to say they are cheating. The Russians can do so much under this treaty to advance and expand their strategic forces over the length of the New START treaty and our ability to determine whether or not they are doing that and whether it violates the treaty is very, very low. The degree of verifiability is very low.

I would assert that an assessment that says it is effectively verifiable would be incorrect. It is also true that the Senate can give its advice and consent to an unverifiable treaty.

4

Disaster Preparedness and Recovery

H1N1 Preparedness[*]

An Overview of Vaccine Production and Distribution

Anne Schuchat

Director, National Center for Immunization and Respiratory Diseases (NCIRD), Centers for Disease Control and Prevention (CDC); Assistant Surgeon General, U.S. Public Health Service, U.S. Department of Health and Human Services (HHS); bachelor's degree, Swarthmore College, 1980; M.D., Dartmouth Medical School, 1984; resident and chief resident in internal medicine, New York University (NYU)'s Manhattan VA Hospital, 1984–88; various positions with the CDC, including chief of the Respiratory Diseases Branch, National Center for Infectious Diseases (NCID); acting director, NCID; director, National Immunization Program (NIP); officer, Epidemic Intelligence Service (EIS), NCID; author of over 150 articles in books and periodicals; recipient of the U.S. Public Health Service (USPHS) Meritorious Service Medal and various other honors.

Editor's introduction: In testimony presented to the U.S. House of Representatives several months after the initial appearance of H1N1, or "swine flu," in the spring 2009, Anne Schuchat reports on the disease's global reach, its persistence throughout the summer in the United States, its early-season onset, and its continued virulence. She details the systems in place to monitor the spread of H1N1, including information-gathering from hospitals and schools, and discusses the Centers for Disease Control and Prevention (CDC)'s campaign to inform the public on how to keep the virus from spreading. While acknowledging delays in the delivery of the H1N1 vaccine, she also predicts it will soon become more readily available and lists the high-risk groups who should be given priority in receiving vaccinations.

---

[*] Delivered on November 18, 2009, at Washington, D.C.

Anne Schuchat's speech: Chairmen Pallone and Stupak, Ranking Members Deal and Walden, members of the subcommittees, thank you for this opportunity to update you on the public health challenges of 2009 H1N1 influenza.

The Centers for Disease Control and Prevention (CDC) and our colleagues throughout the Department of Health and Human Services (HHS) are working in close partnership with many parts of the federal government, as well as with states and localities, under a national preparedness and response framework for action that builds on the efforts and lessons learned from the past few months, this previous spring and influenza preparedness trainings conducted during the last several years. Working together with governors, mayors, tribal leaders, state and local health departments, the medical community and our private sector partners, we have been monitoring the spread of H1N1 and facilitating prevention and treatment, including implementing a vaccination program. CDC also has deployed staff, both domestically and globally, to assist in epidemiologic investigation of the virus and support state, local and territorial health departments with the H1N1 mass vaccination campaign.

Influenza is probably the least predictable of all infectious diseases, and the 2009 H1N1 pandemic has presented considerable challenges—in particular the delay in production and delivery of a vaccine, in part because of the slow growth of the virus during the manufacturing process. Today I will update you on the overall situation, provide an update on vaccination status, and discuss other steps we are taking to address these challenges.

TRACKING AND MONITORING INFLUENZA ACTIVITY

One major area of effort is the tracking and monitoring of influenza activity, which helps individuals and institutions monitor and understand the impact of the 2009 H1N1 virus. Since the initial spring emergence of 2009 H1N1 influenza, the virus has spread throughout the world. H1N1 was the dominant strain of influenza in the southern hemisphere during its winter flu season. Data about the virus from around the world—much of it collected with CDC assistance—have shown that the circulating pandemic H1N1 virus has not mutated significantly since the spring, and the virus remains very closely matched to the 2009 H1N1 vaccine. This virus also remains susceptible to the antiviral drugs oseltamivir and zanamivir, with very rare exception.

Unlike a usual influenza season, flu activity in the United States continued throughout the summer, at summer camps and elsewhere. More recently, we have seen widespread influenza activity in 48 states; any reports of widespread influenza this early in the season are very unusual. Visits to doctors for influenza-like illness as well as flu-related hospitalizations and deaths among children and young adults also are higher than expected for this time of year, and higher than have been observed at any time in many recent flu seasons. We are also already observing that more communities are affected than those that experienced H1N1 outbreaks this past spring and summer.

Almost all of the influenza viruses identified so far this season have been 2009 H1N1 influenza A viruses. However, seasonal influenza viruses also may cause illness in the upcoming months—getting one type of influenza does not prevent you from getting another type later in the season. Because of the current H1N1 pandemic, several additional systems have been put in place and existing systems modified to more closely monitor aspects of 2009 H1N1 influenza. These include the following:

Enhancing Hospitalization Surveillance: CDC has greatly increased the capacity to collect detailed information on patients hospitalized with influenza. Using the 198 hospitals in the Emerging Infections Program (EIP) network and 6 additional sites with 76 hospitals, CDC monitors a population of 25.6 million to estimate hospitalization rates by age group and monitor the clinical course among persons with severe disease requiring hospitalization.

Expanding Testing Capability: Within 2.5 weeks of first detecting the 2009 H1N1 virus, CDC had fully characterized the new virus, disseminated information to researchers and public health officials, and developed and begun shipping to states a new test to detect cases of 2009 H1N1 infection. CDC continues to support all states and territories with test reagents, equipment, and funding to maintain laboratory staff and ship specimens for testing. In addition, CDC serves as the primary support for public health laboratories conducting H1N1 tests around the globe and has provided test reagents to 406 laboratories in 154 countries. It is vital that accurate testing continue in the United States and abroad to monitor any mutations in the virus that may indicate increases in infection severity, resistance to antiviral drugs, or a decrease in the match between the vaccine strain and the circulating strain.

Health Care System Readiness: HHS is also using multiple systems to track the impact the 2009 H1N1 influenza outbreak has on our health care system. HHS is in constant communication with state health officials and hospital administrators to monitor stress on the health care system and to prepare for the possibility that federal medical assets will be necessary to supplement state and local surge capabilities. To date, state and local officials and health care facilities have been able to accommodate the increased patient loads due to 2009 H1N1, but HHS is monitoring this closely and is prepared to respond quickly if the situation warrants.

Implementing a Flu-related School Dismissal Monitoring System: CDC and the U.S. Department of Education (ED), in collaboration with state and local health and education agencies and national non-governmental organizations, have implemented a flu-related school dismissal monitoring system for the 2009–2010 school year. This monitoring system generates a verified, near-real-time, national summary report daily on the number of school dismissals by state across the 130,000 public and private schools in the United States, and the number of students and teachers impacted. The system was activated August 3, 2009. This has helped us to calibrate our messages and guidance and may have contributed to the smaller number of school closings seen in the fall relative to those seen in the spring.

PROVIDING SCIENCE-BASED GUIDANCE

A second major area of effort in support of individuals and institutions is to provide science-based guidance that allows them to take appropriate and effective action. Slowing the spread and reducing the impact of 2009 H1N1 and seasonal flu is a shared responsibility. We can all take action to reduce the impact flu will have on our communities, schools, businesses, other community organizations, and homes this fall, winter, and spring.

There are many ways to prevent respiratory infections and CDC provides specific recommendations targeted to a wide variety of groups, including the general public, people with certain underlying health conditions, infants, children, parents, pregnant women, and seniors. CDC also has provided guidance to workers and in relation to work settings, such as health care workers, first responders, and those in the swine industry, as well as to laboratories, homeless shelters, correctional and detention centers, hemodialysis centers, schools, child care settings, colleges and universities, small businesses, and federal agencies.

With the holidays coming up, reducing the spread of 2009 H1N1 influenza among travelers will be an important consideration.

CDC quarantine station staff respond to reports of illness, including influenza-like illness when reported, in international travelers arriving at U.S. ports of entry. Interim guidance documents for response to travelers with influenza-like illness, for airline crew, cruise ship personnel and Department of Homeland Security port and field staff have been developed and posted online. As new information about this 2009 H1N1 influenza virus becomes available, CDC will evaluate its guidance and, as appropriate, update it using the best available science and ensure that these changes are communicated to the public, partners, and other stakeholders.

In preparation for the upcoming months when we expect many families and individuals to gather for the holidays, we are preparing to launch a national communications campaign to encourage domestic and international travelers to take steps to prevent the spread of flu. Plans are to display public advertisements with flu prevention messages in ports of entry and various other advertising locations, such as newspapers and online advertisements, both before and during the upcoming holiday travel season.

SUPPORTING SHARED RESPONSIBILITY AND ACTION
THROUGH ENHANCED COMMUNICATION

A third major area of effort is to support shared responsibility and action through enhanced communication to individuals. Our recommendations and action plans are based on the best available scientific information. CDC is working to ensure that Americans are informed about this pandemic and consistently updated with information in clear language. The 2009 H1N1 pandemic is a dynamic situation, and it is essential that the American people are fully engaged and able to be part of the mitigation strategy and overall response. CDC will continue to conduct regular media briefings, available at flu.gov, to get critical information about influenza to the American people.

Some ways to combat the spread of respiratory infections include staying home when you are sick and keeping sick children at home. Covering your cough and sneeze and washing your hands frequently will also help reduce the spread of infection. Taking personal responsibility for one's health will help reduce the spread of 2009 H1N1 influenza and other respiratory illnesses.

CDC is communicating with the public about ways to reduce the spread of flu in more interactive formats such as blog posts on the Focus on Flu WebMD blog, radio public service announcements, and podcasts.

Through the CDC INFO Line, we serve the public, clinicians, state and local health departments and other federal partners 24 hours/day, 7 days/week, in English and Spanish both for phone and email inquiries. Our information is updated around the clock so we are well positioned to respond to the needs and concerns of our inquirers. Our customer service representatives get first-hand feedback from the public on a daily basis. In addition to the H1N1 response, we continue to provide this service for all other CDC programs.

PREVENTION THROUGH VACCINATION

A fourth major area of effort is prevention through vaccination. Vaccination is our most effective tool to reduce the impact of influenza. Working in close partnership with industry, HHS has led the process of developing a safe and effective 2009 H1N1 influenza vaccine, but the delivery of vaccine to the public has not been as rapid as hoped or initially estimated. CDC, in collaboration with the Food and Drug Administration (FDA), characterized the virus, identified a candidate vaccine strain, and our HHS partners expedited manufacturing, initiated clinical trials, and licensed four 2009 H1N1 influenza vaccines all within five months. The speed of this vaccine development was made possible due to investments made in vaccine advanced research and development and vaccine manufacturing infrastructure building through the office of the Assistant Secretary for Preparedness and Response (ASPR), Biomedical Advanced Research and Development Authority (BARDA) over the past four years, and in collaboration with CDC, the National

Institutes of Health (NIH), and FDA. The rapid responses of HHS agencies, in terms of surveillance, viral characterization, pre-clinical and clinical testing, and assay development, were greatly aided by pandemic preparedness efforts for influenza pandemics set in motion by the H5N1 virus re-emergence in 2003, and the resources Congress provided for those efforts.

Pandemic planning had anticipated vaccine becoming available 6-9 months after emergence of a new influenza. In fact, 2009 H1N1 vaccination began in early October—just 5 months after the emergence of 2009 H1N1 influenza. Critical support from Congress resulted in $1.44 billion for states and hospitals to support planning, preparation, and implementation efforts. States and cities began placing orders for the 2009 H1N1 vaccine on September 30th. The first vaccination with 2009 H1N1 influenza vaccine outside of clinical trials was given October 5th. Tens of millions of doses have become available for ordering, and millions more become available each week. Although the initial pace of vaccine delivery to the States has complicated the early immunization efforts, vaccine will become increasingly available over the weeks ahead, and will become more visible through delivery in a variety of settings, such as vaccination clinics organized by local health departments, healthcare provider offices, schools, pharmacies, and workplaces.

States have begun executing their plans to provide vaccine to targeted priority populations, and CDC continues to offer technical assistance to states and other public health partners as we work together to ensure the H1N1 vaccination program is as effective as possible. Although we had hoped to have more vaccine distributed by this point, we are working hard to get vaccine out to the public just as soon as we receive it.

H1N1 vaccines are manufactured by the same companies employing the same methods used for the yearly production of seasonal flu vaccines. H1N1 vaccine is distributed to providers and state health departments similarly to the way federally purchased vaccines are distributed in the Vaccines for Children program. Two types of 2009 H1N1 vaccine are now available: injectable vaccine made from inactivated virus, including thimerosal-free formulations, and nasal vaccine made from live, attenuated (weakened) virus.

CDC's Advisory Committee on Immunization Practices (ACIP) has recommended that 2009 H1N1 vaccines be directed to target populations at greatest risk of illness and severe disease caused by this virus. On July 29, 2009, ACIP recommended targeting the first available doses of H1N1 vaccine to five high-risk groups comprised of approximately 159 million people; CDC accepted these recommendations. These groups are: pregnant women; people who live with or care for children younger than 6 months of age; health care and emergency services personnel; persons between the ages of 6 months through 24 years of age; and people from ages 25 through 64 years who are at higher risk for severe disease because of chronic health disorders like asthma, diabetes, or compromised immune systems. In addition, ACIP recommended that local public health authorities may want to prioritize a smaller group of people while supplies are limited, in which case the following groups who are at the highest risk for infection or severe illness should receive the vaccine before others: pregnant women, people who live with or care for children younger than 6 months of age, health care and emergency medical services personnel with direct patient contact, children 6 months through 4 years of age, and children 5 through 18 years of age who have chronic medical conditions. This subset of the five target groups comprises approximately 42 million persons in the United States. These recommendations provide a framework from which states can tailor vaccination to local needs.

Ensuring a vaccine that is safe as well as effective is a top priority. CDC expects that the 2009 H1N1 influenza vaccine will have a similar safety profile to seasonal influenza vaccine, which historically has an excellent safety track record. So far the reports of adverse events among H1N1 vaccination are generally mild and are similar to those we see with seasonal flu vaccine. We will remain alert, however, for the possibility of rare, severe adverse events that could be linked to vaccination. CDC and FDA have been working to enhance surveillance systems to rapidly detect any unexpected adverse events among vaccinated persons and to adjust the vaccination program to minimize these risks. Two primary systems used to monitor vaccine safety are the Vaccine Adverse Events Reporting System (VAERS), jointly operated between CDC and FDA, and the Vaccine Safety Datalink (VSD) Project, a collaborative project with eight managed care organizations covering more than nine million members. These systems are designed to determine whether adverse events are occurring among vaccinated persons at a greater rate than among unvaccinated persons. CDC has worked with FDA and other partners to strengthen these vaccine safety tracking systems and we continue to develop new ways to monitor vaccine safety, as announced earlier this week by the Federal Immunization Safety Task Force in HHS. In addition, based on the recommendation of the National Vaccine Advisory Committee (NVAC), HHS established the H1N1 Vaccine Safety Risk Assessment Working Group to review 2009 H1N1 vaccine safety data as it accumulates. This working group of outside experts will conduct regular, rapid reviews of available data from the federal safety monitoring systems and present them to NVAC and federal leadership for appropriate policy action and follow-up.

More than 36,000 people die each year from complications associated with seasonal flu. CDC continues to recommend vaccination against seasonal influenza viruses, especially for all people 50 years of age and over and all adults with certain chronic medical conditions, as well as infants and children. As of the fourth week in October, 89 million doses of seasonal vaccine had been distributed. It appears that interest in seasonal flu vaccine has been unprecedented this year. Manufacturers estimate that a total of 114 million doses will be brought to the U.S. market.

REDUCING THE BURDEN OF ILLNESS AND DEATH
THROUGH ANTIVIRAL DISTRIBUTION AND USE

In the spring, anticipating commercial market constraints, HHS deployed 11 million courses of antiviral drugs from the Strategic National Stockpile (SNS) to ensure the nation was positioned to quickly employ these drugs to combat 2009 H1N1 and its spread. In early October, HHS shipped an additional 300,000 bottles of the oral suspension formulation of the antiviral oseltamivir to states in order to mitigate a predicted near-term national shortage indicated by commercial supply data. In addition, the Secretary authorized the release of the remaining 234,000 bottles of pediatric Tamiflu® on October 29th. We will continue to conduct outreach to pharmacists and providers related to pediatric dosing and compounding practices to help assure supplies are able to meet pediatric demand for antiviral treatment, and we have updated our guidance relating to general antiviral use as new information has warranted. Finally, CDC and FDA have also worked together to address potential options for treatment of seriously ill hospitalized patients with influenza, including situations in which physicians may wish to use investigational formulations of antiviral drugs for intravenous therapy. The FDA issued an emergency use authorization (EUA) on October 23rd, 2009, for the investigational antiviral drug peramivir intravenous (IV) authorizing the emergency use of peramivir for the treatment of certain hospitalized adult and pediatric patients with confirmed or suspected 2009 H1N1 influenza infection. Physician requests for peramivir to be used under the EUA are managed through a CDC web portal.

CLOSING REMARKS

CDC is working hard to limit the impact of this pandemic, and we are committed to keeping the public and the Congress fully informed about both the situation and our response. We are collaborating with our federal partners as well as with other organizations that have unique expertise to help CDC provide guidance to multiple sectors of our economy and society. There have been enormous efforts in the United States and abroad to prepare for this kind of challenge.

Our nation's current preparedness is a direct result of the investments and support of Congress over recent years, effective planning and action by Federal agencies, and the hard work of state and local officials across the country. We look forward to working closely with Congress as we address the situation as it continues to evolve in the weeks and months ahead.

Again, Mr. Chairman, thank you for the opportunity to participate in this conversation with you and your colleagues. I look forward to answering your questions.

Remarks at International Donors Conference[*]

Towards a New Future for Haiti

Hillary Rodham Clinton

U.S. Secretary of State, 2009– ; born Chicago, IL, October 26, 1947; B.A., Welles-ley College, 1969; J.D., Yale Law School, 1973; postgraduate study on children and medicine at Yale Child Study Center, during which staff attorney at Children's Defense Fund and consultant to Carnegie Council on Children; advised House Committee on the Judiciary, 1974; joined faculty of School of Law at University of Arkansas, Fay-etteville, 1974; joined Rose Law Firm, 1977, became full partner, 1979; First Lady of Arkansas, 1979–1981, 1983–1992; First Lady of the United States 1993–2001; chair, Task Force on National Health Care Reform 1993–94; U.S. senator (D), New York, 2001–09; author: It Takes a Village and Other Lessons Children Teach Us (1996), An Invitation to the White House: At Home with History (2000), Living History (2004).

Editor's introduction: In this address, presented at the United Nations (UN), Hillary Clinton discusses the need for the international community to help rebuild Haiti after the devastating earthquake of January 12. The reasons to help are not only moral and humanitarian, she argues, but also stem from self-interest: If there are no jobs for Haitians in Haiti, they will migrate to other countries, and if the shattered health care system is not repaired, deadly diseases could spread across national borders. She further posits that the crisis poses a challenge not only to Haitians, but to the global community, which must offer aid in smarter and more effective ways.

Hillary Clinton's speech: Thank you very much, Secretary General, and thank you for your leadership and your personal commitment to this international endeavor.

President Preval, to you and the members of your government, we thank you for the extraordinary work that you have done leading up to this point.

To former President Clinton, with whom I first went to Haiti many years ago about two months after we were married, thank you for taking on another assignment from the Secretary General.

And to all of the countries and international institutions represented here, thank you. Thank you for the immediate response to the overwhelming catastrophe that afflicted the Haitian people and thank you for your continuing commitment.

We have had over 140 nations working to support the Government of Haiti in delivering food, temporary shelter, and medical care to thousands of survivors. But the emergency relief is only the beginning of what will be a long road to recovery, as the Secretary General just pointed out; one that will require global support.

Some people wonder, "Why Haiti? Why this great outpouring of international humanitarian concern and commitment to Haiti's future? Why is Haiti's fate of such consequence to the region and the world that it deserves sustained help? Why should we hope that this time, with our collective assistance, Haiti can achieve a better future?" These are questions that deserve answers and I believe that this conference will begin to do so.

The humanitarian need, we know, is great. Therefore, as fellow human beings, we respond from a position of conscience and morality to help those who, but for the grace of God, we could be in a world where natural disasters are often unpredictable, inflicting great costs. Haiti was a country of 9 million people before the earthquake. Today, more than a quarter of a million of those people have died. More than a million are homeless. Hundreds of thousands live in temporary camps without enough food or sufficient access to sanitation. Nearly every government agency has been destroyed along with universities, hospitals, and primary schools, which we know are the foundations to a nation's long-term progress. Close to a million young people were preparing to enter the job market within five years. Now their opportunities have crumbled while the need for jobs has multiplied.

Before the earthquake, Haiti was on a path to progress. The government, led by President Preval, had started enacting critical reforms. Haiti's economy grew by nearly 3 percent last year. Two international chains launched new hotels, a sign of a rising tourism industry. New factories were opening and others had been contracted to begin production. But with the earthquake, the results of much of this hard work were wiped away. But the people of Haiti never gave up. As they mourn their losses, they gathered the resources they had left and began working around the clock to put their lives and their country back together. They relied on the strength and the spirit that have carried them through tough times before. But they need our help. They cannot succeed without the support of the global community, and we need Haiti to succeed. What happens there has repercussions far beyond its borders.

There are two paths that lie before us. If Haiti can build safe homes, its citizens can escape many of the dangers they now face and return to more normal lives. If Haiti can realize broad-based, sustainable economic growth, it can create opportunity across the country beyond Port-au-Prince so Haitians don't have to move to their capital or leave their country to find work. If Haiti can build strong health and education systems, it can give its people the tools they need to contribute to their nation's progress and fulfill their own God-given potentials. If Haiti can create strong, transparent, accountable institutions, it can establish the credibility, trust, and stability its people have long deserved. And if Haiti can do all of those things with our help, it will become an engine for progress and prosperity generating opportunity and fostering greater stability for itself and for countries throughout the hemisphere and beyond.

But there is another path that Haiti could take, a path that demands far less of Haiti and far less of us. If the effort to rebuild is slow or insufficient, if it is marked by conflict, lack of coordination, or lack of transparency, then the challenges that have plagued Haiti for years could erupt with regional and global consequences. Before the earthquake, migration drained Haiti of many talented citizens, many of whom live in our country. If new jobs and opportunity do not emerge, even more people will leave.

Before the earthquake, quality healthcare was a challenge for Haiti. Now, it is needed even more urgently. Haiti has the highest rate of tuberculosis in the hemisphere, the highest rate of HIV, the highest rates of infant, child, and maternal mortality, one of the highest rates of child malnutrition. And with the public health system now shattered, those numbers will climb. The lack of sanitation services could cause outbreaks of lethal illnesses. And the lack of reliable medical services could give rise to new drug-resistant strains of disease that will soon cross borders.

Before the earthquake, hunger was a problem for Haiti. Years of deforestation had stripped the land of its rich topsoil and people struggled to grow or purchase enough food to feed their families. The riots over food that broke out in 2008 toppled Haiti's government. Now, food is even more scarce, and people more desperate.

Before the earthquake, security was a challenge for Haiti, and a United Nations peacekeeping mission, MINUSTAH, helped promote the rule of law. Now the dedicated UN workers in Haiti have suffered terrible losses. So have the Haitian National Police, which were building their ranks and their capacity. With so much destruction and dislocation, security is even more tenuous. Drug trafficking is a half a billion dollar a year industry in Haiti. It thrives on political and social instability. Trafficking in human beings is also rampant. Tens of thousands of children are trafficked in Haiti every year, and now even more are vulnerable.

Now, each of these problems directly affects the people of Haiti, but they indirectly affect us all. And if they worsen, it is not only the people of Haiti who will suffer. Yet I have great confidence in the resilience of the people of Haiti. Their history has tested them and now they are being tested again. So are Haiti's leaders, in whom I also have great confidence. So we are called to do better than we have in the past. Many countries here have helped Haiti in the past. Many NGOs have helped Haiti in the past. We cannot do what we've done before.

The leaders of Haiti must take responsibility for their country's reconstruction. They must make the tough decisions that guide a strong, accountable, and transparent recovery. And that is what they are starting to do with the creation of a new mechanism that provides coordination and consultation so aid can be directed where it is most needed. And we in the global community, we must also do things differently. It will be tempting to fall back on old habits—to work around the government rather than to work with them as partners, or to fund a scattered array of well-meaning projects rather than making the deeper, long-term investments that Haiti needs now. We cannot retreat to failed strategies.

I know we've heard these imperatives before—the need to coordinate our aid, hold ourselves accountable, share our knowledge, track results. But now, we cannot just declare our intentions. We have to follow through and put them into practice. Therefore, this is not only a conference about what financially we pledge to Haiti. We also have to pledge our best efforts to do better ourselves—to offer our support in a smarter way, a more effective way that produces real results for the people of Haiti.

So let us say here, with one voice, we will pass this test for us. To that end, the United States pledges $1.15 billion for Haiti's long-term recovery and reconstruction. This money will go toward supporting the Government of Haiti's plan to strengthen agriculture, energy, health, security, and governance. We are committed to working with the people and organizations throughout Haiti, including civil society groups, private businesses, NGOs, and citizens. And I'm very glad to see so many of them represented here today.

We will also be looking for ways to engage our Haitian diaspora. Haitian Americans have much to contribute to this effort. And we will seek specifically to empower the women of Haiti. I've said this so many times that I know I sound like a broken record, but investing in women is the best investment we can make in any country. And investing in the Haitian women will fuel the long-term economic recovery and progress, not only for them, but for their families.

Over the years, all of our countries have learned many lessons, particularly from the tsunami that the United Nations was instrumental in leading the response to. Now, we must put those lessons to work in Haiti. I'm very excited and very committed on behalf of President Obama, the Government of the United States, and the people of the United States to help Haiti and to help the leaders of Haiti lead a recovery effort worthy of their highest hopes.

Thank you so much, Secretary General.

Congressional Testimony[*]

Tony Hayward

Director, TNK-BP, 2010– ; born Slough, England, May 21, 1957; geology degree, Ashton University, Birmingham, England; Ph.D., University of Edinburgh, Scotland; joined British Petroleum (BP) as rig geologist, 1982; numerous technical and commercial positions, BP, 1982–1990; executive assistant to BP CEO, 1990–92; exploration manager, Colombia, BP, 1992–95; president of operations, Venezuela, BP, 1995–97; director of exploration, BP, 1997–99; group vice president, BP Amoco Exploration and Production, and member of BP's Upstream executive committee, 1999–2000; BP group treasurer, 2000–02; executive vice president, BP, 2002–03; chief executive of exploration and production, BP, 2003–2010.

Editor's introduction: In congressional testimony delivered before the House of Representatives Committee on Energy and Commerce Subcommittee on Oversight and Investigations, BP CEO Tony Hayward expresses contrition for the disastrous explosion and fire aboard the Deepwater Horizon oil rig, which killed eleven workers and resulted in millions of gallons of oil leaking into the Gulf of Mexico. He pledges the full resources of his company to stop the flow of oil and mitigate the leak's environmental effects. He also describes the efforts of BP, along with various other parties, to address the situation, including the digging of relief wells, collecting oil from the water, and treating subsea oil with dispersants, claiming that BP had spent $1.5 billion so far, with much more to come. Hayward's words did little to appease lawmakers, however, who were critical of what they saw as BP's complacency. Hayward had already courted controversy for a comment he made the previous month: "There's no one who wants this over more than I do. I would like my life back." Two days later, on day 61 of the spill, he prompted further outrage by participating in a glitzy yacht race around England's Isle of Wight. But he was not without sympathizers on Capitol Hill: Rep. Joe Barton, Republican of Texas, told him, "I'm ashamed that a private corporation can be subjected to what I characterize as a shakedown."

---

[*] Delivered on June 17, 2010, at Washington, D.C.

Tony Hayward's speech: Chairman Stupak, Ranking Member Burgess, members of the Subcommittee. I am Tony Hayward, Chief Executive of BP plc.

The explosion and fire aboard the Deepwater Horizon and the resulting oil spill in the Gulf of Mexico never should have happened and I am deeply sorry that they did. None of us yet knows why it happened. But whatever the cause, we at BP will do what we can to make certain that an incident like this does not happen again.

Since April 20, I have spent a great deal of my time in the Gulf Coast region and in the incident command center in Houston, and let there be no mistake. I understand how serious this situation is. This is a tragedy: people lost their lives; others were injured; and the Gulf Coast environment and communities are suffering. This is unacceptable, I understand that, and let me be very clear: I fully grasp the terrible reality of the situation.

When I learned that eleven men had lost their lives in the explosion and fire on the Deepwater Horizon, I was personally devastated. Three weeks ago, I attended a memorial service for those men, and it was a shattering moment. I want to offer my sincere condolences to their friends and families—I can only imagine their sorrow.

My sadness has only grown as the disaster continues. I want to speak directly to the people who live and work in the Gulf region: I know that this incident has profoundly impacted lives and caused turmoil, and I deeply regret that. Indeed, this is personal for us at BP. Many of our 23,000 U.S. employees live and work in the Gulf Coast region. For decades, the people of the Gulf Coast states have extended their hospitality to us and to the companies like Arco and Amoco that are now part of BP. We have always strived to be a good neighbor.

We have worked to hire employees and contractors, and to buy many of our supplies, locally.

I want to acknowledge the questions that you and the public are rightly asking. How could this happen? How damaging is the spill to the environment? Why is it taking so long to stop the flow of oil and gas into the Gulf?

And questions are being asked about energy policy more broadly: Can we as a society explore for oil and gas in safer and more reliable ways? What is the appropriate regulatory framework for the industry?

We don't yet have answers to all these important questions. But I hear the concerns, fears, frustrations—and anger—being voiced across the country. I understand it, and I know that these sentiments will continue until the leak is stopped, and until we prove through our actions that we will do the right thing. Our actions will mean more than words, and we know that, in the end, we will be judged by the quality of our response. Until this happens, no words will be satisfying.

Nonetheless, I am here today because I have a responsibility to the American people to do my best to explain what BP has done, is doing, and will do in the future to respond to this terrible incident. And while we can't undo these tragic events, I give you my word that we will do the right thing. We will not rest until the well is under control, and we will meet all our obligations to clean up the spill and address its environmental and economic impacts.

From the moment I learned of the explosion and fire, I committed the global resources of BP to the response efforts. To be sure, neither I nor the company is perfect. But we are unwavering in our commitment to fulfill all our responsibilities. We are a strong company, and nothing is being spared. We are going to do everything in our power to address fully the economic and environmental consequences of this spill and to ensure that we use the lessons learned from this incident to make energy exploration and production safer and more reliable for everyone.

A COORDINATED EFFORT

We have been committed to responding to these tragic events and coordinating with the federal government from the beginning. On April 21, the Administration began holding meetings and regular calls with me and other members of BP's leadership to discuss BP's response effort, as well as federal oversight and support.

Even before the Deepwater Horizon sank on the morning of April 22, a Unified Command structure was established, as provided by federal regulations. Currently led by the National Incident Commander, Admiral Thad Allen, the Unified Command provides a structure for BP's work with the Coast Guard, the Minerals Management Service and Transocean, among others. We are grateful for the leadership of President Obama, members of his cabinet, the state governors, and local officials.

As the scope of the unfolding disaster became more apparent, we reached out to additional scientists and engineers from our partners and competitors in the energy industry, as well as engineering firms, academia, government and the military. Among the resources that have been made available:

- Drilling and technical experts who are helping determine solutions to stopping the spill and mitigating its impact, including specialists in the areas of subsea wells, environmental science and emergency response;

- Technical advice on blowout preventers, dispersant application, well construction and containment options;

- Additional facilities to serve as staging areas for equipment and responders, more remotely operated vehicles (ROVs) for deep underwater work, barges, support vessels and additional aircraft, as well as training and working space for the Unified Command.

Working under the umbrella of the Unified Command, BP's team of operational and technical experts is coordinating with many federal, state, and local governmental entities and private sector organizations. These include the Departments of Interior, Homeland Security, Energy, and Defense, the National Oceanic and Atmospheric Administration (NOAA), US Fish & Wildlife Service (USFW), National Marine Fisheries Service (NMFS), EPA, OSHA, Gulf Coast state environmental and wildlife agencies, the Marine Spill Response Corporation (MSRC) (an oil spill response organization), as well as numerous state, city, parish, and county agencies.

Some of the best minds and the deepest expertise are being brought to bear. With the possible exception of the space program in the 1960s, it is difficult to imagine the gathering of a larger, more technically proficient team in one place in peacetime. And including BP, industry and government resources, more than 27,000 personnel are now engaged in the response in various activities such as booming, skimming, surveying, clean-up operations, wildlife protection and rehabilitation, and claims support. In addition, we are helping to train and organize the more than 19,000 citizen volunteers who have come forward to offer their services. The outpouring of support from government, industry, businesses, and private citizens has truly been both humbling and inspiring.

WHAT WE ARE DOING

Our efforts in response to this incident are focused on two critical goals:

• Successfully stopping the flow of oil; and

• Minimizing the environmental and economic impacts from the oil spill.

These are without a doubt complex and challenging tasks. While we have had to overcome hurdles, we are doing everything we can to respond as quickly and effectively as we can.

From the beginning, we have been committed to a transparent response. We know the public wants as much information as possible about this unprecedented event, and we continue to do our best to provide it so the public can understand the incident and its impacts.

SUBSEA EFFORTS TO SECURE THE WELL

Our first priority is to stop the flow of oil and secure the well.

We are currently drilling two relief wells, which we believe represents the ultimate solution to stopping the flow of oil and gas from the well. The first relief well is currently at a depth of 15,226 feet, and the second relief well is currently at 9,778 feet.

Separately, the goal has been to minimize or stop the flow of oil and gas before the relief wells are completed. From the beginning, we have implemented a multi-faceted strategy, featuring a range of technological approaches. Our efforts to stop the well from the seabed included a number of interventions to the failed BOP, and the 'top kill' procedure. We understand the public's frustration that these approaches did not stop the flow of oil. We, too, were disappointed.

Although we were not able to stop the well at the seabed, our efforts to contain the oil and gas have been more successful. While our first attempt with a Containment Dome was not successful due to gas hydrate formation, we learned lessons that have underpinned subsequent successes. Specifically, we first deployed a Riser Insertion Tube Tool that overcame these gas hydrate problems and captured more than 2,000 barrels per day for ten days. On June 3, we replaced this with the Lower Marine Riser Package Cap, which had increased our collection to about 15,000 barrels per day.

On Wednesday morning, we were in the early stages of increasing oil and gas collection through our next containment step, the Q4000 Direct Connect. It utilizes much of the subsea 'top kill' equipment and takes oil directly from the failed BOP to the Q4000 on the surface. We expect to optimize collection over the next few days to levels well above what was previously accomplished.

It is important to keep in mind that these techniques have never before been attempted 5,000 feet under water. On the seabed, we have made unprecedented use of ROVs for a variety of tasks, including working on the BOP, positioning riser cutting devices and slings, connecting hoses, positioning containment devices and providing extensive surveying and monitoring. We cannot guarantee the outcome of these operations, but we are working around the clock with the best experts from government and industry.

We continue to do more to increase our operational flexibility and collection capability. This includes securing vessels with greater processing and storage capacity, adding shuttle tankers for transporting oil, procuring spares of critical equipment, installing permanent riser systems, and replacing the containment cap with a more secure system. We will not rest with our containment efforts until the well is permanently killed. I know it feels like this all takes a long time but we are compressing operations that normally take months into days.

In addition to these containment operations, and with the approval of the Unified Command and in conjunction with the EPA, we continue injecting dispersant subsea using ROVs. Dispersant acts by separating the oil into small droplets that can break down more easily through natural processes before they reach the surface. Use of dispersant subsea reduces the amount of oil traveling to the surface, which, in turn, reduces the amount of spray dispersant required at the surface. In addition, dispersant use at the source requires approximately one quarter of the amount of dispersant that would be necessary for use on the surface. Sonar testing and aerial photographs show encouraging results.

There has been a lot of discussion about the use of dispersants. On June 4, a federal panel of experts studying this issue recommended continued use of dispersants after analyzing potential risks and benefits for the environment. The dispersant we are using—Corexit—is on the National Contingency Plan Product Schedule, which is maintained by the EPA. We will continue to work closely with the EPA to try to identify alternative dispersants and to monitor the situation closely. We will only use dispersants in ways approved by the Unified Command, supported by the EPA and other relevant agencies.

CLEAN UP EFFORTS

BP is a "responsible party" under the Oil Pollution Act. This means that federal law requires BP, as one of the working interest owners of Mississippi Canyon 252, to pay to clean up the spill and to compensate for the economic and environmental impacts of the spill. Let me be clear: BP has accepted this responsibility and will fulfill this obligation. We have spent nearly $1.5 billion so far, and we will not stop until the job is done.

It is important to understand that this "responsible party" designation is distinct from an assessment of legal liability for the actions that led to the spill. Investigations into the causes of the incident are ongoing, and issues of liability will be sorted out separately when the facts are clear and all the evidence is available. The focus now is on ensuring that cleanup, and compensation for those harmed by the spill, are carried out as quickly as possible.

Our cleanup efforts are focused on two fronts: in the open water and at the shoreline.

ON THE WATER

On the open water, more than 4,200 response vessels are in use, including skimmers, storage barges, tugs, and other vessels. The Hoss barge, the world's largest skimming vessel, has been onsite since April 25. In addition, there are 49 deepwater skimming vessels, which includes ten 210-foot MSRC Oil Responder Class Vessels, which each have the capacity to collect, separate, and store 4,000 barrels of oily water mix. To date, over 400,000 barrels of oily water mix have been recovered.

As part of our response efforts, over 2,000 "Vessels of Opportunity," independent vessel owners throughout the Gulf Coast are using their boats in a variety of oil recovery activities, including towing and deploying booms, supporting skimming and burn operations, finding and recovering tar balls and transporting general supplies and personnel.

Also on the open water, with the Coast Guard's approval, we are attacking the spill area with EPA-approved biodegradable dispersants, which are being applied from both planes and boats.

ACTIONS TO PROTECT THE SHORELINE

Near the shoreline, we are implementing oil spill response contingency plans to protect sensitive areas. According to the Coast Guard, the result is the most massive shoreline protection effort ever mounted.

To support rapid response, we have made available a total of $175 million to Louisiana, Mississippi, Alabama, and Florida, as well as $70 million to assist these states in tourism promotion efforts.

To date, we have deployed over 2.5 million feet of containment boom and over 3.0 million feet of sorbent boom in an effort to contain the spill and protect the coastal shoreline. The Department of Defense is helping to airlift boom to wherever it is currently needed across the Gulf coast.

Highly mobile, shallow draft skimmers are also staged along the coast ready to attack the oil where it approaches the shoreline.

Wildlife clean-up stations have been mobilized, and pre-impact baseline assessment and beach clean-up has been completed in many locations. Shoreline cleanup assessment teams (SCAT) are being deployed to affected areas to assess the type and quantity of oiling, so the most effective cleaning strategies can be rapidly applied.

Our largest single project commitment to date is to fund the $360 million cost of six berms in the Louisiana barrier islands project. On June 7, we announced that we will make an immediate payment of $60 million to the state of Louisiana to allow the state to begin work on the project immediately. BP will make five additional $60 million payments when the Coastal Protection and Restoration Authority of Louisiana certifies that the project has satisfied 20%, 40%, 60%, 80%, and then 100% completion milestones. The entire $360 million will be funded by the completion of the project.

In addition, BP is committing up to $500 million to an open research program studying the impact of the Deepwater Horizon incident, and the associated response, on the marine and shoreline environment of the Gulf of Mexico. The program will investigate the impacts of the oil, dispersed oil, and dispersant on the ecosystems of the Gulf of Mexico and coastal States.

COMMUNICATION, COMMUNITY OUTREACH, AND ENGAGING VOLUNTEERS

We are also working hard to keep the public and government officials around the country informed of what is happening. We are regularly briefing federal, state, and local officials, and we are holding town hall sessions to keep affected communities informed.

BP is also supporting volunteer efforts related to shoreline clean-up. We have partnered with existing volunteer organizations in each of the states to ensure efficient registration and deployment of volunteers to the areas where they can help most.

Untrained volunteers are not being used for any work involving contact or handling of oil, tar balls, or other hydrocarbon materials. This work is being carried out by trained personnel. In some cases, volunteers who receive more intensive training on the safe handling of hazardous materials and vessel operation for laying boom can become contract employees (Qualified Community Responders).

There are twenty-five BP community-outreach sites engaging, training, and preparing volunteers in Alabama, Florida, Louisiana and Mississippi. A phone line has also been established for potential volunteers to register their interest in assisting the response effort.

We recognize that beyond the environmental impacts there are also economic impacts on many of the people who rely on the Gulf for their livelihood. BP will pay all necessary cleanup costs and all legitimate claims for other losses and damages caused by the spill.

The BP claims process is integral to our commitment to do the right thing. To date, BP has already paid out over $90 million on the more than 56,000 claims that have been submitted. While the initial focus has been on individuals, we are now moving funds on an expedited basis to business owners with nearly $16 million to be paid out this week to businesses alone.

To ensure the process is as fair and transparent as possible, an independent mediator will be appointed to provide an independent judgment in cases in which BP and a claimant are in disagreement. The mediator will be fully independent of BP, and claimants who disagree with the mediator's judgment will retain all rights under the Oil Pollution Act of 1990 either to seek reimbursement from the Oil Spill Liability Trust Fund or to file a claim in court.

Thirty-two walk-in claims offices are open in Alabama, Florida, Louisiana, and Mississippi. Our call center is operating 24 hours a day, seven days a week. We also have in place an on-line claims filing system. Nearly 700 people are assigned to handle the claims, including almost 600 experienced claims adjusters working in the impacted communities. Claim forms can be filled out in English, Spanish, or Vietnamese, and Spanish and Vietnamese translators are available in many offices.

We are striving to be efficient and fair and we look for guidance to the established laws, regulations and other information provided by the US Coast Guard, which oversees the process.

We will continue adding people, offices and resources as necessary.

INVESTIGATING WHAT HAPPENED

The question we all want answered is "What caused this tragic accident?"

A full answer to this and other questions must await the outcome of multiple investigations now underway, including a joint investigation by the Departments of Homeland Security and Interior (Marine Board) and an internal investigation by BP itself.

Our internal investigation was launched on April 21, 2010 and is being conducted by BP's Head of Group Safety and Operations.

The investigation team's work thus far suggests that this accident was brought about by the apparent failure of a number of processes, systems and equipment. While the team's work is not done, it appears that there were multiple control mechanisms—procedures and equipment—in place that should have prevented this accident or reduced the impact of the spill. The investigation is focused on the following seven mechanisms:

1. The cement that seals the reservoir from the well;

2. The casing system, which seals the well bore;

3. The pressure tests to confirm the well is sealed;

4. The execution of procedures to detect and control hydrocarbons in the well, including the use of the blowout preventer (BOP) and the maintenance of that BOP;

5. The BOP Emergency Disconnect System, which can be activated by pushing a button at multiple locations on the rig;

6. The automatic closure of the BOP after its connection is lost with the rig; and;

7. Features in the BOP to allow ROVs to close the BOP and thereby seal the well at the seabed after a blowout.

I understand people want a simple answer about why this happened and who is to blame. The truth, however, is that this is a complex accident, caused by an unprecedented combination of failures. A number of companies are involved, including BP, and it is simply too early to understand the cause. There is still extensive work to do.

LESSONS LEARNED

There are events that occurred on April 20 that were not foreseen by me or BP, but which we need to address in the future as lessons learned from this terrible tragedy. With ongoing investigations into the incident and continuing efforts to secure the well, we are in the early stages of trying to learn from this incident.

But, as I see it, there are already lessons to be learned, and I wanted to share two of them with you today.

Lesson 1: Based on the events of April 20 and thereafter, we need to be better prepared for a subsea disaster. It is clear that our industry needs to significantly improve our ability to quickly address deep-sea accidents of this type and magnitude.

The industry has made significant strides in preparedness measures before, and we will do so again. Following the Exxon *Valdez* oil spill, the industry recognized the need to enhance its capacity to address oil spills. The result was the MSRC, an independent, nonprofit company which maintains a significant inventory of vessels, equipment and trained personnel, complemented by a large contractor work force. The work of MSRC and other contractors has been central to the surface spill response efforts in the Gulf.

But based on the events of April 20 and thereafter, it is clear that this is not enough. We now need to develop a similar capability for dealing with large undersea spills. We have no doubt that others in the industry will join us in efforts to develop this capability.

Lesson 2: Based on what happened on April 20, we now know we need better safety technology. We in the industry have long relied on the blowout preventer as the principal piece of safety equipment. Yet, on this occasion it apparently failed, with disastrous consequences. We must use this incident as a case study to avoid a similar failure in the future.

Since the April 20 explosion and fire, BP has been carefully evaluating the subsea blowout preventers used in all our drilling operations worldwide, including the testing and maintenance procedures of the drilling contractors using the devices. We will participate in industry-wide efforts to improve the safety and reliability of subsea blowout preventers and deep water drilling practices. And we will work closely with other interested parties as we do so.

CONCLUSION

We understand the seriousness of the situation. We know the world is watching us. No one will forget the 11 men who lost their lives in the explosion on the Deepwater Horizon. We hear and understand the concerns, frustrations, and fears that have been and will continue to be voiced. I understand that only actions and results, and not mere words, ultimately can give you the confidence you seek. We will be, and deserve to be, judged by our response.

I give my pledge as leader of BP that we will not rest until we stop this well, mitigate the environmental impact of the spill and address economic claims in a responsible manner. No resource available to this company will be spared. We and the entire industry will learn from this terrible event and emerge from it stronger, smarter and safer.

Testimony to the Congressional Black Caucus[*]

Focus on Haiti

Paul Farmer

Chair of the Department of Social Medicine, Harvard Medical School, Chief of the Division of Global Health Equity at Brigham and Women's Hospital in Boston, and Deputy Special Envoy for Haiti at the United Nations (UN), 2009– ; born October 26, 1959, North Adams, MA; A.B., Duke University, 1982; Ph.D., anthropology, Harvard University, 1990; M.D., Harvard Medical School, 1990; founder, Boston-based Partners in Health, 1987, where he has worked since; recipient of a John D. and Catherine T. MacArthur Foundation "genius award," 1993; author of numerous articles and the books AIDS and Accusation: Haiti and the Geography of Blame *(1992);* The Uses of Haiti, *(1994);* Infections and Inequalities: The Modern Plagues, *(1999).*

Editor's introduction: In this address, delivered before a hearing of the Congressional Black Caucus entitled "Focus on Haiti: The Road to Recovery—A Six Month Review," doctor and anthropologist Paul Farmer testifies that one of the primary tasks of development assistance in the aftermath of the earthquake must be to strengthen Haiti's public sector, since many well-intentioned nongovernment organizations (NGOs) have not succeeded in solving Haiti's problems. Farmer points out that the weakness of the public sector owes partly to the foreign policy of the United States and other nations, which in opposition to the presidency of Jean-Bertrand Aristide starved Haiti of aid. Comparing the situation in Haiti to that in the United States during the Great Depression, Farmer quotes Franklin Delano Roosevelt in calling for an extensive program of job creation.

Paul Farmer's speech:

1. Acute-on-chronic

---

[*] Delivered on July 27, 2010, at Washington, D.C.

The six-month anniversary of the earthquake, which many Haitians have taken to calling, simply, "the catastrophe," will cause soul-searching in some circles, grim determination in others, and bitter recriminations from still other quarters. I will not contribute here to these veins of commentary, although we all know they're important and inevitable. Instead I will use my time to comment on a few large but soluble problems now before us and to make two distinct and complementary recommendations. Indeed, most of these problems have long faced all those of good will who seek to stand in solidarity with the Haitian people, which is why, as physicians, we know that what happened on January 12th is aptly described as an "acute-on-chronic" event.

Though by some reports and some "macro" indicators there had been slow improvements in Haiti in the year prior to the quake, the problems we're struggling with today are longstanding, if much aggravated by the worst natural disaster to befall the world in recent centuries. Whether we look at health, education, potable water, or safe, affordable housing, we can draw similar conclusions: first, great weakness in the public sector makes it exceedingly difficult to deliver basic services at significant scale; second, not enough of the pledged earthquake relief has reached those in greatest need.

Although Haitians are rightly tired of having their country labeled "the poorest in the western hemisphere," it is nonetheless true that the country has poor health indicators, was a few years ago deemed the most water-insecure nation in the Americas, has low levels of literacy, and now, with up to 1.6 million in IDP camps, has enormous, almost overwhelming, housing instability. Into the breach have come a large number of well-intentioned NGOs, which have sought, with some local success, to provide basic health and educational services, and, on an even smaller level, access to potable water and improved housing. I am myself from this sector, since I've been a life-long NGO volunteer and work for a U.S. medical school as a teacher and clinician. But I would like to argue here that my own earnest engagement in this arena has taught me that one of the primary tasks of development assistance, including that delivered by NGOs, must be to strengthen Haitian public-sector capacity, especially in the arenas of health, education, water, and housing—which some refer to as basic social and economic rights. Our historical failure to do so is one of the primary reasons that trying to help the public sector now is like trying to transfuse whole blood through a small-gauge needle or, in popular parlance, to drink from a fire hose.

Why the public sector? Before answering, I'm not suggesting here that NGOs and the private sector are not part of the solution; far from it. But there is a pragmatic and humble point to be made here: the profusion of NGOs—and some have estimated that Haiti, a veritable Republic of NGOs, has more of them per capita than any other country in the world—has not led to adequate progress in provision of basic services to all who need them nor to a functioning safety net for the poorest. Case in point: over 85% of primary and secondary education in Haiti is private, and Haiti is, as mentioned, plagued by illiteracy; over 500,000 school-age children were not in school prior to the earthquake.

There are transient ironies, too. Sometimes bursts of attention can improve a terrible situation; some blood does get through the too-small needle. Take water insecurity: by some reports, it has lessened since the earthquake led many groups to focus on bringing clean water to the displaced. One survey in Port-au-Prince suggested that diarrheal diseases had by last month *dropped* 12% below the pre-earthquake level. But is the massive importation of bottled water readily sustained? Is it the way to improve water security for all?

There is also a more philosophical point behind a plea for attention to the public sector: How can there be public health and public education without a stronger government at the national and local levels?

2. Why?

I have argued that the quake dramatically worsened a bad situation. I could focus on statistics, noting that some 17–20% of federal employees were killed or injured in the quake, or that 27 of 28 federal buildings were destroyed. And I would note that few public personnel were able to perform well within the buildings prior to the earthquake. Some of the best doctors and nurses I know are struggling to perform in the public sector without the tools of our trade—diagnostics and medications, for example, but also anything approaching adequate salaries. In a hearing like this one, it is important to ask why this is so, and I have previously done so before both houses of our Congress. It is not a pretty story, for the decline of Haiti's already feeble civil service is tightly tied, and has been for a century, to internecine strife but also to U.S. policies. Other powerful countries have played unhelpful roles, too.

Let me take only the last decade. Beginning in 2000, the U.S. administration sought, often quietly, to block bilateral and multilateral aid to Haiti, having an objection to the policies and views of the administration of Jean-Bertrand Aristide, elected by over 90% of the vote at about the same time a new U.S. president was chosen in a far more contested election. How much influence we had on other players is unclear, but it seems that there was a great deal of it with certain international financial agencies, with France and Canada; our own aid, certainly, went directly to NGOs, and not to the government. Public health and public education faltered, as did other services of special importance to the poor. I noted in a book written in those years that the budget of the Republic of Haiti, nine million strong, wasn't much different from that of the city of Cambridge, Massachusetts, with 100,000 citizens; neither amounted to a quarter of the budget of the Harvard teaching hospital, a single one, in which I trained and now work.

Without resources, it was difficult for public providers to provide; many left to work in NGOs, which did not have a mandate to serve all citizens, and others left the country altogether. Choking off assistance for development and for the provision of basic services also choked off oxygen to the government, which was the intention all along: to dislodge the Aristide administration.

But the coup, simply denied as such by some in the so-called international community, did not really take. The U.S.-selected caretaker government was unpopular, unrest continued to grow, and Port-au-Prince became the kidnapping capital of the world in spite of a very large U.N. presence. Again, the so-called forces of order, the police, were weak or corrupt—as pale a reflection of what the force should have been as were public health and public education.

Some efforts to reverse this ruinous policy of squeezing the public sector, which was often and correctly denounced by Congresswomen Lee and Waters and many other members of the CBC, have been palpable over the past year, although progress has been slow. And then came the earthquake, which further decreased the capacity of the public sector to provide meaningful services, leaving once again a growing number of NGOs and other non-state providers to fill the breach. Allow me to give two more data points: on January 27th, it was noted in the *Washington Post* that less than 1% of all U.S. quake aid was going to the Haitian government. (Almost as much went, even, to the Dominican government.) My colleagues at the U.N. are tracking these numbers, and also pledges made and disbursed, and here's one of the latest: of $1.8 billion for earthquake relief sent to Haiti, less than 2.9% has so far gone to the government.

I argued here in 2003, in testimony to the Senate Committee on Foreign Relations, that it is difficult, without real and sustained commitments to strengthening the public sector—including its regulatory and coordinating capacity, so that the quality of the services offered by NGOs and others will not be all over the map—to monitor funds and to use them efficiently. This remains true today. *Thus are the Haitian people still tasting the bitter dregs of the cup we prepared for them as we weakened, or failed to strengthen, the public sector over the past decades.*

During these years, unfair international trade policies cut Haitian farmers off at the knees, accelerating the complex and vicious cycle of urban migration and deforestation that set the stage for the food insecurity that was to follow, for the extreme vulnerability to heavy rains and storms, and for the massive overcrowding and shoddy construction revealed to all late in the afternoon of January 12th.

3. What is to be done?

This is where we are at the six-month mark, as hurricane season approaches. Less than five percent of the rubble has been cleared. People are going to camps for shelter and for other services that all of us humans need to get by. Gender-based violence worsens the "structural violence" to which the poor, in general, are subjected. The good news is that the enormous generosity and solidarity of the world after the earthquake was and is real: it's estimated that more than half of all American households contributed to earthquake relief. Speaking as a volunteer for PIH, I can proudly announce that we have, along with the Ministry of Health, already broken ground on a huge new teaching hospital in central Haiti. We know from experience, as my colleague Loune Viaud will report, that it's possible to get a great deal done in rural Haiti, and these services and jobs will also pull people out of the city and contribute to the decentralization so desperately needed.

But there needs to be a shift, especially in how we plan and deliver basic health, education, and other safety-net services: a commitment to move at least some of the assistance (including private money) into public hands, which has not been at all the favored approach to assistance to Haiti. This is increasingly recognized as the right thing to do, as Paul Weisenfeld, Haiti Task Team Coordinator for USAID, who reported the falling rates of water-borne diseases noted above, observed recently: "I think it's key to us that if we're going to have sustainability we are going to have to work through Haitian institutions, which requires strengthening them. Obviously [they've] been weakened tremendously by this earthquake, so at the same time that we implement reconstruction programs, we need to strengthen government institutions so that we can work through them."[1] We have also just worked with the American Red Cross to support performance-based financing of medical and nursing staff in Haiti's largest public hospital. These efforts will not be easy, but they are necessary.

This shift will not be a panacea for Haiti but could be coupled with a powerful and complementary focus on another movement of capital, this time from public to private and from wealthy to poor: a focus on job creation and on strengthening the hand of those trying to farm (and reforest) the land and also on young people, especially young women, living in poverty. We need a greater sense of urgency. And the most urgent task of all is the creation of jobs that will confer dignity to those in greatest need. As FDR said early in the Depression, "The Nation asks for action and action now. Our greatest primary task is to put people to work."[2]

As it was during the Great Depression, there are innumerable public-works jobs imaginable, from reforestation and rubble removal to preparing for back-to-school (*la rentrée*), which must put kids back in schools, safe schools, with the books and uniforms they need and a nutritious lunch during the day. As for health, Haitians need a real health system. This will require a massive investment in new clinics and hospitals, staff to run them, and health insurance at a time when only 300,000 families have it. These are indivisible tasks, as FDR noted at the outset of the Depression: "Public health . . . is a responsibility of the state as [is] the duty to promote general welfare. The state educates is children. Why not keep them well?"[3]

Job creation and improved health and educational services, with greater investment in the public sector: this should be a big part of the mantra. I do not mean to suggest that this transfer of capital, resources, etc., is easy. We know it's not, because we're in direct contact with the representatives of large multilateral and bilateral agencies, which have to follow laborious processes in order to disburse funds. But let us ask, in the face of urgent need, if we are well served by the fetishization of process now retarding the flow of capital into the hands of families in greatest need. The International Commission for the Reconstruction of Haiti, which is now being born, needs to be swift and nimble; the rules of the road for development assistance need to be rewritten, not to favor contractors and middlemen and trauma vultures, but to favor the victims of the quake. Right now there are shovel-ready projects, which could create tens of thousands of jobs and perhaps more. There are plenty of people living in poverty, including the market women who have never had access to capital or financial services and who have been working against an undertow of unfair trade policies, who are as entrepreneurial as anyone else in the world. Projects of all sorts can be greenlighted, but will move sluggishly if the funds seep into the ICRH too slowly and if projects cannot be moved forward because of strangling strictures on how the money is to be used.

People in this country know it's possible to move forward with a sense of urgency. During the Depression, job creation and improved services from health care to education to rural electrification were the focus of many efforts. FDR, then the governor of New York, called for "workfare" and welfare through the Temporary Emergency Relief Administration (TERA). This call was made on August 28, 1931, and it was up and running by winter: The crisis had finally imposed some discipline of responsibility even on the Republican legislators, who with uncharacteristic docility did what the governor asked. (The New York voters would overwhelmingly approve the bond issue in November 1932.) Faithful to romantic notions of rural life, Roosevelt had TERA subsidize the resettlement of as many unemployed as possible on marginal farmland, with tools and instruction on how to cultivate it. In six years TERA assisted five million people, 40 percent of the population of New York State, at a cost of $1,555,000. At the end of the period, 70 percent of these were no longer reliant on government assistance.[4]

Later these lessons were taken to scale in many programs, including the Civil Works Administration, which created millions of jobs and moved billions into the public sector through public works and into the hands of the previously unemployed.

Certainly Haiti's need is no less great than that faced by the States during the Depression. Let us hope it can build a more just tax base, even though its IRS, like its Ministries of Health and Education, has been destroyed. In the meantime, the world has responded generously and now it is incumbent upon us to move these resources into the hands of the Haitian people, especially those directly affected, in these two complementary ways. Again, this is not a choice between public and private sectors, any more than this is a choice between strengthening local agriculture and rebuilding infrastructure, but rather a plea to focus resource distribution on the poor and displaced by providing basic services and through job creation. There is no evidence whatsoever that this is an impossible mission.

FOOTNOTES

1 Remarks by Paul Weisenfeld, USAID Haiti Task Team coordinator, at a media roundtable on July 19, 2010. Available at: http://www.usaid.gov/press/speeches/2010/sp100719_1.html

2 Roosevelt, Franklin D. First Inaugural Address. March 4, 1933.

3 Black, Conrad. *Franklin Delano Roosevelt: Champion of Freedom.* New York: PublicAffairs, 2003. Page 194.

4 Black, pages 216-217.

5

The State and Future of Philanthropy

Why on Earth Would a Foundation Try to Get Rid of All of Its Money?*

Gara LaMarche

President and CEO, The Atlantic Philanthropies, 2007– ; born Westerly, RI, August 26, 1954; B.A., Columbia College, 1976; staff associate, American Civil Liberties Union (ACLU), 1976–79; associate director, New York ACLU, 1979–1984; executive director, Texas ACLU, 1984–88; associate director and director of Free Expression Project, Human Rights Watch, 1990–96; vice president and director of U.S. Programs, Open Society Institute (OSI), 1996–2007; author of numerous articles on human rights and social justice issues; adjunct professor, John Jay College of Criminal Justice, 1982–84, The New School, 2000–03, and New York University (NYU), 2006– ; serves on a number of boards, including the PEN American Center, The White House Project, and the Leadership Council of Hispanics in Philanthropy.

Editor's introduction: In this address, presented at the Annual Meeting of Delaware Valley Grantmakers, Gara LaMarche outlines the reasons behind the decision to spend all of The Atlantic Philanthropies' endowment and thus terminate the foundation by 2017. This resolution, LaMarche explains, is based partly on the philosophy of Charles Feeney, the organization's founder, who believed in dedicating sizable resources to counteract emerging problems early on, before they grew into full-blown crises. LaMarche goes on to discuss historical precedents for the spend-down model, his organization's place in the history of philanthropy, and the ways that the spend-down philosophy affects the organization's programs.

Gara LaMarche's speech: My talk this afternoon poses the question, which I will spend the next fifteen minutes or so attempting to answer, "why on earth would a foundation try to get rid of all of its money?" It is the aspect of The Atlantic Philanthropies, I find, that most people are intensely interested in. Not the fact that we are one of the largest foundations in the world—in fact the largest private funder in every one of the seven countries in which we operate, outside the United States. Not that we have a legal status that permits us to be extensive and vigorous

---

* Delivered on January 8, 2009, at Philadelphia, PA. Reprinted with permission.

funders of advocacy. Not our comprehensive approach to evaluation and learning and somewhat rare, for our field, in-house unit for carrying it out.

No, what is most fascinating to observers of The Atlantic Philanthropies is that our board, following the wishes of our donor, Chuck Feeney, is committed to spending our endowment and ending the foundation as we know it in the next eight years. By the time we are done, we will be the largest spend-down foundation in history. What, people want to know, is it like to give away money at that pace? How does it make your strategies and practices different from foundations trying to manage their assets to exist in perpetuity? And how, they always ask with a laugh, can they help us spend it faster?

Well, in the last few months the market has been doing a fine job of helping us get closer to zero, thank you very much. It is suddenly a different and stranger climate in which to be talking about spending down, when several of our colleague foundations have in recent weeks literally gone out of business, involuntarily and with terrible impact on grantees left struggling to deal with the effects of cancelled payments. But Atlantic still has over three billion dollars left, and yes, it is a weighty responsibility. Why did we take this less-traveled route?

It started with our donor, Chuck Feeney, who believes strongly in a philosophy he calls "giving while living." By the 1980s, Feeney had already transferred virtually all of his vast wealth to the foundation, and has lived since quite modestly, owning no home or car. He remained on the Atlantic board, and a few years ago, when the foundation's future was being discussed, Feeney, who was heavily influenced by Andrew Carnegie's "Gospel of Wealth," and Carnegie's belief that a man who dies wealthy dies disgraced, sent a rare note to the Atlantic Trustees, saying: "I believe that people of substantial wealth potentially create problems for future generations unless they themselves accept responsibility to use their wealth during their lifetime to help worthwhile causes."

The idea is that the world has many pressing problems, and if we can focus resources on them today, through an investment approach, we will minimize the need for dealing with them more urgently and less thoughtfully as crises later on. That lens guides in the first place the selection of issues that the Atlantic board identified—the challenges of aging societies, the needs of disadvantaged children and youth, systemic abuses of human rights, the delivery of health care to underserved regions and populations—but it could be applied as well to other issues, like climate change.

Spending down your assets is not for everyone, and recognizing the pluralism of philanthropy, we understand that most foundations will probably not choose to follow us. We have no desire to preach or scold others for choosing to remain perpetual institutions. There are many positive reasons for assuring strength and continuity over generations.

Yet we hope to provide advice and examples to those who are considering the path we have taken. And there will be more. Despite the current economic distress, it is safe to predict that in the next twenty years, as in the last twenty, significant new sources of philanthropic wealth will come into the picture. While Ford,

Carnegie, Rockefeller and a few other 75-and 100-year-old perpetual foundations continue to play extremely significant roles on the philanthropic scene, a number of today's largest and most talked-about foundations—Gates, now buttressed with the Buffett contribution; George Soros's Open Society Institute, for which I used to work; the Google and Omidyar Foundations; and Atlantic itself—did not exist a few decades ago. Some, like Atlantic, will disappear, but others not yet born will emerge and become leaders and innovators.

The spend-down approach to philanthropy is just beginning to receive scholarly attention, and Atlantic has itself supported two research initiatives, one by the Urban Institute and the other by the Aspen Institute. We also participate in a few oral history and documentation projects focusing on our choices and process. The leading historical model for spending down is the Julius Rosenwald Foundation, established in 1917, not long after Carnegie and Rockefeller, by the founder and President of Sears Roebuck. According to the recent biography of Rosenwald by his grandson, Peter Ascoli, he came to feel that endowments were often created by well-meaning donors for purposes whose significance waned over time, such as orphan asylums, which even by Rosenwald's day had come to be seen as outmoded institutions.

Julius Rosenwald also had an activist bent, and an aversion to bureaucracy characteristic of visionary living donors—take it from me, I have worked for two of the four biggest, George Soros and Chuck Feeney—Rosenwald wrote to his board that:

> I am not in sympathy with . . . perpetuating endowment and believe that more good can be accomplished by expending funds as trustees find opportunities for constructive work than by storing a large sum or money for long periods of time. By adopting the policy of using the fund within this generation, we may avoid these tendencies toward bureaucracy and a formal or perfunctory attitude toward the work which almost invariably develops in organizations which prolong their existences indefinitely. Coming generations can be relied upon to provide for their own needs as they arise.

Or, as Waldemar Nielsen put it in his book *Inside American Philanthropy*, "time is not the friend of foundation vigor and effectiveness. In fact, with the passing of years, decay and stagnation are quite common, if not endemic."

So Julius Rosenwald played a large role in the University of Chicago and a variety of Jewish organizations, but perhaps his biggest legacy was the construction of schools serving rural African-Americans in 15 southern states, cooperatively built with local communities, and the strengthening of key black institutions of higher education, among them Tuskegee and Howard universities. He also created 1,000 scholarships and fellowships for African-American students. The human capital energized by this generosity is incalculable. But because Julius Rosenwald cared little about the credit, and did not leave behind a perpetual foundation bearing his name, his impact is much less well known than that of the Carnegies, Rockefellers and Fords. That may be one reason, perhaps, why the spend-down course is not often followed, since in my experience ego is not in short supply among the wealthy and successful.

While Rosenwald's is the largest previous spend-down foundation, there are others, and Atlantic is trying to learn from their experiences. Irene Diamond and her husband Aaron created a foundation, named after Aaron, who died before it got off the ground, and over ten years in [the] 1980s and 1990s it spent its assets on a set of focused initiatives, leaving at least two significant legacies, an AIDS research center headed by Dr. David Ho, who was named *Time*'s Man of the Year in 1996 for his critical role in creating anti-retroviral therapy; and a set of successful small high schools in New York City, which formed the basis for a much broader school reform effort eventually joined in by Gates, Carnegie and OSI and institutionalised in New York and elsewhere. Not a bad monument.

I knew Irene Diamond, who died in 2003 at the age of 92, and like Rosenwald, Feeney and Soros, she was an impatient person. Vincent McGee, who led her foundation, recalls that she didn't have much tolerance for process or long learning curves. "Look, you have youth and time to talk about process," she once said to him. "I don't. I'm the fire engine driving your process down the street."

Vinny, who is an activist himself, now works for Atlantic and is a tremendous resource for our spend-down process. We also just hired Bill Roberts, the longtime leader of the other most prominent and effective spend down foundation of recent years, The Beldon Fund, which over ten years concluding in 2008 was a major force in creating state organizing capacity for environmental protection. Bill's experience will also be helpful to Atlantic, since he knows first-hand, as he told *Beyond Five Percent*, a recent publication of Northern California Grantmakers and the New York Regional Association of Grantmakers, how difficult it is to implement and complete a spend-down plan. "To get a clear, focused, staffed strategy humming in less than two years is optimistic," Bill said. "Then you're on the street, looking for grants to make, explaining the strategy, which can take another year or two. All pistons don't fire until year three or four. Then you make a mid-course correction in year five or six, so now you have maybe three years where you're at full tilt—the sweet spot."

One spend-down foundation whose departing staff we didn't hire, since it's at an opposite ideological pole from Atlantic, is the John M. Olin Foundation, though I admire its discipline and its leadership very much—a story told in John Miller's *A Gift of Freedom*, a book I assign to my philanthropy and public policy class at New York University's Wagner School. Olin was influenced by Julius Rosenwald, but his own interests focused on preservation of the free enterprise system that had allowed him to build his fortune, and the conservative law and economics movement, not to mention the Federalist Society, which shaped Reagan and Bush justice policies, including the life-tenured federal judiciary, can be counted among Olin's legacies.

Of course, there are a number of avenues available to foundations between preserving themselves forever and going out of business. In 1999, the Charles E. Culpepper Foundation turned over its assets to the Rockefeller Brothers Fund and merged trustees and operations. Raymond C. Smith, a food store heir, merged his foundation into the Community Foundation for Southeastern Michigan when he died at the age of 97. The HKH Foundation has established flexible payout rates to permit it to rise to opportunities that call for stepped-up spending, for instance increasing its giving by a third to promote civic engagement before the 2004 elections, in the same spirit that Atlantic and the Open Society Institute have announced plans to spend tens of millions of dollars together to take advantage of the enormous policy opportunities presented by the new Obama administration.

Now, finally, to the question of how it affects the choices Atlantic makes and the ways in which we carry out our work. There are three principal areas to look at: investments, human resources, and programme.

Atlantic's investment team has one of the most unusual challenges in its field. We want those managing our funds to maximize the return on our assets while we work steadily to reduce them. In our shorthand description of this, it means getting to zero by the end. Briefly put, our Investment Team and Committee have been charged with managing our money to assure that we can pay our current commitments (currently in the neighborhood of $900 million), commit a further annual amount of approximately $360 million a year, and pay for our operating costs. The grant commitment target has been set so as to be challenging, but achievable, and we hope to be able to increase the commitment rate over time if returns are good, being more conservative—as at the current moment—when conditions are challenging.

These are all policy decisions, of course—we could decide to alter our spending plan, making more grants now and fewer later, or end the foundation earlier than 2017—but given our current plan of assuring a steady flow across the remaining years, we are on track.

I was pleased upon coming to Atlantic in 2007 to find that we had a good plan in place for encouraging key staff to remain in place carry out the work of the foundation until the end, and dealing with them fairly. In the absence of such a plan, there would be a natural tendency for staff to seize opportunities that arise in order to plan for their careers and their families, and they'd be justified in doing so. I certainly plan—unless my employers decide otherwise—to be the one to turn out the lights at Atlantic. And if we are faced with gaps in staff capacity in the final years, I think we could attract the necessary talent by tapping accomplished people seeking "encore" careers, in the fashion of our chairman Fritz Schwarz, who followed a successful corporate and civic legal career to take a senior role at the Brennan Center for Justice, or young people, who would see spending a few years at Atlantic as a valuable opportunity, and in some cases academics and other professionals, who could come to us on leave or private-sector consultants seconded to us for a time.

I don't worry too much about the human resources side of spend down, not only because of the tools we have put in place, but also because virtually all staff at Atlantic are mission-driven. When people are principally motivated by advancing their social values, as our staff at all levels are, and when you treat them well and with respect, their loyalty to the enterprise is strong.

On the most important program side, we are just concluding a months-long process of what Bill Roberts called "mid-course correction," and there are two key results of that which may at first seem contradictory, but which I think are in fact complementary. The first is to take what was already a highly-focused foundation, with clear strategic objectives in our four program areas and seven geographies, and make it even more so. We will move out of several areas where we don't have sufficient traction, and drill down further into those where we do. At the same time, we have shifted more money to a "Venture Fund" which will allow us to move quickly to take advantage of short-term opportunities, particularly in the policy realm which is, to borrow another Bill Roberts phrase, our "sweet spot." You might call it strategic opportunism, and it has permitted us to make the largest-ever grant for advocacy to a health care coalition that is now poised to work with the new president to repair the largest gap in the U.S. social safety net, and to work with Barbara Hogan, the progressive new health minister who is ending years of AIDS denialism in South Africa.

If there is another shift in Atlantic as we enter the last eight years or so of our grantmaking, it is that we have considered what our legacy means and come up with a somewhat different answer than when we first thought about it some years ago. Originally we thought that our limited time-horizon obligated us to take on only those issues where we could have a reasonable chance of success within that span—not ending poverty, for instance, but abolishing the death penalty or strengthening indigent defense systems in three selected states. Our earlier goals had the virtue of specificity and up or down measurability, and that is attractive. But policy successes come and go—we thought we had abolished the death penalty, for all practical purposes, in the U.S. in the early 1970s, only to have it come roaring back. What is enduring, though, is the strengthening of institutions and the building of leadership that will be strong and able to take on the challenges of human rights or disadvantaged youth or public health or aging long after today's fleeting policy battles, and long after Atlantic is gone. So operating within an explicit framework of promoting social justice in all we do, Atlantic will deepen the already significant commitment it has to building the capacity of key institutions and movements in the fields we have chosen to focus on.

Mark Twain famously said, of the prospect of death by hanging, that it "powerfully concentrates the mind," and that is surely true for the death of an endowment. Everything weighs more, and counts more. But that seems a dark spot on which to end this talk, for what I have found most true is that it is fun to approach this challenge—indeed, liberating. So I will close instead with the words of my friend Lewis Cullman, a vigorous patron of arts, education, democracy and human rights who with his wife Dorothy is busily spending their fortune on philanthropy. "What I learned as a little boy from my mother," Lewis says, "I don't care what people say about me when I'm dead. I won't be around to hear it. Why not get the joy out of spending your money while you're alive?"

Nonprofits, Philanthropy and Public Policy[*]

Are We at a Critical Moment?

Steven Rathgeb Smith

Professor, Evans School of Public Affairs, University of Washington, 2004– ; professor of public policy, Georgetown University, 2010– ; B.A., Brown University, 1973; M.S.W., Washington University, St. Louis, 1978; Ph.D. political science, Massachusetts Institute of Technology (MIT), 1988; assistant professor, Washington University, St. Louis, 1987–88; assistant professor, Sanford School of Public Policy, Duke University, 1988–1996; assistant professor, 1996–1997, associate professor, 1997–2004, Nancy Bell Evans Professor of Public Affairs, 2007–09, Evans School of Public Affairs, University of Washington; visiting professor, Georgetown Public Policy Institute, Waldemar A. Nielsen Chair in Philanthropy, Georgetown University, 2009–10.

Editor's introduction: In this address, part of a series of discussions on philanthropy held at Georgetown University's Center for Public and Nonprofit Leadership, Steven Rathgeb Smith offers a detailed history of the relationship between the government and philanthropic organizations. To buttress his point that we are, in fact, at a critical moment, especially in view of the global financial downturn, Smith makes some observations and recommendations on how government and philanthropic organizations can work together.

Steven Rathgeb Smith's speech: As I was preparing this speech, it seemed especially fitting that I would be giving this presentation at this moment, given the important public policy challenges and issues currently being debated here in Washington and around the country. Wally Nielsen spent his entire professional career deeply interested in the intersection of government and public policy and philanthropy and nonprofit organizations. He worked in the early post war period in the implementation of the Marshall Plan in Europe and then moved to a role as a program officer at the Ford Foundation in the 1960s with responsibility for grants to Africa where he was immersed in the intersection between

---

[*] Delivered on October 8, 2009, at Washington, D.C. Reprinted with permission.

philanthropy—through Ford Foundation grants—and US public policy on the ground. He subsequently wrote three highly regarded books on his experiences in Africa. But the work that brought him wider acclaim and recognition was a series of books starting with *The Big Foundations* in 1972 and then *The Endangered Sector* in 1979. In these books and others, he was what you might call a friendly critic of foundations and organized philanthropy. He admired the pioneering and innovative philanthropy of the big foundations such as Rockefeller and Ford. But he also lamented that foundations were often too cautious in engaging urgent public problems and sometimes steered away from controversial issues and problems. In essence, he believed that foundations—while they had a proven capacity to address urgent public problems—they also had great untapped potential that could be used for the betterment of society, especially its more disadvantaged citizens.

However, he also worried that changes in the role of government and public policy contained the risk of overwhelming foundations and philanthropy. In particular, he wrote *Big Foundations* in the immediate aftermath of the landmark 1969 federal legislation that imposed new regulations on foundations including mandated payout levels and strict prohibitions on political activity. He was also very concerned that the overall growth of the American state contained the risk of swamping the efforts of philanthropy, making them irrelevant or ineffective, and by blurring the boundaries between government and nonprofit or Third Sector as called it—a term in common currency today in Europe, Australia, New Zealand and many other countries. As a result, he thought foundations and nonprofit organizations in general were at a critical transition point.

By calling attention to the growth of the American state and the increasing interconnections between government, public policy, and nonprofit organizations, he was acknowledging the transformation in the role of government and its relationship to the nonprofit sector as well as his concerns for the future of philanthropy given the new role of government. With this observation as a starting point, let me offer some thoughts on the historical development of this government-philanthropy and nonprofit relationship, in order to place in context the contemporary situation. During colonial times, churches and early nonprofit organizations including universities and hospitals were critical and often prominent components of the social structure were central the provision of valued public services such as health care and education, to the extent that is was provided.

But the initial structure of the American state—with its decentralization, limited resource base, and minimal federal government role in domestic policy—created powerful incentives for a distinctly local nonprofit sector with relatively little ongoing funding support or direction from government. Thus, nonprofits providing services were dependent upon a mix of private donations, fees, and very modest public subsidies. But as noted by Robert Putnam, Gerald Gramm, Theda Skocpol and others, many nonprofits during this period were associations and clubs rather than what we today regard as public charities in fields such as health, education or social services.

Subsequently, the late 19th and early 20th century witnessed a steady expansion in nonprofit organizations engaged in providing services to the citizenry, especially services for children and the poor. Indeed, many of the more prominent and notable of these organizations remain with us today: Catholic Charities, the YMCA, Lutheran Social Services, the Salvation Army, Goodwill Industries, and the Boys and Girls Clubs. The establishment of these service agencies was part of a wave of new national, federated organizations with chapters in local communities throughout the country. Nonetheless, most local nonprofits were churches, social clubs and associations such as the Masons, the Elks, and the Grange, rather than public charities offering social, educational and health services to the public. The latter was a relatively small part of the nonprofit sector and continued to be primarily reliant on private donations, fees, and very modest public subsidies. Indeed, many nonprofit agencies such as settlement houses and emergency assistance programs were entirely dependent upon private charitable donations.

This period also witnessed the emergence of wealthy philanthropists and the big foundations bearing their names including the Rockefeller and Ford foundations. These foundations were also very much engaged in public policy issues including the urgent public health problems in the US and abroad. And, Andrew Carnegie in particular won a lasting place in the annals of philanthropy with his support of the establishment of public libraries throughout the country.

In the early 20th century, another major new development within organized philanthropy was the creation of the Community Chest, the forerunner of today's United Way. Started in Cleveland, the Community Chest quickly spread throughout the country so most communities of significant size had a Community Chest organization by the end of the 1920s. Essentially, the Community Chest was a membership organization of leading nonprofit service agencies in local communities, although the specific mix of agencies varied across the country. The member agencies agreed to pool their resources and solicit donations through payroll deduction through a combined campaign. For many agencies such as the chapters of the YMCA or the American Red Cross, the Community Chest quickly became one of their major sources of revenue. Importantly, though, most of these Community Chest agencies viewed their mission as quite separate and distinct from government and relatively few agencies received public subsidies.

These agencies though were overwhelmed during the Depression in the 1930s with many agencies accepting emergency relief funds. Many local nonprofits failed entirely or merged with other nonprofits. The Depression of course had dramatic consequences on the role of the federal government in many areas of American life including income maintenance programs such as pensions, welfare, and regulation. But surprisingly, the involvement of government, notably the federal government, in the regulation and funding of nonprofit service agencies remained quite limited or temporary for two reasons: many Depression-era funding programs were on an emergency basis and quickly ended after the start of World War II; and the federal government assumed at least part of the responsibility for poor relief, freeing at least some agencies from the direct cash and in-kind support for poor people.

Consequently, nonprofit agencies in the late 1940s and 1950s remained largely dependent upon private donations (especially Community Chest funds) and fees. Some nonprofits with programs such as foster care received modest, limited public subsidies. Overall, the restricted character of nonprofit revenue sources meant that most agencies were relatively small and lacked extensive professionalization or infrastructure.

In essence, the many major and important New Deal initiatives of the 1930s did not to fundamentally alter the funding role of the federal government as it pertained to nonprofit service agencies. Public policy for direct social and health services remained largely decentralized to state and local government. To be sure, the federal government provided grant-in-aid support during the 1950s in some policy areas such as child welfare and hospitals through the Hill-Burton Act of 1946 which authorized construction grants and loans. However, these federal programs were quite targeted and/or limited so most nonprofit service agencies such as the YMCA or local family service agencies were largely unaffected.

Many scholars including Wally Nielsen as well as policymakers and practitioners have noted the dramatic shift in the relationship between government and the nonprofit sector which occurred in the 1960s and 1970s. Four key developments stand out as major breaks or turning points: First, the federal government provided ongoing funding support for local nonprofit service agencies through grants to the state and local governments who then contracted with nonprofit organizations or through new direct federal grants to nonprofit agencies at the local level.

Second, this new federal funding allowed and encouraged the creation of thousands of new nonprofit agencies outside the existing networks of established Community Chest agencies. As a result, new channels of support were opened for minority and previously marginalized community based organizations. This major development in turn led to profound changes in the United Way and the Combined Federal Campaign, including much more open eligibility for funding. The long term consequence has been the continued division of public and private funding into smaller and more unpredictable revenue streams.

Thirdly, the federal government also expanded its new regulatory reach and authority that provided the basis for a more assertive monitoring and evaluation role for government vis-à-vis the nonprofit sector including foundations through the 1969 Tax Reform Act.

And fourth, the American state grew rapidly and devoted substantially more resources in a host of important policy areas such as health care, poverty, humanitarian assistance, and medical research. The influx of federal funding rapidly changed the government-nonprofit relationship. Many longstanding agencies that had previously depended upon Community Chest funds became substantially dependent upon government funds. Entirely new nonprofits such as community action agencies and community mental health centers were created. And state and local governments invested in new capacity to manage the expansion of contracts to nonprofits. New public funding now dwarfed the collective efforts of foundations in areas such as poverty and health care.

This restructured government-nonprofit relationship was controversial. Many scholars and nonprofit executives feared that government funding would undermine the distinctive character and autonomy of nonprofit agencies. Many policymakers were also worried about the potential loss of accountability for public funds as more and more services were contracted to private, largely nonprofit agencies. And many scholars, commentators and nonprofit personnel were concerned that the reach of the federal government had become too extensive and far-reaching, potentially compromising the distinctive character of the nonprofit sector including foundations and community based organizations. As Nielsen noted in his 1979 book, *The Endangered Sector*, "A time of planned, governmentalized, officially subsidized, and guided pluralism is upon us. Nonprofit institutions, as one element of a society in radical transformation, will never again be the same in status, relative scale, function or autonomy." These sentiments were echoed at the time in the writings of other scholars including Nathan Glazer, Peter Berger and Richard Neuhaus.

To an extent, some of the trends Nielsen and others identified have continued. In particular, the state has grown tremendously in the last 30 years, despite the efforts of a succession of presidential administrations to devolve responsibility to the states and localities and curtail the growth of government and the federal government in particular. Big federal health insurance programs such as Medicare and Medicaid have escalated rapidly. New and/or expanded programs in child welfare, personal assistance services, community care, low-income housing, community development, drug and alcohol treatment, and workforce development were created at the federal level. Welfare reform in 1996 had the effect of creating greater demand for nonprofit services while at the same time shifting federal and state funding substantially away from cash assistance through Temporary Aid for Needy Families (TANF) to social services to support poor and disadvantaged individuals. Until the financial crisis, many states also increased their support of key services such as community care. The diversity of government funding support for the nonprofit sector also increased through the expanded use of vouchers, tax credits, and tax-exempt bond money.

For instance, Congress created an entirely new network of largely nonprofit low-income housing organizations in 1986 when they authorized the creation of the Low-Income Housing Tax Credit which has been used to support the building and renovation of thousands of low-income housing units nationwide.

In short, government funding support for nonprofit organizations (as well as other organizations) through contracting and other types of so-called policy tools such as tax credits—has increased greatly, helping to spur the continued growth of nonprofit organizations, although several other factors are at work in the sharp rise in the number of nonprofits including: rising incomes, increased demand for an array of services provided by nonprofits, changing views of government, and growing interest in corporate social responsibility. Reflecting these many factors, the number of charitable nonprofit 501 c 3 organizations has almost doubled since 1995 to almost 1 million.

One other particularly important public policy development that has played a key role in the rising prominence of nonprofit organizations and their role in addressing social problems was the establishment by Congress and the Clinton administration of AmeriCorps and the Corporation for National and Community Service in 1993. The recent precedents for AmeriCorps date to the 1960s with the establishment of the Peace Corps and VISTA. But these programs were relatively modest in scope. Also, President George H. W. Bush inaugurated his now well-known "Points of Light" campaign to champion volunteer and community initiatives around the country, primarily through private funds with federal encouragement. The launching of AmeriCorps in the 1993 put the federal government squarely in support of community service, service learning, and a more extensive role for nonprofit organizations in helping their communities.

Throughout the Clinton Presidency, the Corporation was politically embattled and was at times in danger of defunding and elimination. However, the Corporation did survive and has offered an assertive role for government in regards to nonprofits in ways that are quite different than the contracting and regulatory role for government that emerged in the 1960s. The Corporation and AmeriCorps has funded thousands of AmeriCorps volunteers who have in turn worked in thousands of different community organizations providing staff support to mostly newer organizations in a wide range of service fields—from social welfare to the environment to early childhood education. In the process, AmeriCorps volunteers have generated publicity and support for local organizations that has proven useful in fundraising and generating broader based community support.

Arguably, another very important long-term effect of the Corporation and AmeriCorps is direct and indirect support to an array of new nonprofit organizations based upon a social entrepreneurship and community service model such as City Year, Teach for America, Citizen Schools, the Harlem Children's Zone, and Youth-Build. These organizations tend to have partnerships with public agencies, foundations, and corporations and actively seek growth and deeper program impact, aided in part by foundation grants and funding from the Corporation for National and Community Service. These organizations are also major backers of the recently enacted Edward M. Kennedy Serve America Act of 2009 and the Office of Social Innovation. These organizations have in turn inspired a whole new generation of young people to engage in community service and work in public service more generally, especially through nonprofit organizations rather than government. Many of these young people have even created their own nonprofit organizations to further their goals.

In general, the newer nonprofit organizations with close working relationships with AmeriCorps and the Corporation tend to be quite different organizations than the nonprofits engaged in contracting for public services. For instance, the big growth areas in contracting in the last 25 years (until the financial crisis) have been in services such as home care and home health, foster care, community care for the developmentally disabled and the mentally ill, low-income housing, community development, and child care. The agencies providing these services are primarily professional, staff-driven organizations with relatively few volunteers, except for board members. Some of these services are highly complex involving many different types of professionals and the legal system, consequently it is much more difficult to engage these organizations in various types of volunteer or community service activities.

Nonprofit community agencies contracting with state and local government for important public services also tend to have quite different levels of engagement with advocacy and public policy. Many community agencies face formidable challenges in their capacity to engage in public policy advocacy on behalf of their organizations and the individuals who benefit from their services including a lack of resources and a worry about the potential implications of public policy advocacy for their organizations. Consequently, many local agencies have sought to work through intermediary organizations such as a regional association of service providers, especially in their specific service field such as child welfare or housing.

By contrast, many of the newer social entrepreneurial organizations are less likely to have these types of state and local networks. Many new social entrepreneurial organizations tend to eschew engagement with government or contracting while others have grown substantially through extensive partnerships with foundations, government, and corporations.

Yet, many of the newer social entrepreneurial and community service organizations also share an important characteristic: they are relatively young and of modest size at a time of funding cutbacks by foundations, corporations and government. Many organizations have been forced to rethink their strategic plans and reinvent themselves in order to sustain their organizations amidst the financial crisis.

Importantly, the combination of the financial crisis and the new Obama administration puts nonprofits and government at a very important historical moment. Government support for community service and volunteering is at an all-time high. Interest among young people in AmeriCorps, the Peace Corps, and service-oriented nonprofits such as Teach for America is intense and growing. The contemporary nonprofit sector is remarkably diverse on many different dimensions. The federal stimulus money has at least the potential to directly or indirectly help many nonprofits at the local level.

Nonetheless, nonprofit agencies providing an array of public services through contracts around the country are suffering through a wave of cutbacks, although the severity of the situation varies tremendously depending upon the state or locality or specific service provided. Moreover, many state and local governments are increasing their regulatory and monitoring efforts, requiring nonprofits to invest in more capacity to comply with government contract expectations.

Thus, the Obama administration and state and local governments need to take advantage of this broad popular support for voluntarism and community service and recognize that the nonprofit infrastructure requires an ongoing investment and commitment from government and private funders. The Corporation for National and Community Service provides direct support for thousands of volunteers but generally does not support the infrastructure and capacity of the nonprofit organizations themselves. The risk is that without a vibrant nonprofit infrastructure, AmeriCorps volunteers may not have a satisfactory experience or maximize their potential value to their communities. This infrastructure support should also include adequate funding for existing services.

More generally, the expanded role of AmeriCorps also calls attention to the evolution of the federal government relationship to nonprofits and philanthropy since the 1960s. The advent of extensive government contracting with nonprofits in the 1960s and 1970s greatly reduced the dependence of nonprofit service agencies on private philanthropy. Likewise, the creation of the Corporation for National Service essentially freed voluntarism and community service, at least in part, from its dependence on private funding and smaller scale state and local efforts.

Yet, the combined effects of extensive contracting and government support of community service means that more than ever the citizen encounters with public services—either as service recipients or deliverers—will be through a nonprofit organization, rather than government. This is at a time of serious financial strain on many nonprofit organizations due to declines in public funding and foundation grants as well as increased competition for the remaining public and private grants. Moreover, many nonprofit organizations are relatively new and at a point in their life-cycle where their initial source of funding—whether it is a foundation or corporate grant or a government contract—is in decline and their founding board and staff are looking to transition out of the organization. And this situation is occurring at a time of growing expectations by government and foundations on accountability and performance.

Because of the confluence of these circumstances, we are at a important transition point in terms of the relationship of nonprofit service agencies and organized philanthropy including foundations and federated fundraising organizations such as the United Way to public policy, creating the opportunity for community-based service agencies, organized philanthropy and government to think differently and creatively about their increasingly intertwined relationship.

With this situation in mind, I would offer the following suggestions and observations for next steps by government, nonprofit service organizations, and organized philanthropy, especially foundations. Government, for its part, has an obligation to ensure that nonprofit services are provided equitably and adequately in order for citizens to be in a position to achieve full social and political citizenship. This effort by government should include an investment approach to nonprofits by policymakers that emphasizes accountability and results as well as sound governance and community engagement. This investment approach requires the following:

1) Ongoing support with technical assistance and capacity building. Many newer organizations are not well-positioned to compete for government contracts and funding or to respond to the expectations of private foundations on evaluation and performance assessment. Government can thus be an especially valuable resource in supporting the infrastructure and capacity needs of nonprofits.

2) A recognition of the potential and limits of performance contracting strategies with nonprofits especially contracting approaches that focus on narrow per-

formance targets. In my view, government needs to develop performance measure-
ment approaches with nonprofits that also include attention to governance and
community and citizen engagement concerns. In particular, many newer nonprofits have small boards and relatively small staffs and do not have strong linkages to
local external stakeholders. Government could play a positive role by encouraging
nonprofits to develop and enhance their community relationships and support.
Rethinking performance management approaches to nonprofit organizations is
also important because it can affect the diversity of the sector, potentially lead to
unwanted consequences for some agencies including inappropriate professionalization, unnecessary costs and a shift away from their core competency in programming.

3) A third point is that policymakers—with the support of nonprofits and organized philanthropy—should seek structured ongoing forums for the discussion
and possible resolution of issues of mutual concern such as funding levels, rates,
regulations and new program initiatives. Indeed, other countries have created their
types of forums. For instance the United Kingdom has created a formal "Com-
pact" between the government and the nonprofit sector that provides a structured
ongoing opportunity for the two sectors to discuss important issues and jointly
develop new programs and policies. More informal efforts have been tried in the
US, especially at the state and local levels. Given the many interconnections between nonprofits and government, these more structured opportunities for dialogue should be developed and explored in a more concerted fashion.

4) Government also needs to support through its own policies the representative
role of nonprofit organizations. A major reason that we value nonprofits is for their
potential to represent citizen interests and provide valued feedback to policymakers
on important public policy matters. But unless government is supportive of this
representative role, nonprofits will face serious internal and external constraints to
engaging policymakers in important advocacy on behalf of citizens and their communities. Let me be specific. Many cities across the country including Portland
and Seattle directly and indirectly support the participation of neighborhood organizations on important municipal policy issues. Some states have directed their
state agencies to create liaisons to the nonprofit sector. In jurisdictions, state and
local agencies work collaboratively with nonprofit associations and encourage their
input and ongoing participation in the policy process. Government administrators
and legislators can seek nonprofit input and comment on proposed regulations
and policies. In short, an assertive and supportive government can greatly enhance
the potential of nonprofit agencies to effectively represent local communities and
their citizens.

Nonprofit organizations for their part also can take several steps that will position them to provide effective and sustainable services and programs. These steps
include:

First, nonprofit organizations could usefully rethink their governance. Many
nonprofits—especially newer, more community-based organizations—have small
boards that are mismatched with the needs of the organization. A larger and more

broad-based board with diverse members would help to ensure the sustainability of the organization and promote greater accountability and effectiveness.

Second, nonprofits—including the board members, staff and volunteers—also could do more to engage the policy process, broadly defined. This can include participation in local community events and organizations to membership in coalitions and associations to active engagement in important policy concerns affecting nonprofits and their communities. I would argue that this engagement is especially critical today given the financial crisis, the increased demands for accountability by nonprofits, the enhanced scrutiny of nonprofits by policymakers, especially at the federal level, and the greater competition for public and private grants. Given the funding crisis of state and local government, nonprofits should also strive to hold government accountable for its own obligations to adequately fund key public services delivered by nonprofit service agencies.

Third, and, importantly, to cope with the current funding and regulatory environment, nonprofits will need to be creative and innovative in programming, organizational structure and their relations with other organizations. Already, some nonprofits have created affiliated 501 c 4 organizations to engage in the policy process. In addition, many larger nonprofits have established affiliated c 3 organizations to help with their fundraising.

In many communities, nonprofits are working together to reduce expenses including the co-location of services. Some foundations are helping with this effort by funding the purchase of buildings that can then be used by many local community organizations who can also pool their resources to defray expenses. Many nonprofits have also found benefit in creating targeted advisory committees to broaden their community support, strategic planning, and fundraising capacity. Many other examples exist including various types of hybrid nonprofit and for-profit structures, especially among the newer more social entrepreneurial types of nonprofit organizations.

Foundations are also central to the evolving role of the relationship of nonprofit organizations to public policy and the unfolding effects of public policy on nonprofits themselves. As I noted, we value nonprofits for their role in representing citizen interests and providing valued public services—from foster care to low-income housing to community development to environmental advocacy. Foundations can take several concrete steps to help nonprofit organizations in these efforts and to aid them in coping with the current funding crisis.

First, foundations can support advocacy by nonprofits. To be sure, foundations are constrained by law from supporting both lobbying and partisan political activity, but foundations could provide valuable support to nonprofit coalitions and intermediary associations representing nonprofits as well as nonprofit advocacy organizations engaged in public education and policy analysis on critical policy concerns such as poverty, tax reform, the environment, and affordable housing.

Second, most foundations do not have the resources to effectively tackle many important policy problems on their own. However, foundations could partner with other foundations, corporations, and government to provide a more extensive response to local problems. Many examples of this type of collaboration exist around the country today. For example, in Baltimore, a nonprofit public-private partnership, East Baltimore Development Inc., is a collaborative effort of the federal, state and local government, local foundations such as the Annie E. Casey Foundation and the Goldseker Foundation, and local corporations including leading banks. Their mission is to revitalize the East Baltimore neighborhood and provide needed public services to the local citizenry. This type of model directly engages foundations in local policy issues and promotes an ongoing relationship with key public, philanthropic and corporate leaders on important policy matters.

Third, foundations need to think creatively about their own grantmaking. As many scholars and nonprofit leaders have noted, many nonprofit organizations—especially newer community organizations—can face serious constraints on their ability to raise capital. Foundations can help nonprofits through expanded use of "program related investments" that allow foundations to invest their endowment funds in organizations which are related to the foundation's mission. For instance, foundations have loaned money to intermediary organizations in the low-income housing and community development fields—which then loan the money directly to local provider agencies to help with their capital needs. Expanded use of these program-related investments could also help foundations support nonprofits' sustainability, especially in these difficult economic times. These investments are part of a broader push for mission-based investing by foundations that calls for aligning the investments and grantmaking of the foundation with the mission and goals of the foundations.

Fourth, foundations should weigh the desire to have impact with the importance and value of supporting the local nonprofit infrastructure. Many community organizations may be providing valuable services to the community but they are not good candidates for going to scale and expansion beyond the boundaries of their own community or region. Moreover, many of these organizations are providing more routine—but nonetheless essential—services. Thus, foundations need to balance specific program impacts with the need to sustain local community organizations.

More broadly, foundations and nonprofit organizations should think comprehensively about their contributions to society. In recent years, there has been a tendency to think narrowly about program impact—as typified in certain types of performance contracting regimes, program evaluation models, and the focus in current discourse on the charity care levels of nonprofit hospitals as a condition of their tax status. In my view, nonprofits need to think creatively about governance and their connections to their community and the policy process in order to contribute broadly to their local communities. Nonprofit organizations can provide many potential benefits to the polity that go beyond specific program impacts. Peter Frumkin has noted the importance of expressive benefits—the opportunity to create organizations and responses that are reflective of deeply held values and commitments such as the many and varied faith-based organizations.

Moreover, nonprofits can help build social capital and foster a sense of community and engagement that can have lasting impact on the citizenry and their communities. Funding constraints and expectations can sometimes create serious obstacles to the ability of nonprofits to engage their communities in a meaningful way; foundations and government should help support these community oriented roles of nonprofits.

Surprisingly, though, nonprofits, foundations and their supporters have often found it difficult to find legitimate forums for this sort of policy exploration and decision making on the contemporary and potential contributions of nonprofits and foundations. To be sure, many national intermediary associations can sometimes play this role but it is difficult to sustain this effort given the funding challenges. In addition, associations representing sub-sector groups such as hospitals and universities may do a very fine job in their particular field. But for the nonprofit sector as a whole, an absence of forums exist which hampers effective oversight, the development of appropriate public policies and more successful self-regulation by the nonprofit sector themselves. For this reason, more structured opportunities for dialogue and policy analysis on key policy issues affecting nonprofits is especially important.

In sum, I do believe that we are at a particularly important juncture in the evolution of the relationship between nonprofits including foundations and public policy, given the financial crisis, the priorities and support of the new Administration, the broad enthusiasm throughout the country for community service and voluntarism and the urgent policy problems that need attention. To effectively respond, nonprofit service agencies and foundations will need to think creatively and constructively about their roles and responsibilities to the citizenry and acknowledge and support the active partnership with government in successfully addressing social problems and local community needs.

"The Three Ls"*

Chris "Ludacris" Bridges

*Rap artist and actor; born Champaign, IL, September 11, 1977; studied music man-
agement at Georgia State University, 1998–99; discography:* Back for the First Time
(2000), Word of Mouf *(2001),* Chicken-n-Beer *(2003),* The Red Light District
(2004), Release Therapy *(2006),* Theater of the Mind *(2008),* Battle of the Sexes
(2010); film and screen appearances include Crash *(2004),* Hustle and Flow *(2005),*
and Law and Order: Special Victims Unit *(2006–07).*

Editor's introduction: In this presentation, delivered at a National Press Club
Luncheon, rap artist and actor Chris "Ludacris" Bridges describes his philanthropic activities, which take place under the umbrella of the Ludacris Foundation.
Arguing that America's promise is unfulfilled, he outlines the areas in which his
foundation works and gives examples of its activities. He says that he hopes each
of his issue-related musical releases might spark a movement, and points out that
even the much-maligned hip-hop community was quick to give back when floods
hit the Atlanta area. While some might be skeptical of celebrity philanthropy as
merely a publicity stunt, Bridges expresses a belief in its potential: When the event's
moderator later asked, "What do you think could be done if all young celebrities
started foundations like you did when you were only 24 years old?" Bridges answered, "I feel like there would be no more issues in America whatsoever. I feel like
we would almost be on our way to living the perfect lives in a perfect United States
of America."

Chris Bridges's speech: Thank you. Thank you very much for that wonderful introduction. She is definitely right, I did write my first song when I was nine years
old. But to let everybody know, I don't still have the audio. But just let you know,
when I was nine years old, my first song I wanted to rhyme with girlfriend, so the
rap was called, "I'm Cool, I'm Bad, I Might be Ten, But I Can't Survive Without
My Girlfriend." So once I actually turned ten years old, I could say that song with

---

* Delivered on October 23, 2009, at Washington, D.C. Reprinted with permission.

the utmost confidence ever. So just letting you know, that was my first song. So thank you very much.

First of all, I want to thank, of course, the NPC and the general public. The general public, make some noise. Where's the general public at? All right. It feels good for the general public to come out and support me. This is my first time doing this. This is our first time doing our annual foundation dinner here in Washington, D.C. Of course, we want to connect with all the policymakers and the movers and shakers of the United States of America. So that's why I'm here. It's definitely my first time doing this luncheon and I'm very, very proud and I feel like the gratitude is out of this world right now, just for accepting me and having me do this.

So real quick, I want to thank everybody for this honor. Of course, like I said, I want to thank you for inviting me to speak to this special group of truth seekers, the recorders of the industry and all of the change agents. You, the press, have a very special responsibility, and that is to be a mirror for us to see ourselves, our communities, our country, and of course the rest of the world. And I truly respect the role that you play in our system.

I'm sure that some of you are asking, "Now, why would I want to speak at the National Press Club in Washington, D.C.? And why would they invite me?" To some, I'm just an entertainer, and of course I make my living by stringing together verses or playing a part in some movie or television series that you all may have seen, "Law and Order," by the way. I don't know if you saw that. "The Gamer" is also out at the movie theaters. In case you haven't seen it, go check it out.

Well, what would Ludacris have to say, what would I have to say about leadership? Well, I'm here to let you know, I'm going to say a lot of different things. So take what I say word for word. Immediately, you wonder if I'm planning to run for office, maybe for president in 2012. I'm here to let everybody know you don't have to worry about me doing that, for sure. But in fact, when I speak of leadership, I'm talking about leadership that is apolitical, leadership that is very basic and that starts with self. There's a cry for it. In fact, that is what the last election was all about. People were saying that we need something fresh, we need something new, we need something that defies convention. America has a great promise, but to me it's a promise that's unfulfilled. Not everyone gets an equal chance at it, and some never get a chance at all.

Not everyone believes that tomorrow can be better than today, or that the promise is even meant for them at all. Now, it's not right with all of our resources, every citizen is not afforded the opportunities to be the best that they can be if they want. And it was once said to treat people as if they were what they ought to be, and you help them become what they are capable of being. That is a promise fulfilled, in my opinion. Our communities need fixing. Our systems are badly broken. We can't wait on the government, the institutions, social programming and policies alone to fix our communities. We have to look at other sources, and that's why I'm here today.

In today's world, we have new issues and new challenges. The old way of looking at these issues and challenges have not rendered the outcomes that I feel we want.

Trust bonds have been broken. Logical thinking, while necessary, is not sufficient. We need lateral thinking. And by that, I mean thinking outside our current frame of reference. We need a new type of leadership. And that's why maybe I will run for president in 2012.

But currently, people are looking in a different direction for philanthropic leadership. There's a call for everyday people to take leadership roles within philanthropy in order to help the communities in which they work and live. And that's something I feel like I've done to the fullest of my capabilities. When I say leading by example, that's exactly what not only myself but the Ludacris Foundation has done. With my mother, of course, the Ludacris Foundation was formally established in December of 2001 to sustain my commitment to make a difference in the lives of the youth, the families and communities throughout the United States of America. Now, my foundation inspires you through education and memorable experiences to live their dreams, thereby uplifting families, communities, and fostering economic development.

We have three key program focus areas, and I call them the three Ls. This is what I came up with. The first is leadership and education, the second is LudaCares, and the third is living healthy lifestyle, which is something very similar to what Mrs. Obama is doing right now. So let me share these with you.

Leadership and education is preparing everyone and all the youth to be successful with an emphasis on why education matters and making a lifelong difference. Not only education, but educating yourself. LudaCares, insuring that communities and its residents know that we care about them. I feel like I do that by leading by example and continuing to go to these communities, because if I weren't there, they wouldn't know how much we care about them.

Living healthy lifestyles. As I said, this is geared towards youth to learn about healthy eating, to address issues like nutritional health and childhood obesity, provide preventative health services and education to underserved youth. We help young people achieve their dreams through the encouragement of the principles of success. We aim to show young people in America that they are the builders of their own future. And it's not necessarily the cards that they're dealt, but how they play their cards.

Now since 2001, the Ludacris Foundation has donated well over $2 million to support organizations that work to help families and communities. Our programs and support initiatives have directly impacted thousands upon thousands of lives. And what I'm more proud of is the fact that we have over 10,000 hours of invested hands-on service. That means that I don't just cut the checks and I tell everybody else to do the work for me. I'm there personally to make sure I know exactly where not only my money, but anybody who donates their money is going. And that's extremely important to me.

I'm going to give you an example. As a result of Hurricane Katrina's devastation, approximately over 20,000 families were relocated or migrated to the city of Atlanta. And I, along with my foundation, my mother, and Ebony Sun Entertainment, donated over $100,000 in support of families victimized by the hurricane.

We provided housing, we provided housing assistance, we provided counseling assistance, we provided job referral assistance to 15 impacted families relocated to the Atlanta area. Each of these 15 families received four months of free rent, free furnished housing, a refrigerator full of food, clothing, toiletries, linens, all because not only did we dedicate our own supplies to these people, but we partnered up with a local radio station to ask the rest of the city of Atlanta to come and donate things that they don't need and that they would be willing to help out with.

Another example, in 2006 I released a song, "Runaway Love," which depicted children running away from a very dysfunctional life situation. As a follow-up to the song, my foundation partnered with the National Runaway Switchboard, and that's something I feel very important. Any song that I put out, I want to make it a movement, not just a single. There's a whole story behind it. But we partnered up with the NRS to help bring awareness to the problems facing runaway youth in America. Last year for November's National Runaway Prevention Month, I started a new public education campaign including a new PSA that was distributed to TV stations across the country. The initiative was spearheaded by the NRS with seven support from Greyhound to increase their awareness of issues facing America's runaways and educate the public on solutions and the role they can play in preventing youth from running away.

This year, we are continuing those efforts, and a lot of people don't even understand that over a million kids run away from home each and every year. I feel like this is one of those problems that a lot of people don't really understand about, and because I came out with this song I wanted to make everyone at how serious of a problem that that is, and how that can lead to so many other problems that we see in America today.

Yet another example, last Christmas, or LudaCrismas, as I would put it, we hosted a LudaCrismas event in the four cities for over 500 disenfranchised children, ages ranging from six to seventeen years old. Each event was tailored to the specific age of the youth involved, but the common theme was to create a fun and memorable experience for all of them. Children attending the events were treated to games, entertainment, of course great food, and at some locations, the children were also able to outfit a teddy bear and take pictures with Santa. These children were selected from communities throughout each city's metropolitan area by partnering with that community based and municipal organizations.

Now recently, we were able to offer our own—I'm extremely proud about this, and I'm sure a lot of you heard about it—but we offered our own metro Atlanta stimulus package. A LudaCares stimulus package of the sort, so to speak. We partnered with the local dealership and gave away 20 cars to individuals that needed a hand up during these tough economic times. And that's something that's extremely important to me. I feel like we give a hand up, we don't give a hand out. I only like to help people that want to help themselves, not people that are just going to take it and just take advantage of the situation. That is what I love to do. So having a vehicle to get back and forth to work and daycare would make the difference in getting and keeping a job, especially in these hard economic times. And it touched my heart to be able to personally give the key to these cars to these individuals and to hear their stories.

We got over 5,000 different letters, and out of those 5,000 you can understand how hard it could possibly be for us to pick 20 out of those 5,000. So when I sit here and say that we always wish that we can do more, I honestly say that and I feel like with more power and more influence and the more that I do, the more that I can give back. And the reason I'm up here today is just to let everybody know I try to lead by example in that I feel like I have a certain amount of power and influence. I feel like that there are others that have more power and influence than I have, and there are some that may not feel as if they have as much power and influence as I have. But that doesn't mean that they can't do their part in giving back.

Now to give you another example, two weeks ago we raised over $100,000 to support flood survivors in the Atlanta area. T.I., who's another rapper, and myself, we reached out to our friends in the hip-hop entertainment community for help. And I know a lot of people, they like to criticize the hip-hop community, but let me tell you exactly what the hip-hop community did within one hour of myself and T.I. reaching out to them to help our community. First of all, I donated $10,000, T.I. donated $10,000 and he was actually incarcerated at the time, and he still donated $10,000 towards the cause because he feels just as important about giving back to his community as I do. And then we turned to friends and colleagues for help, and they didn't hesitate. We made over $80,000 in eight hours from the hip-hop community. And it's as simple as that.

So with everything that I'm sitting here trying to tell you today, all the facts that I'm giving you, all of my personal insight, to me this is the new philanthropy that I'm talking about. Operating as an organization at the community level day to day. It's not your typical corporate institutional giving, just a group of likeminded individuals pooling their efforts to make a difference. Changing the social landscape one frame at a time.

Secondly, because there are new challenges in education, as we all know, there are new challenges in health care, as we all know, and other deep social issues that affect our youth, families and communities. Now, I feel like we have to approach these challenges with a new language. A form of communication that everyone knows about, a new technological platform and a broader view of community and globalism. Social networks and digital platforms are critical to reaching donors and communicating with constituents. Tweeting, Facebook, MySpace, YouTube, they're all essential tools in this new philanthropic environment.

Now third, the call for new philanthropic leadership is also a call for new relationships of trust. Understanding these communities in need and garnering their trust and the trust of donors that their contributions will make a direct and positive impact is extremely important to me, which is why all of the examples I've given you I was very hands on with, I was there in person with, and people know. They're starting to call me—I have many different nicknames, but Luda FEMA is one of them. I'm here to let you know. That's because I'm hands on. Please believe me when I tell you.

Now, I take the responsibility of leadership and giving back very seriously, as you can tell. I have a deep-rooted tradition of service that has only broadened with my celebrity status. If I have more, I will try to do more, as I've said before. I mention these things not to pat myself on the back or brag, but to underscore the responsibility I feel like we all have to turn back, to reach back and give back to our communities. This period in our history should be a time of reflection for all of us to appreciate what we have and what we have given to those in need of our help.

This year, I chose D.C. to host my 6th Annual Ludacris Foundation Dinner, and I wanted to reach a national audience about service and a new call for leadership. We are recognizing five outstanding individuals for their tireless work and strong commitment to community service. Honorees are selected in acknowledgement of the excellence and integrity embodied in their work, as well as their willingness to support and participate in programs benefiting their community.

Now this year's honorees include, I call him my godfather, Mr. Quincy Jones, the Chairman's Award goes to, of course, Mr. Quincy. Kevin Liles, the President's Award, Debra Lee, BET Networks, the Corporate Award, and DC WritersCorp, accepted by Kenny Carroll, the community service award.

In addition, this year in honor of the foundation's first Washington, D.C. gala, Congresswoman Maxine Waters will be bestowed the first Ludacris Foundation Congressional Leadership Award. All of this, I say, to make you understand that when we leave Washington, the work of the foundation will carry on stronger than before. Thanks in part to success of the benefit dinner, of course, our partners and the opportunity that you have afforded me today to get our message across.

In the coming months, we look forward to expanding our footprint and doing more in the D.C. area, as well as everywhere else. And in closing, I just want to say, again like I said before, the task is not so much to see what no one yet has seen, but to think what no one yet has thought, about that which everybody sees. We have to have a paradigm shift regarding issues and possible solutions. And I shouldn't have to tell you all that, because you know it. Thank you very much.

Remarks to Council on Foundations[*]

2010 Family Philanthropy Conference

Ben Cameron

Program Director for the Arts, Doris Duke Charitable Foundation, 2006– ; born High Point, NC, October 18, 1953; B.A., University of North Carolina at Chapel Hill, 1975; M.F.A., Yale School of Drama, 1981; associate artistic director, Indiana Repertory Theater, 1981–84; literary manager, PlayMakers Repertory Company, 1984–86; literary manager, National Endowment for the Arts (NEA), 1988–1990; director, Theater Program, NEA, 1990–92; senior program officer, Dayton Hudson Foundation, 1993–97; manager, community relations, Target Stores, 1997–98; executive director, Theatre Communications Group, 1998–2006; author of various articles and columns on theater.

Editor's introduction: In this speech, delivered at a conference of family philanthropic organizations, Ben Cameron describes the growth of the nonprofit arts sector throughout the United States as a signal achievement of philanthropy. After the National Endowment for the Arts (NEA) came under fire in 1989 over its funding of controversial art and artists, arts advocates found themselves under siege, forced to justify the value of their contributions to society at large. In the years since, the sector has not only held its ground, but made steady headway, and Cameron offers a rousing defense of the arts, heralding not only their economic importance, but their developmental, spiritual, and social value.

Ben Cameron's speech: Given the conversation of the last several days, I'd like to begin by looking at one of the great success stories of organized philanthropy—the growth of the nonprofit arts sector. Spearheaded by the Ford and Rockefeller Foundations in the late 1950s and '60s; joined by government in 1965 with the creation of the National Endowment for the Arts in 1965 and the subsequent cre-

[*] This speech was first presented at the Council on Foundations' 2010 Family Philanthropy Conference in San Diego, California, on February 2, 2010, and has been reproduced and reprinted with permission of the Council on Foundations and Ben Cameron. Copyright © 2010 Ben Cameron and Council on Foundations. All rights reserved.

ation of local arts agencies in many communities and state arts councils in every state; expanded through both corporate foundations—AT&T, Dayton Hudson and Philip Morris, to name a few—and deepened by innumerable family foundations and by individual donations, philanthropy exploded the arts beyond the major metropolitan areas of New York, San Francisco and Chicago, to cities and communities as far flung as Blue Lake, CA, Whitesburg, KY, and Douglas, AK—all homes to major arts entities today. Designed to professionalize the arts, improve the economic fortunes of artists, and expand the base of arts audiences and consumers across the country, this effort succeeded beyond our wildest dreams—truly catalytic philanthropy at its best.

The 1989 NEA controversies involving the works of Andres Serrano and Robert Mapplethorpe came as a shock. Assuming that the role of the arts as central to civilized community was broadly understood, arts leaders and philanthropists, while quite capable of discussing critical and aesthetic theory, were often unprepared to address challenges that were based, not in issues of quality, but in value. "What is the value of these images for my community?" critics asked in essence. "What is the value of supporting the arts? Indeed, what is the value of the arts at all?"

These controversies marked a turning point for many of us in arts philanthropy. Ever since, the arts community has worked diligently to quantify its value—value commonly now framed as economic, educational and social.

The arts are indeed critical to local and national economic vitality. Arts advocates often cite local economic impact studies which prove that arts organizations typically leverage an additional, $3–5 or $5–7 for the local economy for every dollar spent on a performing arts ticket—dollars for local restaurants, parking, and gift shops, for local printers who print programs, for fabric stores where the cloth is bought for costumes, for the piano tuners who tune the instruments, for the caterers who run the concessions. And more. Today, in fact, the more than 104,000 nonprofit arts and culture organizations generate $166.2 billion in economic activity. Where the arts are imperiled, entire local small business communities and governments feel the aftershocks as well.

These economic arguments were especially powerful for us when I worked at Target Stores (or Tarzhay)—arguments enhanced by our recognition of the role the arts play in creating livable communities to attract and retain potential workers. Moreover, during my time at Target Stores, I came to appreciate that our competitive advantage was essentially an arts advantage. Imagine for a moment trying to walk through a Target Store, divesting it of the work of artists and the influences of arts instruction and exposure. The music over the loud speakers clearly is the first thing to go (something not everyone admittedly may regret, but there you are); next to follow are the audio and entertainment departments. The book section has to go, as does the entire fashion division. Those Michael Graves teapots are out; the colorists and visual artists whose work has informed makeup and jewelry means that those departments too have to go. Designers have also crafted much of the furniture and lighting fixtures—those all go now—both those in the retail space and those in the "backstage" area where the offices are. At the rate we're going, we're only going to have household solvents and fertilizer left, but we will need to re-package those without design labels and special holders—some paper bags will do. Frankly, it's a miracle we've found the store: we need to eliminate the advertising, the copy writing, the clever TV commercials with actors that engender consumer curiosity and loyalty, the branding graphics of the Target image itself. Indeed, we really have no store at all, since architects, those folks who got their start largely in arts classes in schools, suddenly haven't been there to create the designs. In short, we're out in a field, where no one can find us or be aware we exist, trying to sell generic products in unappealing packaging. Those of us who follow Target are aware of its rapid ascent into the American consciousness, its place at the center of New York fashion and advertising industries even though there is no Target store in Manhattan. Clearly, Target has competitors—WalMart and Kmart among oth-ers (both of whom arguably have advantages of lower price points)—but Target's upscale image, its trend forward fashions, its hip advertising, its in-house lines of designer- and artist-lines like those Michael Graves teapots—suggest significantly that the competitive edge stems from having better design, better imaging, better use of language, better art, better artists than their competitors—artists who began to hone their skills in creative writing classes, in sculpture and painting classes, in music—orchestra, band and chorus—classes, in acting classes long ago as chil-dren.

But the arts value is more than economic. With the advent of new research, we have become increasingly sophisticated about quantifying our value in other dimensions as well. Social behavioralist Shirley Brice Heath of Stanford Univer-sity—not an arts researcher—was among the first to study the arts in the broader context of after school programs—girl scouts, sport teams, and more. In working with highrisk students in inner city East Palo Alto, Heath was admittedly surprised to find that it was the arts students who dramatically outperformed their peers in significant ways. It was the arts students who are four times more likely to win aca-demic awards and four times as likely to participate in math and science fairs, who showed significant reduction in disciplinary infractions, who performed better on verbal and math SAT scores—a differential of 80–120 points in some studies—and who are more than eight times more likely to graduate than students without arts experiences. These studies have been reinforced by a Harvard study focusing on students working with Shakespeare, work that promotes greater complexity in thinking, greater verbal acuity, tolerance of ambiguity, interpretive skills and increased sense of self-discipline and self-esteem.

Academics notwithstanding, arts nurture healthy communities—and not just through links between creation of cultural districts and crime reduction. A UCLA study proves that high school seniors who participated in the creation of theatre are 40% less likely to tolerate racist behavior than kids who were not theatre partici-pants, and was I the only one who noticed the *New York Times* features on Colum-bine in the aftermath of school shootings—features where the students repeatedly said the ONLY place they felt a sense of community, where the cliques lost their power, and the disenfranchised felt welcome was in the performing arts center?

For these reasons, those of us who work in the arts can now stand proudly and confidently in front of civic leaders and government officials and say, "If you care about economic prosperity, you must care about the arts. If you care about educational achievement for your children, you must care about the arts. And if you care, perhaps most significantly, for harmonious race relations and a more inclusive, cooperative society, you must care about the arts."

In spite of these arguments the last 10 years have witnessed a gradual erosion of arts philanthropy—regular declines in the percentage of the philanthropic dollar attached to the arts, the inability of arts giving to keep pace with inflation, the disappearance of major national arts funders like the AT&T, and Philip Morris aka Altria Foundations, and the elimination of discrete arts programs altogether, not only at the local small foundation level but at Rockefeller, Ford and many many others. With the national economic collapse, local and state arts giving are under assault, corporate philanthropy has largely abandoned the field and individual donors, who have far less disposable income, are pulling back in ways that affect both contributed and earned revenues.

But I would suggest that the real crisis the arts face is not economic.

Our world today is most dramatically marked by a host of shifting demographics in age, geographic distribution, gender and more; thrillingly by our increasing diversity—moving as we are to a nation defined by plurality rather than majority—and by the advent of technology. For the arts in particular, these shifts have already brought enormous challenges—challenges to the historically Eurocentric orientation of the institutional arts, with special challenges to forms like opera, ballet, and symphonic music. Technology for its own part is radically changing how we think, how we behave, how we congregate, even how our economy works. Together, these forces are provoking a fundamental realignment of cultural expression and communication—a realignment that is shaking the newspaper and television industries, the publishing and book industries, and (in an indication of what may be yet to come) has left the recorded music and music distribution industries in disarray.

Far from making the arts irrelevant, diversity and technology promise to make the arts more critical than ever. As we stand on the brink of an age in which the ability to think and to behave creatively will be paramount, arts cannot be viewed as part of the need: they must be viewed as part of the solution, whatever your larger goals may be.

Chris Anderson, editor of *Wired* magazine and author of a book entitled *The Long Tail*, for example, sees in technology the unleashing of a veritable tsunami of creative energy. With the invention and now affordability of cell phones, mini cams, computer software and more, he notes, the means of artistic production have been democratized for the first time in human history. In the 1930s, people who wished to make a movie had to work for Warner Brothers or RKO, for who could afford cameras, lighting equipment, editing equipment and more? Now who among us does not know a 14-year-old hard at work on her second, third or fourth film?

Furthermore, the means of artistic distribution have been democratized. Again, in the '30s, the major studios played that role; now upload your film onto You-Tube or Facebook, and you have instant worldwide distribution with the click of a button.

This double impact is occasioning a massive redefinition of authorship and the cultural market. Today everyone is a potential author—and while the market for traditional arts audiences may be eroding, the market for arts participants—those citizens who dance or write poetry, who paint or sing, who make their own films or—as our very first speaker, Arthur Brooks, happily noted, play the French horn—is exploding as indeed the market paradigm shifts from consumption to broader participation in which attendance is only one option. It is in embracing this shift that the possibilities—the necessities—for a new chapter in arts philan-thropy arises. Indeed, the Solomonic question facing us all may well be, "How do we reward the hopes, dreams and aspirations of a new generation, without disman-tling the still-vibrant seminal achievements of the past?"

Let me be clear: I for one believe that the historic institutions that we have funded to date will continue to be worthy of our investment. They represent the best opportunities for lives of economic dignity for many artists, and the logical place where artists who need and deserve to work at a certain scale can find an ap-propriate home. Whatever we do as a funding community, we must continue to nurture and promote these groups, and especially support their efforts to adapt and change to the larger world.

But to see these institutions as synonymous with the totality of the arts is far too limiting. The most dramatic recent development in the arts is the rise of the hybrid artist, the artist who works in multiple arenas—who works in science or technol-ogy, prison reform or education, AIDS awareness or environmental reform, not for economic survival (although that may be a benefit) but because of a deep organic belief that the work she or he is called to do cannot be accomplished in the tradi-tional hermetic environment of an arts institution but can only be accomplished through deep engagement with other fields.

Today's dance world is defined, not only by the great companies of New York City Ballet and Alvin Ailey, but by companies like Liz Lerman's Dance Exchange, a multigenerational company with dancers in age from 18 to 79, who collaborate with genomic scientists to embody and explore the DNA strand or nuclear physi-cists at CERN in Geneva.

Today's theatre world is defined, not only by great institutions like the Steppen-wolf of Chicago, Arena Stage of Washington DC or New York's Public Theatre but by a dense network of small ensembles and groups dedicated to community build-ing and social action—groups like Cornerstone Theatre of Los Angeles, whose faith-based project brought together 10 religious communities—Bahai, Jewish, Muslim, Catholic, Native American and even gay and lesbian believers—to work, both within faiths and collaboratively across faiths, to create plays to bring diverse religious congregations together to explore common belief and engage in social healing in the aftermath of 9/11.

Today's museums embrace, not only great visual artists working in traditional media, but groups like Stan's Cafe, who use grains of rice to graphically embody and contrast the distribution of population and wealth—one grain of rice for every African with HIV next to a pile with one grain of rice for every African—powerful embodiments and depictions that serve as preludes to substantive action and policy reform.

Today's leading poets work, not merely in the isolation of the study or the retreat, but actively with Iraqi war veterans to help them translate and articulate their experiences as a part of healing, while today's playwrights work, not only with directors and actors, but with youth gangs, helping them articulate, channel and represent their experiences as alternatives to violence.

Indeed, however important the arts have been to date, they will be even more important as we move into the future.

The arts will be increasingly important to economic vitality and business success, especially as creative industries explode: witness the recent explosive growth of iPods, the emergence of the computer gaming industry—which now outsells music and film recordings combine—neither of which any of us foresaw a decade ago. Leaders of these and other new and emerging industries will benefit from arts exposure as well: as author Daniel Goldman, in his book *Working with Emotional Intelligence*, notes, the primary indicators of success in leading include empathy, the ability to listen to others and motivate, commitment, integrity; the ability to communicate and influence, to initiate and accept change—the very principles that lie at the heart of creating art, the very abilities instilled by arts instruction. Not surprisingly, both the Harvard and Yale Business schools have recently restructured their curricula to promote critical and creative thinking.

The arts will play an increasingly pivotal role—if we let them—in educational and cognitive reform. Traditional emphasis on science and math, while critical, falls short of the advanced integrated thinking of left and right brain demanded by the future—a shift articulated by, of all people, Mike Huckabee, who compared science and math-only education to creation of a data base without a server. Already, we see a dramatic move within colleges and universities to embrace and seize the power of the arts to promote deeper reflection and awareness—an entire Creative Campus movement typified by Dartmouth University's two-year campuswide examination of class and privilege, involving the political science, psychology, economic, humanities, sciences and business departments—with artists like director Peter Sellars and Anne Galjour, who interviewed local citizens and recreate their experiences in a play squarely at the center—a success that now has placed the arts at the table in Dartmouth's strategic long-term planning.

The arts will be increasingly critical as we move to a democratic pluralistic society. As Francois Materasso observes, the arts enable people with nonmajority values, ideas or lifestyles to represent themselves to the majority, to become subjects of their own characterization rather than the object of characterizations by others. How has our understanding of the injustices of the criminal system been expanded by *The Exonerated*, the play about prisoners on death row performed across the country and at state capitols; of Iraqi war refugees reshaped by *Aftermath*, currently touring the nation, or of the experience of women through *The Vagina Monologues*? How did the film *Philadelphia* and productions of *The Normal Heart* and *The Laramie Project* humanize the HIV positive and gay community for an indifferent nation?

Ever since Charles Dickens novels produced changes to child labor law, and *Uncle Tom's Cabin* galvanized the abolition movement, the arts have been critical to social change. Those of us who remember the Vietnam war protests—protests that always began with singing "Blowing in the Wind"—or the civil rights movement—where we always sang "We Shall Overcome"—cannot be surprised by the power of the music to form instant community posed to move together. Arts can be a massive force for social change.

And the arts is an arena where family foundations have a special role to play. The essential local nature of many arts groups means that the bulk of arts funding will always come from local sources. Given that the huge majority of cultural organizations have budgets of less than $1 million, grants of modest or even relatively small size can have an extraordinary impact financially and emotionally—especially given the value that the imprimatur of a grant from your foundation can bestow. Whether you might choose to support a theatre or orchestra or ballet or another cultural organization or to support arts programs at a Boys and Girls Club or support prison and health care reform through the lens of arts interaction, engaging with the arts will expand your creative sense of the possibilities of the future, expand your multiple generation reach, and build communities in new ways—communities informed by deep listening, by creative expression and by mutual respect, which all too often today are in shockingly short supply.

I for one am optimistic about the future of our nation and of the arts. As a Luddite who still regards his computer as a typewriter with a screen, I decided three years ago to plunge myself into the belly of the proverbial beast and attended Pop Tech, an annual conference in Camden, ME, for 500 high tech folks, bringing them together to listen to—and interact with—high level thinkers of every stripe and description. Contrary to my expectations, this was not a conference designed to talk about startups or financing or survival, but about how we will change the world. How we will solve global warming. How we will solve AIDS. How we will leave the world a healthier, ecologically balanced, less poverty-ridden place. Indeed, the unspoken agenda was that there is nothing that we cannot do, and in the world of high tech, truly anything is possible. You might call this folly of youth—and indeed, many of the participants are young.

You may call it hubris.

But what became clear to me is that within this world of infinite possibilities, there is infinite value to be found in the arts.

Artists are embraced at every level at PopTech—they speak on the same panels as scientists and social activists, and virtually every session is followed by performances by live artists—artists like young African American Vanessa German who blew the roof off with her powerful spoken word evocation of passions and feeling;

like a physically challenged hip hop dancer who danced on his crutches, shattering our sense of what the human body could and could not do; like the gospel choir of HIV+ Africans from the African continent, whose singing said more about the complex intersection of faith and disease than any report could ever suggest. I was encouraged that this group of high tech leaders fought to get there. Camden, ME, is not an easy place to access, and if any community can convene virtually, this one can. Yet through PopTech and TED and even through conferences like the one we all attend today, communities insist on coming together because of the unique value of live, face to face, collective experience, of conspiring—meaning to breathe together, breathing the same air. And throughout PopTech, a minor chord, a palpable hunger throbbed in the background—a hunger that the arts meet, not in the extrinsic or instrumental values they offer, but in the intrinsic—in the realm of emotions and spirit. This group was desperate to slow down, to lead less frenetic lives, to find experiences that promote contemplation, captivation, focus and extended surrender, that resonate emotionally, delight, provoke curiosity, enhance spiritual value—the very intrinsic domain that the arts always occupy.

Especially now, in a moment when we all must confront the fallacy of a market orientation uninformed by social conscience, we must embrace the role of the arts in the formation of our collective and individual characters, particularly the character of the young, who are increasingly subjected to "bombardment" of sensation through violent film and video. And in an age of demonization and fear of difference, of intolerant social policies and politicians who encourage us to view our fellow human beings with fear and hostility and suspicion—we must nurture the arts—the arts which gather audiences to look at our fellow human beings with curiosity and generosity. God knows, if we have ever needed that capacity in human history, we need it now.

We are here today, joined by common cause. We work together to promote a healthier, more vibrant world, to ameliorate human suffering and nurture a more thoughtful, empathic and substantive and yes economically prosperous society.

I invite you to embrace arts in your efforts and to be animated by new possibilities. I promise you that a hand of friendship is extended not only from the Doris Duke Charitable Foundation but from Grantmakers in the Arts to help you think through this work, both now and for years to come; and I thank you for your kindness and patience in listening to me this morning. Thank you and Godspeed.

Cumulative Speaker Index: 2000–2009

A cumulative speaker index to the volumes of Representative American Speeches for the years 1937–1938 through 1959–1960 appears in the 1959– 1960 volume; for the years 1960–1961 through 1969–1970, see the 1969–1970 volume; for the years 1970–1971 through 1979–1980, see the 1979–1980 volume; for the years 1980–1981 through 1989–1990, see the 1989–1990 volume; and for the years 1990–1991 through 1999–2000, see the 1999–2000 volume.

Index

About the Editor

Currently a member of the editorial staff of *Art in America* magazine, BRIAN BOUCHER earned a bachelor's degree in art history at Vassar College and a master's degree from the Williams College Graduate Program in the History of Art. To his knowledge, he has no relation to the famous hockey player of the same name. In addition to numerous reviews and articles in *Art in America* and other art publications, he has also written, for *New York* magazine, the unlikely story of his cross with a wanted man on the run from the law: "My Roommate the Diamond Thief: He Found Me on Craigslist; I Found Him on America's Most Wanted." He lives in New York City.